EVERYDAY INSPIRATION
from
GOD'S CREATION

BARBOUR
PUBLISHING

© 2011 by Barbour Publishing, Inc.

ISBN 978-1-62416-683-9

eBook Editions:
Adobe Digital Edition (.epub) 978-1-62836-365-4
Kindle and MobiPocket Edition (.prc) 978-1-62836-366-1

Scripture quotations marked KJV are taken from the King James Version of the Bible.

Scripture quotations marked NIV are taken from the HOLY BIBLE, NEW INTERNATIONAL VERSION®. NIV®. Copyright © 1973, 1978, 1984, 2010 by Biblica, Inc.™ Used by permission. All rights reserved worldwide.

Scripture quotations marked NLT are taken from the *Holy Bible*, New Living Translation, copyright © 1996, 2004. Used by permission of Tyndale House Publishers, Inc. Wheaton, Illinois 60189, U.S.A. All rights reserved.

Scripture quotations marked NASB are taken from the New American Standard Bible, © 1960, 1962, 1963, 1968, 1971, 1972, 1973, 1975, 1977, 1995 by The Lockman Foundation. Used by permission.

Scripture quotations marked MSG are from *THE MESSAGE*. Copyright © by Eugene H. Peterson 1993, 1994, 1995, 1996, 2000, 2001, 2002. Used by permission of NavPress Publishing Group.

Scripture quotations marked ESV are from *The Holy Bible, English Standard Version*®, copyright © 2001 by Crossway Bibles, a publishing ministry of Good News Publishers. Used by permission. All rights reserved.

Scripture quotations marked NCV are taken from the New Century Version of the Bible, copyright © 2005 by Thomas Nelson, Inc. Used by permission.

Scripture quotations marked CEV are from the Contemporary English Version, Copyright © 1991, 1992, 1995 by American Bible Society. Used by permission.

Scripture quotations marked NKJV are taken from the New King James Version®. Copyright © 1982 by Thomas Nelson, Inc. Used by permission. All rights reserved.

Scriptures marked ASV are taken from the American Standard Version of the Bible.

Scripture quotations marked AMP are taken from the Amplified Bible, © 1954, 1958, 1962, 1964, 1965, 1987 by The Lockman Foundation. Used by permission.

Scripture quotations marked NLV are taken from the Holy Bible, New Life Version, Copyright © 1969, 1976, 1978, 1983, 1986, Christian Literature International, P.O. Box 777, Canby, OR 97013. Used by permission.

Scripture quotations marked NET are from the NET Bible® copyright © 1996–2006 by Biblical Studies Press, L.L.C, http://bible.org. Scripture quoted by permission. All rights reserved.

Scripture quotations marked TNIV are taken from the Holy Bible, Today's New International® Version, TNIV®. Copyright 2001, 2005 by International Bible Society®. Used by permission of International Bible Society®. All rights reserved worldwide. "TNIV" and "Today's New International Version" are trademarks registered in the United States Patent and Trademark Office by International Bible Society®.

Scripture quotations marked RSV are from the Revised Standard Version of the Bible, copyright 1946, 1952, 1971 by the Division of Christian Education of the National Council of the Churches of Christ in the USA. Used by permission.

Scripture quotations marked HCSB have been taken from the Holman Christian Standard Bible © copyright 2000 by Holman Bible Publishers. Used by permission.

Scripture quotations marked CJB are taken from the Complete Jewish Bible, copyright 1998 by David H. Stern. Published by Jewish New Testament Publications, Inc. Distributed by Messianic Jewish Resources Int'l. All rights reserved. Used by permission.

Scripture marked GNT taken from the Good News Translation—Second Edition, Copyright © 1992 by American Bible Society. Used by Permission.

All scripture quotations marked DARBY are taken from the Darby Translation of the Bible.

Published by Barbour Publishing, Inc., P.O. Box 719, Uhrichsville, Ohio 44683, www.barbourbooks.com

Our mission is to publish and distribute inspirational products offering exceptional value and biblical encouragement to the masses.

Member of the
Evangelical Christian
Publishers Association

Printed in the United States of America.

Especially for

_____

From

_____

Date

_____

Creation speaks— will you listen?

Out on a country path with my dog this morning, I crossed a railway bridge. Pausing at the top, I looked around at the fields, farms, roads, houses, and the mountains in the distance. "Thank You, God," I whispered.

Right then two dozen goldfinches rose from a bush to my right. I thought I'd startled them, but they didn't fly away. They swooped down in front of me, almost touching the asphalt before rising and disappearing into the bushes on the other side. A second later they repeated the maneuver in reverse, this time landing in a bush just a foot or so farther down the path. Then back again. And back again.

Twittering happily, they "laced up" the path I was walking on, moving ahead of me just out of reach. At the bottom of the hill the little golden flock rose up against the blue sky and did one last twirl before flying away.

Now I'm not saying God laid on a procession for me as His way of saying, "You're welcome," but. . .

This world is just too wonderful to be the accidental result of a big bang. *Everyday Inspiration from God's Creation* brings together a bunch of those moments and thoughts that show just how extraordinary the most ordinary thing in nature can be.

The earth was here before we arrived, and if we want to know more about ourselves and where we came from, we could do worse than look around at the home provided for us. The answers are here, there, and everywhere, if we have eyes to see. If we have ears to hear, then we should listen, with every expectation of being surprised and delighted!

Creation speaks all the time, and these 365 stories with scriptural verses should help remind us who is really doing the talking—and who we might like to say, "Thank You" to!

DAVID MCLAUGHLAN, EDITOR

Enjoying God's Love

> "The LORD your God is with you, the Mighty
> Warrior who saves. He will take great delight
> in you; in his love he will no longer rebuke you,
> but will rejoice over you with singing."
> ZEPHANIAH 3:17 NIV

. . . .

Have you ever thought of a naturally beautiful place—a river, a lake, a mountain—as yet another demonstration of God's love? One avid fly fisherman put it this way:

"One day when I was out on the river, it was as if I heard the voice of God telling me that He put that river there *for me*, that He created the fish I was trying to catch *for me*. . .that He was there *for me*. For the first time in my life—standing waist deep in that river—I came to know God as a loving Father who truly enjoys spending time with me while I was doing one of the things I love most."

Enjoy the beauty of God's creation when you spend a day at your favorite stream. Enjoy the natural beauty, the peace and solitude, and the fish. But remember, your heavenly Father is there, enjoying those things *with you*!

. . . .

*Father God, remind me that the beauty I enjoy when
I'm streamside is Your special gift for me to enjoy—
simply because You love me!*

Starting Out Small

*For you see your calling, brethren, that not
many wise according to the flesh, not many
mighty, not many noble, are called.*

1 CORINTHIANS 1:26 NKJV

. . . .

Near Yosemite National Park stands a grove of old-growth trees, rising like lofty towers, lifting their arms to heaven all day long.

These mammoth trees are hundreds of years old, having weathered fire and famine, parasites and people. Look around, and you'll see other, smaller trees—about the size of a person—dotting the area. There's nothing special about them, their slender trunks contrasting sharply with the breathtaking girth of the colossal trees nearby. But every giant in the grove started out just like those young trees.

As Christians, we too have a towering destiny ahead of us. The contrast between what we are now and what we've been called to is so striking that we might shake our heads in disbelief. But God intentionally chose the weak, not the mighty, for great things. Let's look ahead with anticipation, boasting now of what the Lord will do.

. . . .

*Lord, I'm encouraged that You have
prepared a great future for me!*

The Rocks Cry Out

*Let everything that has breath praise
the LORD. Praise the LORD.*
PSALM 150:6 NIV

. . . .

As Jesus rode into Jerusalem, His followers began cheering Him. The Pharisees, grumpy as always, told Jesus to silence the crowd. But Jesus answered that if the people stopped praising Him, the very rocks would cry out.

Imagine that! Everything that exists in nature—trees, grass, rivers and seas, clouds, mountains, even the rocks underfoot—testify to God's majesty.

If you look at the rocks around you, you'll notice that they're composed of a variety of minerals. Certain kinds are harder than others. Some are huge boulders; others are tiny bits of gravel. There are white rocks, brown rocks, gray rocks, multicolored rocks.

Those rocks are a picture of humanity. There are many sizes, shapes, styles, and colors of people. But we all have the ability to recognize that our Creator is worthy of praise.

So what are you waiting for?

. . . .

*Lord, I thank You for the constant reminders all
around me that You are the God of all creation.*

From the Depths of the Earth

*Though you have allowed me to
experience much trouble and distress,
revive me once again! Bring me up once
again from the depths of the earth!*

PSALM 71:20 NET

. . . .

Mammoth Cave, in Kentucky, is the world's largest cave system. It has over 360 miles of tunnels and is still not fully explored and mapped.

As we walk, crawl, and wiggle through a maze of twisting little passages, all seemingly alike, it is easy to become claustrophobic. When all lights are extinguished, we experience true darkness like we've never "seen" before. Hands waved in front of faces are indistinguishable. Fears can quickly bubble up to the surface and, left unchecked, can become panic.

Life can often be like Mammoth Cave. Are we in a fix? We probably descended by our own free will. But now, how are we going to get out? We definitely need the Light.

God sometimes allows us to get into trouble. But He will never be far from us.

. . . .

*Lord God, I've experience much trouble of my
own making in this life. Please bring me up
out of the depths. Have mercy on me!*

The Vastness of God's Creation

Thus the heavens and the earth
were completed in all their vast array.
GENESIS 2:1 NIV

. . . .

Theodore Roosevelt often invited his friend William Beebe, the American naturalist and author, to spend time with him at his home in Cove Neck, New York. The two enjoyed spending time out on the lawn in the dark of night, and Roosevelt would point to the skies and recite, "That is the Spiral Galaxy in Andromeda. It is as large as our Milky Way. It is one of a hundred million galaxies. It consists of one hundred billion suns, each larger than our sun." Once he made that observation, Roosevelt would smile and say, "Now I think we are small enough! Let's go to bed."

If you've ever spent a night outdoors, away from the city lights, you might have observed the same things Roosevelt and Beebe did decades ago. There's something about the beauty and vastness of the heavens that reminds us of just how small we really are—but more importantly just how big and awesome the God who created every one of the countless galaxies, stars, planets, moons (and the list goes on) really is.

. . . .

Lord God, I thank You for showing me just a
small glimpse of Your greatness by allowing
me to see the vastness of Your creation.

Nesting at God's Altar

Yea, the sparrow hath found an house, and the
swallow a nest for herself, where she may lay
her young, even thine altars, O LORD of hosts,
my King, and my God.
PSALM 84:3 KJV

. . . .

For thousands of years, farmers have awoken to find deer in their wheat fields and rabbits in their gardens. These days, as suburbia encroaches upon the wilderness, many wild animals have learned to coexist with us: raccoons rummage around our back alleys, hawks nest in our skyscrapers, and squirrels live in our walnut trees.

A touching incident of the wild invading human cities is described in the psalms, when sparrows and swallows built their nests in the sides of God's altar. The psalm writer describes his longing to be as constantly close to God as those birds were. But he couldn't—perhaps he was a poor laborer who had to work all day, perhaps he lived too far away.

These days, we don't need to travel to Jerusalem to worship God. But the lesson remains: just as those birds chose to dwell close to God, so too should we.

. . . .

Help me, Lord, like those birds,
to always stay close to You.

Daniel Boone's Religion

"Love the LORD your God. . .and. . .
love your neighbor as yourself."
MATTHEW 22:37–39 NKJV

. . . .

On Sundays, young Daniel Boone walked with his mother to the Quaker meetinghouse, carrying an old English gun for protection against wild animals and Indians. On the gun's butt was carved, D. BOON. 1746. MY MOTHER CHIRCH GUN.

Daniel Boone grew up on a frontier farm in Pennsylvania. From his father he learned to hunt, farm, tan leather, use carpenter's tools, and work a blacksmith's forge. From his mother, Daniel inherited the religious convictions that stayed with him all his long life.

A restless pioneer, Boone walked westward with his family, blazing a trail called the "Wilderness Road," building the first fort (Boonesborough) on the Kentucky River, mapping routes through the wilds of North Carolina, Tennessee, and Virginia—and at the age of eighty-two was seen hunting alone in Nebraska.

As an old man, in a letter to his sister-in-law, Daniel Boone expressed his faith and life's code: "I am as ignorant as a Child. All the Religion I have is to Love and fear God, believe in Jesus Christ, Do all the good to my Neighbors and my Self that I can. . .and trust in God's mercy for the Rest."

. . . .

Thank You, Father, for the simplicity of "true religion."

Great Achievements

But God made the earth by his power;
he founded the world by his wisdom and
stretched out the heavens by his understanding.
JEREMIAH 10:12 NIV

. . . .

As human beings, we love to build, and throughout history, we've engineered some truly amazing things. The "Lost City of the Incas," Machu Picchu, was built high in the Peruvian Andes against horrific conditions. The pyramids at Giza still defy explanation as to how they were constructed so precisely. More recently, Mount Rushmore stands as one of the grandest stone carvings ever conceived.

Observing these spectacles, we're likely to use words like *brilliant, incredible, fantastic,* or *magnificent.* Isn't it interesting, though, that when God created our world and everything in it, He used a much simpler word to describe His own efforts. God simply called them "good."

With that in mind, just imagine what God considers *genius* or what He would call *brilliant.* In fact, we could *never* conceive such things—they're too far beyond our mental reach. That's the kind of majesty only our Creator can produce, and simply by speaking it into existence.

Our most remarkable achievements pale in comparison to those of our almighty God.

. . . .

Lord, help us to keep our own intelligence, creativity,
and ability in their proper perspective.

Boast in the Lord Alone

*May the LORD silence all flattering
lips and every boastful tongue.*
PSALM 12:3 TNIV

. . . .

Some fishermen are notorious for bragging. Who hasn't heard a particularly boastful angler talking with pride after catching the most fish and the biggest one of the day?

The humble angler, on the other hand—and the one most of us enjoy fishing with—is the one who loves seeing others enjoy similar success. . .and who realizes that everything, even a successful day of fishing, is a gift from God. God can use anything to illustrate biblical truth—including a day of fishing with your friends.

Remember that there's no better day of fishing than the one in which everyone comes out of it grateful to God for successes enjoyed. And remember to follow the apostle Paul's instructions: "Let those who boast boast in the Lord" (2 Corinthians 10:17).

. . . .

*Father, may I never forget that any success I enjoy
is Your gift to me. May I boast only in You.*

There are places where, in a single day, it's possible to enjoy coffee and rolls while watching the sun rise over the mountains. . .take a winding drive through spectacular old-growth forests. . .stop for a picnic with a view of a breathtaking waterfall. . .enjoy supper around a fire on a beach. . . and watch the sun set into the ocean. Looking up into the night sky makes for a star-studded grand finale.

The incredible beauty of our world and the awesome expanse of the universe may cause us to think that they're somehow permanent—that they always were and always will be. Biblically, that's not true, though the scope of nature can remind us of how small and short lived we humans are.

What part of us will last forever? We know our souls live on after death. But what is the legacy we'll leave on earth? Will any part of our lives stand the test of time, like the mountains, forests, beaches, or stars?

Today, let's make a conscious effort to exemplify faith, hope, and love—those three things that will last forever.

. . . .

Lord, may my life demonstrate faith,
hope, and love—especially love.

. . . .

There's a feeling that mountain climbers get when they step onto a summit they never thought they'd reach. Bicyclists get the same sensation when they push through exhaustion to a point where they feel they could pedal all day. Sailors feel the joy, when they pass through the discomforts of being cold and wet to become one with the wind.

We've all had our own version of that incredible feeling. You know when and how it happened, but the words to describe it probably failed you. These are the moments we rise above this world and briefly touch a joy beyond our understanding.

Always remember that heaven will be far better than even our most exhilarating moments on this earth. Don't you think that's worth any hardships we face now?

. . . .

Father, I know the road to heaven is a tough one.
In my moments of weakness, please remind
me that I am coming home—and that the
destination is well worth the journey.

Living off the Land

And David remained in the strongholds in the
wilderness, in the hill country of the Wilderness
of Ziph. And Saul sought him every day, but
God did not give him into his hand.

1 SAMUEL 23:14 RSV

. . . .

There is something appealing about a rugged band of soldiers following a chosen leader, living off the land and surviving by hunting, raiding, and foraging. God had anointed David to be Israel's next king, but King Saul was furious about that. As a result, David and his men lived in exile in the wilderness, constantly on the move.

For years Saul led his army in search-and-destroy missions. Like a cunning fox, David used his wits and wilderness savvy to elude Saul—but there were so many spies, so much danger, that only God could prevent David from being caught. "Saul sought him every day, but God did not give him into his hand."

Saul was determined to kill David, but God was even more determined that *His* will for David's life come to pass—and it did. This same God is watching over us today. Let's pray for Him to watch over us, to bring His will for *our* lives to pass.

. . . .

God, I thank You for watching over me and
for not handing me over to my enemies.

And the angel of Jehovah appeared unto him in
a flame of fire out of the midst of a bush: and
he looked, and, behold, the bush burned with
fire, and the bush was not consumed.
EXODUS 3:2 ASV

. . . .

If you happen to drive along South Dakota's Highway 244, you'll undoubtedly see an amazing sight—giant, sixty-foot-tall carvings of the faces of four presidents—on Mount Rushmore. From that moment, you'll be hooked. You'll have no choice but to drive into the national memorial park for a closer look at the massive sculpture.

Centuries ago, Moses also saw a sight that moved him to draw near. How could that burning bush he noticed not be consumed? The spectacle caught his eyes, and then God captured his heart. With a mandate from the Lord, Moses agreed to lead the Israelites out of Egypt.

Have you seen any unusual "sights" lately? Is there a nagging thought or dream in your mind? Could it be that the Lord is tapping you on the shoulder in love?

. . . .

Lord, I'm sometimes bewildered by the things I "see."
Please open my eyes to perceive what
You are doing in my life.

The Need to Turn Around

But those who want to get rich fall into
temptation and a snare and many foolish and
harmful desires which plunge men into ruin and
destruction. . . . But flee from these things, you
man of God, and pursue righteousness, godliness,
faith, love, perseverance and gentleness.

1 TIMOTHY 6:9, 11 NASB

. . . .

Along the brushy edges of fields, foxes are first-class hunters. Using their eyes, ears, and noses, they are alert to everything that moves, makes a sound, or gives off a scent. They present an image of graceful control as they travel at an easy trot in search of dinner.

Foxes are wise in the ways of their world, too—but a hunter can fool them by imitating the sound of a small animal in trouble. It's a rare fox that will not abandon its plans and come on the run for the free meal it thinks is waiting.

That's when a fox is vulnerable. But let him get one glimpse of the hunter and he'll forget all about that free meal. He'll reverse course without a second thought and sprint away to put as much distance as possible between him and the danger. The fox doesn't hesitate, thinking how good a rabbit dinner would be. He just runs for it.

We do well to make a similar retreat as soon as we recognize spiritual danger.

. . . .

Lord, help us to remember Your precepts and flee
temptations as soon as we recognize them.

. . . .

A few generations back, one author captured childhood imaginations like few others: Richard Halliburton, a 1930s adventurer who flew from one nerve-racking exploit to the next in a biplane named The Flying Carpet.

Among Halliburton's exploits were a swim through the Panama Canal (for a fee of thirty-six cents) and spending the night alone with a mummified pharaoh in a tomb of the Great Pyramid of Giza. Halliburton was a personal friend of Lawrence of Arabia, and fraternized with the French Foreign Legion in Timbuktu. In eighteen months, Halliburton circumnavigated the globe, logging nearly thirty-four thousand miles and visiting thirty-four countries.

On March 3, 1939, Halliburton undertook a new adventure—to sail a Chinese junk across the Pacific Ocean to San Francisco. But later that month, communication with Halliburton stopped. He was declared dead October 5, 1939.

The adventurer once bragged, "There is no book of marvels like my Books of Marvels." He was wrong. There are sixty-six marvelous books of wonder and truth in God's Book, the Holy Bible.

. . . .

When I read Your Word, Father, bring fresh wonder
to my heart; let me find refreshment for my day.

A God of Restoration

He makes me lie down in green pastures,
he leads me beside quiet waters,
he refreshes my soul.
PSALM 23:2–3 NIV

. . . .

Ask several outdoorsmen and women what they like most about their time outside, and you're likely to receive several different answers. Some enjoy the peace, some the solitude, others the sense of being close to the Lord in a natural, God-created setting.

Alone in the wilderness, a person is in a place where one can learn things about God that could never be learned amid the busyness and stresses of everyday life. An individual can get to know God as the One who restores the mind, the body, and the spirit—and all of that through simple fellowship with the Holy Spirit.

When you're enjoying your favorite activity in a peaceful, natural outdoor setting, remember that God wants to use that time to fellowship with you, to teach you, and to restore you as only He can.

. . . .

I thank You, loving Father, that You are a God of love,
of compassion, of provision. . .and of daily restoration.

kingdom and speak of your might.
PSALM 145:10–11 NIV

. . . .

Sometimes authors write in such believable detail that scientists actually study to see if the fictional ideas are possible. Michael Crichton's book *Jurassic Park* is an example: scientists have run experiments and made calculations to learn if cloning long-extinct creatures from well-preserved DNA is possible.

Technologies seen in entertainment such as *Star Trek* and *Star Wars* have been discussed and debated within scientific circles, too. Laser guns, swords made of light, flying machines, and high-tech communication devices are being researched and tested.

Whatever realities we create from science fiction dreams, they will never compare to the creation God reveals to us every day. We may find different ways to use what we already have—but only God can create a physical universe from nothing.

. . . .

Lord, may I never make the mistake
of confusing creation and invention.

Prepare for Sudden Squalls

*LORD, how they have increased who trouble
me! Many are they who rise up against me.*
PSALM 3:1 NKJV

. . . .

No matter what we like doing outdoors, we're wise to check the weather before we start.

Boaters need to beware of violent lakes or seas. Hikers should know when a possible downpour could create a flash flood. Mountain climbers must avoid those areas where violent winds and snowstorms could ruin their adventure.

But we don't have to be outdoors to encounter stormy weather. An argument at home, competition at work, a bully at school—all these "squalls" can blow up suddenly and create difficult, dangerous situations for us.

Thankfully, we have an escape. By prayer and the indwelling power of God, we can stay even keeled in even the most troubled waters and come through them unharmed.

Blessed are the peacemakers in the midst of the storm!

. . . .

*Lord, I should probably expect trouble today.
Please guard my mouth, strengthen my heart,
and give me the humble spirit of Jesus.*

He answered, "I tell you, if these were silent,
the very stones would cry out."
LUKE 19:39–40 ESV

. . . .

When you were young, did you ever spend time skipping stones across a pond—maybe during a fishing trip or hike with your dad? Those stones, the flatter the better, would bounce and skip and jump as many as a dozen times before gravity would finally win the battle and pull the rock underwater.

Stones are good for more than just skipping. They also provide fossil records that help us understand history. But they do even more than that. Stones have the ability to cry out when God's people fail to praise Him. The minute Jesus gave up His spirit on the cross, several remarkable things happened—including an earthquake and the splitting of rocks (Matthew 27:51). Man crucified Christ and the rocks cried out for His glory.

The next time you take a walk, pick up a stone, look closely, and marvel over the fact that God can use such an object to glorify Himself.

. . . .

Father, I am awed by the knowledge that
even a stone can bring glory to Your name.

An Ever-Helpful Sidekick

*Yea, though I walk through the valley of the
shadow of death, I will fear no evil: for thou art
with me; thy rod and thy staff they comfort me.*
PSALM 23:4 KJV

. . . .

The lowly hiking staff is a versatile implement of a thousand and one uses. Well, at least seventy-eight.

It functions as a sturdy "third leg," helping us maintain stability when maneuvering over uneven terrain. It slows our momentum when the path leads downward, and helps push us forward when the trail ascends. We can use the staff to probe surrounding vegetation for unpleasant surprises, or to test soft ground too dangerous to walk on. With only a little ingenuity, we could create an emergency fishing rod from it.

Like the hiking staff, there's another trusty Helper at our side as we travel through life. Our God is ever present to help us past every obstacle—emotional, mental, or spiritual. His power will get us up the mountains and carry us through the dark valleys of trouble and strife. His wisdom is always on call for moments both mundane and challenging.

Don't go anywhere without Him!

. . . .

*Lord, I thank You for the reminder
that You are with me always.*

. . . .

You never know when clicking through the channels will become a worthwhile activity. The news?—A young California condor has been sighted on the North Rim of the Grand Canyon.

Why is that exciting? In the 1980s, less than thirty such birds remained in the wild. Thanks to conservation, within two decades there are almost two hundred condors in the western United States into Mexico.

Isaiah probably never saw a noble condor with its six-foot wingspan, but at a time when the children of God were becoming smaller in number—were almost indistinguishable from the populace around them—the prophet selected a winging metaphor to illustrate man's need to soar in his spirit.

We all have that need, for the presence of the Lord lifting us above the mind-set of a fallen world. Today's let's hope in the Lord—and soar on wings like eagles.

. . . .

The world is just too much for me, Father.
Lift me up in my spirit, so I can look into
Your face and see the person I can be.

Listen to the Silence

Then Jesus said, "Whoever has
ears to hear, let them hear."
MARK 4:9 NIV

. . . .

On a still winter night in the country, the silence might surprise you. The almost complete lack of noise somehow clears the mind and points us to deeper thoughts.

We think we know what silence is, but most of us automatically tune out the noise of distant traffic, the heating system, even the television and radio as they play.

Sadly, it's easy to do the same thing in our Christian life. We "tune out" the little sins that creep into our day, and we think we're doing all right. But when we're truly silent before God, those little sins cry out like a chainsaw roaring through the still winter air—a shock that compels us to do something about them.

Find some real silence, which refreshes the soul. Without any other distractions, spend some time listening to God. "Hear" what He has to say specifically to you—and become more and more the child He wants you to be.

. . . .

Lord, help me not to kid myself. May I
deal with the sin in my life, knowing that,
with Your help, all things are possible.

. . . .

An old pastor, a World War II veteran, had survived a kamikaze attack on his destroyer. The explosion on board threw him into the Pacific. He was in one piece, but the thought of being in the water unnerved him. Not a Christian at the time, prayer was unfamiliar. He struggled and fought the waves for some time.

After a while, though, his training came to mind. He remembered he was wearing a flotation jacket, and realized his struggling was in vain. It would only exhaust him, make him weak, and likely lead to his death. But if he relaxed and let the jacket hold him up, he had a better chance of rescue. The vest could do for him what he couldn't do for himself.

Later, after he'd become a Christian, he shared this story with others going through rough times. We can fight it in our own strength and wear ourselves out, or we can relax in the Lord, letting Him keep us afloat until He brings us through.

. . . .

*Lord, teach me to rest in You and not
to struggle against my circumstances.*

Beyond Our Furthest Limits

The eyes of the LORD are in every place,
beholding the evil and the good.
PROVERBS 15:3 KJV

. . . .

In 1953 Edmund Hillary and Tenzing Norgay were the first people to set foot on the summit of Mount Everest. Within minutes of reaching this never-before-occupied corner of the earth, Hillary dug a hole in the snow and buried a cross there. Given the deep freeze conditions on the top of the mountain, the cross might still be there more than half a century later.

One thing is sure. Before these men reached that summit, before the cross was buried there, God was already there. After all, He made the place!

We don't need to take God with us on our adventures, whether they be organized expeditions or personal explorations. Instead, as we approach those bleak, wonderful, dangerous, awe-inspiring places, we should walk in faith, knowing that He is already there, waiting for us.

. . . .

God, there is no place in this world—or in
our lives—that You have not already "explored."
Help us remember that when we need to exceed our
limits, You have none and there is no better guide.

kindness, humility, gentleness and patience.
COLOSSIANS 3:12 NIV

. . . .

There's a certain science to dressing for a cool- or cold-weather adventure.

"Layering" is designed to balance temperature and moisture levels both inside and out. The inner or base layer, often a polyester item, is supposed to draw sweat away from the skin. The middle or insulating layer, typically wool or fleece, keeps the body warm. The outer or shell layer keeps the worst of the wind and rain away from the other clothing. Together, each layer contributes to the wearer's comfort and protection.

The Bible often likens our Christian preparation to a wardrobe—whether the "armor of God" as described in Ephesians 6 or the "adornment. . .of a gentle and quiet spirit" mentioned in 1 Peter 3. In Colossians 3, the apostle Paul suggested the layering of such spiritual clothes as compassion, kindness, humility, gentleness, and patience.

If we're dressed like that, we'll be safe and comfortable no matter what storms blow around us.

. . . .

*Lord God, may I dress my spirit as
carefully as I do my physical body.*

The Awesome Aurochs

*"Will the wild ox consent to serve you? Will it
stay by your manger at night? Can you hold it to
the furrow with a harness? Will it till the valleys
behind you? Will you rely on it for its great
strength? Will you leave your heavy work to it?"*
JOB 39:9–11 NIV

. . . .

The wild ox—the aurochs—was the ancestor of modern cattle but was far larger, stronger, and more ferocious than bred-down domestic oxen. Aurochs bulls weighed over 2,200 pounds, and as Julius Caesar wrote, "Their strength and speed are extraordinary; they spare neither man nor wild beast." The ancients could only dream of harnessing the power of such creatures.

Aurochs once roamed free throughout Europe and the Middle East. Hunting them was considered such a test of courage and manhood that, over the millennia, they were hunted to the point of extinction. The last wild ox died in Poland in 1627.

In today's utilitarian, results-oriented world, we try to find a practical use for everything, some purpose to justify its existence—but some things just *are*. Some wild creatures exist simply to cause us to consider the power and majesty of the God who created them.

. . . .

*Lord, thank You for creating powerful, magnificent beasts
like the aurochs to strike men with awe and wonder.*

will receive the crown of life that the Lord
has promised to those who love him.
JAMES 1:12 NIV

. . . .

Hikers often find that the first half hour of any walk is the hardest. That's when most trekkers drop out. But the experienced hiker knows better times are ahead. After those initial aches and pains a new energy arises. The body steps up a gear, allowing comfortable walking for much of the day. Beginners who persevere find themselves completing routes they wouldn't have contemplated before.

The walk of faith is not the easy stroll some expect it to be. In fact, it can be rockier than many mountain trails—and a lot of people give up before they really get started.

But, eventually, the wind will be at your back—a new, God-given energy will propel you along the path. You'll do things for Him you could never have imagined at the beginning of your walk—if you just keep going.

. . . .

Dear Lord, You made us capable of great things—
please convince me of that! Through Your work
I am better than I ever realized I could be.

Blessed in Hard Times

*Though hail flattens the forest and the city is
leveled completely, how blessed you will be,
sowing your seed by every stream, and letting
your cattle and donkeys range free.*

ISAIAH 32:19–20 NIV

. . . .

We've been living through extraordinary times: landmark banks and financial institutions are collapsing, rock-solid manufacturers are going bankrupt, the unemployment rate is rising sharply, and thousands upon thousands of mortgages are going into foreclosure. The nation is being shaken to its economic foundations. At times it's difficult to believe it's all really happening.

Through its history, Israel suffered stunning disasters that left her people shocked and anxious: foreign invasions, lengthy droughts, locust plagues, and destructive hailstorms. Yet God promised to provide for His people during such difficult times. He said, "How blessed you will be"! (*Blessed*, mind you, not necessarily rich.)

There are always ways to provide for your family, even in the aftermath of a forest-flattening, city-leveling disaster. In fact, changing times open up new opportunities. The forestry jobs may disappear, the business district may be wiped out—but God can bless you anywhere He pleases.

. . . .

*God, please lead me to new opportunities
in these difficult, changing times.*

A Father's Love

Endure your suffering as discipline;
God is treating you as sons. For what son
is there that a father does not discipline?
HEBREWS 12:7 NET

. . . .

The outdoors are wonderful, but there are risks. One of them is getting bitten by wild animals.

Rabies shots are given quickly to anyone who's even suspected of having been exposed to this animal-borne disease. The shots don't use large needles, but for the 40 percent of people who experience headache, nausea, abdominal pain, muscle aches, and dizziness from them, the series of three to five shots can be an agony. What parents would put their child through such pain—especially when, most of the time, the animal turns out not to have been infected?

If untreated, rabies is 100 percent fatal to humans—and by the time symptoms appear, it's too late to start the shots. So now we ask, what parent wouldn't love their child enough to force them to have treatments?

A youngster might not understand why Mom or Dad is causing such pain. But it is clearly *love* that motivates a parent to hold the squirming child while a doctor administers the shot.

. . . .

Father, I thank You for loving us enough to allow us
some short-term pain to avoid long-term consequences.
And I thank You for being there, holding me when I hurt.

Details of Creation

For you created my inmost being; you knit me
together in my mother's womb. I praise you
because I am fearfully and wonderfully made;
your works are wonderful, I know that full well.

PSALM 139:13–14 NIV

. . . .

Macro photography zooms in on the smallest details of a flower, a butterfly, a bee, or even a spider in a web. Such scenic work is a wonderful way to inspect the intricate workmanship of God's creation.

Though we as human beings were engineered with the same kind of care and detail, depression, low self-esteem, and low self-worth often rob us of the value we have in God's eyes. But who could truly study the intricacies of a monarch butterfly, an Oriental lily, or a rose in close-up detail and not see the majesty of God's creative hand? The painstaking detail of each creation—including ourselves—should bring us to an admiration of His handiwork.

Each of us is "fearfully and wonderfully made" by the great Creator of the universe. Who knows how much time He spent designing each one of us before the foundation of the world in the secret place? His thoughts toward us outnumber the grains of sand.

. . . .

Lord, You have a plan for my life, a purpose for me.
Help me to see my value through Your eyes.

Simplicity and Godliness

*Now John [the Baptist] wore a garment of
camel's hair and a leather belt around his
waist, and his food was locusts and wild honey.*
MATTHEW 3:4 ESV

. . . .

From the wilderness of Judea, John the Baptist appeared, preaching about the kingdom of heaven. Everything about him pointed to a rough, outdoorsy lifestyle—from his plain style of clothing to the food he ate. Probably, many people expected the Messiah's forerunner to arrive with more pomp and circumstance. But that wasn't the case.

John's simple lifestyle allowed him to focus solely on the kingdom. One Bible commentator suggests that John was so consumed with spiritual things that he couldn't even find time for a set meal. So a quick snack of locusts and wild honey was just fine.

Do you feel overwhelmed by a lengthy to-do list and desire to spend time with God, free from the concerns of this world? Why not stuff a small backpack and head out into the wilderness this weekend? Embrace simplicity—and listen for God's voice.

. . . .

*Lord, I long to hear Your voice and sense
Your presence. Lead me into a wilderness
where I might draw closer to You.*

Pole, Pole

The race is not always won by the swiftest,
the battle is not always won by the strongest.
ECCLESIASTES 9:11 NET

. . . .

Mount Kilimanjaro rises 19,340 feet above the African plain. Many flock to the challenge of climbing Africa's highest peak.

"Kili" may be climbed without technical skills, but the guides constantly remind the climbers, "*Pole, pole. . .*" It means "slow, slow" in Swahili. The guides know that those who start the day hiking fast and passing others will later be found by the side of the trail gasping for breath in the thin air. Those who succeed in reaching the summit of the world's highest freestanding mountain are those who have learned the secret of just putting one foot in front of the other, thousands and thousands of times in succession.

Our daily life is much like Kilimanjaro. God doesn't need us to be bottle rockets, making a loud pop but quickly fading away. Instead, He wants long-term faithfulness and growth. Truly rising in Christian maturity requires us to be steady and constant, weathering life's peaks and valleys.

. . . .

God of mountains and valleys, help us remember day
after day that "slow and steady" wins the race.

Our God Is Unique

*"No one is holy like the LORD, for there is none
besides You, nor is there any rock like our God."*
1 SAMUEL 2:2 NKJV

. . . .

A t nearly six miles in circumference, Australia's Uluru is
probably the largest rock in the world.

What else sets Uluru, also known as Ayers Rock, apart?
How about its apparently changing color scheme—including
silvery-gray, brown, orange, and red—depending on the sunlight and weather conditions? Known by geologists as an *in-
selberg*, or "island mountain," local Aborigines see the massive
rock as sacred.

The Bible describes our God as a "sacred rock." There is no
other God like Him. His many names and titles—including
Abba Father, *Bridegroom*, *Friend*, *High Priest*, *I Am*, *King of
Kings*, *Mediator*, *Only Begotten Son*, *Redeemer*, *Savior*, and
Strength—indicate the incredible breadth of His personality and
power.

Unique landmarks are interesting—but our God is truly
special. Whatever trouble, sorrow, or frustration we're experiencing, our God is big enough to cover them all. That's what
makes our Rock so unique and valuable!

. . . .

*Lord, please forgive when I look beyond
You for help. You are always available,
and powerful enough for all my needs!*

Created for a Purpose

He who created the heavens, he is God;
he who fashioned and made the earth,
he founded it; he did not create it to be
empty, but formed it to be inhabited.
ISAIAH 45:18 NIV

. . . .

The Bible reveals God as One who doesn't typically do things just to show His own awesome power, but who has a purpose in what He creates and does. That purpose includes the natural wonder of the earth we have the privilege of enjoying. And it also includes you!

God made the earth and everything in it with a special purpose in mind—namely, that we humans could live here, have dominion, and enjoy it all as His special gift to us. So next time you're out fishing, hunting, camping—you name the activity—take a moment to think about God's purpose for the piece of creation you're enjoying. . .and His special purpose for *you*.

. . . .

Father God, I thank You for creating the earth—
and me—for a special purpose: to glorify You!

Fear Not—God Knows

*"Are not two sparrows sold for a cent? And yet
not one of them will fall to the ground apart
from your Father. . . . So do not fear; you are
more valuable than many sparrows."*
MATTHEW 10:29, 31 NASB

. . . .

Woodland birds sometimes seem unconcerned about a quiet observer. That's when we get to see them pursue their patient, unhurried search for food. They don't seem to be worried about success. They just stick to the job until they have what they need.

It can be amusing to see a sparrow stop hopping along a rotten log to flip a maple leaf onto the ground. When it repeats the action with another leaf, we begin to give the bird a little more credit: it seems to be making decisions.

God knows what's going on in that bird brain—and He knows what's going on in our lives. So we don't need to worry about having enough to eat or what the national economy will do. God knows our needs, and He's promised to supply.

He counts us more valuable than many sparrows.

. . . .

*Great God, I thank You for giving us examples
of Your care for Your creation. Thank You for
assuring us that You value us and are aware of
all our needs. Strengthen our faith in Your care
so that we will confidently trust in You.*

Nature Laughs as Well

He brought me forth also into a large place:
he delivered me, because he delighted in me.
2 SAMUEL 22:20 KJV

. . . .

Nature is harsh! It's "red in tooth and claw." It's survival of the fittest.

Yet, nature is so much more. Ask the dog that runs full tilt after a low-flying swallow without any hope of catching it—but loving the chase! Ask the swallow as it flies in wide circles, just low enough for the dog to think he might nip a tail feather. Watch as it tightens those circles, slowly, but deliberately, until the dizzy dog trips over its own legs.

Watch as the dog gets to its feet and the swallow comes back, and the game starts again.

Life, like nature, can be hard, but it was made to be so much more. Both were made to make the human heart sing. Life was made to be lived to its fullest.

. . . .

Father, we know that difficulties are put in our life
for a reason. They are a means to an end, not an
end in themselves. They are sent to make us better,
and we are never better than when we join with
nature in singing Your praises.

But Can You Fly?

*"The wings of the ostrich wave proudly, but are
her wings and pinions like the kindly stork's?"*
JOB 39:13 NKJV

. . . .

Four thousand years ago, ostriches flourished in the land of Uz, east of Canaan, on the fringes of the Arabian Desert. Later, wealthy Arabs hunted ostriches for food and for sport. The introduction of motor vehicles and firearms in the early twentieth century spelled the birds' demise, and the last Arabian ostrich died in Jordan in 1966.

Flocks of black storks, by contrast, still migrate annually over the Middle East, flying thousands of miles from Europe to Africa. The stork is a significantly sized bird, and while not as large as the ostrich, it has one distinct advantage: the ostrich merely waves its wings proudly as it runs, but the "kindly stork" can actually rise up on its wings and fly.

Many of us might choose to be a powerful heavyweight like an ostrich, with the speed and power to outrun hounds and horses and arrows. But ostriches can't escape big guns. When a trouble too fast to outrun comes along, it's better to be a lightweight stork that can spread its wings and rise into the heavens for refuge.

. . . .

*Dear God, help me to be like a
kindly stork, not like a proud ostrich.*

No Cause for a Curse

Like a flitting sparrow, like a flying swallow,
so a curse without cause shall not alight.
PROVERBS 26:2 NKJV

. . . .

If you watch a swallow swoop through the sky, pursuing insects, you marvel at how it seems to stay airborne all day long. For hours it never touches earth. The same with a flitting sparrow or a hovering hummingbird—they never seem to land.

Once when King David and his army were fleeing Jerusalem, an enemy named Shimei came out and began calling down curses upon David. The king's nephew wanted to kill Shimei, but David replied, "Let him curse. . . . It may be that the LORD will. . .repay me with good for his cursing this day" (2 Samuel 16:11–12).

David had the right attitude. He knew he had done nothing wrong and that no curse would come upon him. He was suffering a temporary setback, but God was with him and had promised to bless him.

For the same reason, Jesus told us, "Bless those who curse you" (Matthew 5:44). We are to respond to hatred and cursing with love and blessing. If someone curses us for no reason, we can be certain that it won't alight on us.

. . . .

God, I thank You that I don't need to
fear the curses of those who hate me.

Joy in the Accomplishment

*All Judah rejoiced over the oath, for they had
sworn it with all their mind. They had sought
Him with all their heart, and He was found by
them. So the LORD gave them rest on every side.*
2 CHRONICLES 15:15 HCSB

. . . .

There's a special feeling of accomplishment we get when we reach the end of a difficult trail or the peak of the mountain. We experience the full satisfaction of having met our goals.

Having pursued our destination to the end—without breaking a leg or breaking up our marriage—we can relax and drink in the outdoor splendor. Rest feels good when all our hard work has paid off.

God also gives a wonderful rest when we've sought Him with our whole heart. The children of Judah had entered into a covenant to seek God, making a commitment to put Him first. It took work on their part, but they rejoiced greatly when they reached their goal.

On our own difficult journey, haven't we felt God strengthening us when we didn't give up? When we reach the point of rest, let's experience the joy of giving ourselves back to Him.

. . . .

*Lord, You've been so good to me.
I want to follow You wherever You go.*

The Black Widow

The fear of the LORD is the beginning of wisdom;
a good understanding have all those who do His
commandments; His praise endures forever.
PSALM 111:10 NASB

. . . .

The most venomous spider in North America is the black widow. It generally lives in the warmer, southern states, hiding in woodpiles, garages, and other dark places. Its venom is said to be fifteen times more poisonous than a rattlesnake's, and works by disrupting the central nervous system.

Those bites are relatively rare, though, as the spiders prefer to hide or run away rather than tangle with a person. If you leave them alone, they'll likely never bother you. Black widows really give us little to fear, but much to respect.

Does that sound like our "fear" of God? The fear of the Lord is all about respect and reverence. We need not be frightened of Him—He loves us! But the respectful reverence we give God in all things is the basis of our whole relationship with Him.

. . . .

Lord, remind me again and again to
observe and respect Your almighty power.

Hiacoomes, the First

Not many wise. . .not many mighty,
not many noble, are called.
1 CORINTHIANS 1:26 KJV

. . . .

Homely and speech impaired, Hiacoomes was an outcast among the Indians of Martha's Vineyard. When some English families settled on the island in 1642, Reverend Thomas Mayhew, their minister, invited the Indian to his home every Lord's day. Hiacoomes gave his heart to Christ—the first fruit of God among the natives.

Enduring ridicule among his own, Hiacoomes grew in grace and courage, and preached the gospel to them. When a tribal sorcerer struck Hiacoomes in the face, he didn't retaliate. "I had one hand for injuries," he said, "and another hand for God. I received wrong with the one, and held even tighter to God with the other."

The sorcerer was later struck by lightning and fell unconscious into a fire. Badly burned, he recovered, renounced his evil spirits, and became a worshipper of God through Jesus Christ. The gospel spread.

By 1675, nearly all the natives of Martha's Vineyard confessed Christ. There were three Indian churches, ten Indian preachers, and six services on the island each Sabbath. Nearby Chappaquidick and Nantucket were Christianized also. The total number of "praying Indians" on the islands was approximately two thousand.

And it all started with a simple invitation.

. . . .

Here I am, Lord—use me!

When Winter Ends

*See! The winter is past; the rains are over
and gone. Flowers appear on the earth;
the season of singing has come, the
cooing of doves is heard in our land.*
SONG OF SOLOMON 2:11–12 NIV

. . . .

In ancient times, just like today, winter was a hard time, a season to be endured. Of course, winter in Israel was not usually accompanied by the subzero temperatures and heavy snows common to much of North America.

Still, spring, when it came, was a time of rejoicing. The cold winter rains had passed and signs of life were appearing. Flowers began to bud. Birds began mating. The low, contented cooing of doves could be heard. It was a happy time, "the season of singing."

Like it or not, all of us go through winter seasons, times of prolonged sorrow or moments when we're nearly overwhelmed by feelings of hopelessness and despair. But God's promise remains true: "Weeping may stay for the night, but rejoicing comes in the morning" (Psalm 30:5).

Winter will always give way to spring. Just don't give up hope!

. . . .

*Lord, help me to trust that hard times will pass—
and that joy will be mine once again.*

Prepared for the Journey

*The rabble with them began to crave other
food, and again the Israelites started wailing
and said, "If only we had meat to eat!"*
NUMBERS 11:4 NIV

. . . .

The Boy Scouts have a list of backpack essentials as long as your arm.

They include a pocketknife for slicing cheese, whittling, tightening screws, and cutting a bandage down to size. A first-aid kit is always handy, along with extra clothing, a water bottle, a flashlight, and plenty of high-energy food for the upcoming trek. The Scouts' big idea, of course, is to be prepared—for every problem, including hunger pangs.

Long ago, the Israelites—under God's direction—prepared for a trip across a desert. As they left Egypt, God caused their neighbors to give them clothing and jewelry. The Israelites herded sheep and cattle, and carried the unleavened dough they'd brought from their land of captivity.

But it was a long trip, with some six hundred thousand mouths to feed. When the people's provisions ran out, God provided for them—miraculously, in spite of their bad attitudes.

We, too, can rest assured that God carries what we cannot. He leads, and He will provide for our journey. Let's not complain like the Israelites, but thank God for His daily provision.

. . . .

*Lord, feed me with Your Word,
and satisfy me with Your presence.*

Into the Dark

And God saw the light, that it was good:
and God divided the light from the darkness.
GENESIS 1:4 KJV

. . . .

Snorkeling off an atoll can be a beautiful and relaxing experience—on the inside of the reef! That's where the water is shallow, the visibility good, and the multicolored fish seemingly unconcerned by your presence.

But venture through a gap in the reef and everything changes. The currents are stronger, the water colder, and the marine life more menacing. Often, the seabed disappears into an inky abyss. It can be a fascinating and enticing world—but venture in without a guide and you're taking a big risk.

Our whole world is like that. From above, where Christians should be, some of those "lower things" can seem awfully enticing. But when we really look, we see they're dark and dangerous.

In this life, we won't always have a protective coral reef surrounding us. But if we have to venture outside, let's take the Lord Jesus as our guide.

. . . .

Jesus, Savior, I am often attracted to those lower things
of life. Remind me today that what truly matters is
within the encircling arms of Your love.

Arrowheads

Let God transform you into a new
person by changing the way you think.
ROMANS 12:2 NLT

. . . .

Long before gun and archery shops, men had to make their own tools for hunting.

Arrowheads, spearheads, and knives were "knapped" from various stones. A skilled knapper could take raw material and hammer away bits and flakes with another stone, creating a sharp, finished point that was attached to an arrow or a spear for hunting. Primitive men armed with stone-tipped spears could bring down much larger, more dangerous animals, which they used for food and clothing.

God "knaps" us in much the same way. He takes us, pieces of rough, raw material, and lovingly works us, bit by bit and flake by flake, into a perfect tool He can use for His purposes.

He already knows what He wants to do with us. Through our many life experiences, we can be knapped for His perfect ways—if only we'll trust Him and allow Him to work.

. . . .

Lord, I commit myself into Your hands today.
Please shape me into what You want me to be.

Seeing Humor in the Outdoors

A merry heart doeth good like a medicine.
PROVERBS 17:22 KJV

. . . .

Sometimes during our time in the outdoors, we can open our eyes and ears to observe what's going on around us. . . and burst into laughter.

It's not difficult to find humor in the natural world. The overprotective blackbird scolding you and buzzing your head as it defends its nest against a perceived threat. . .the beaver that lifts its head out of the water, sending you a bucktoothed grin. . .the river otters playfully seeking a creative angle of attack on their mates. And who can't see the humor in being kept awake on an overnight camping trip by a romantic male bullfrog calling out to the opposite sex?

God created everything we see in the outdoors, and He allows us to enjoy it all. He also created humor—and if we pay close enough attention, we might just find a good laugh in the world of nature. When you do, think of God smiling and laughing with you at some of nature's most humorous sights and sounds.

. . . .

Father, I thank You for allowing me to see the lightness and humor You've strategically placed throughout creation—just for Your children to enjoy!

The Storehouse of Snow

*"Have you entered the storehouses of the
snow or seen the storehouses of the hail,
which I reserve for times of trouble,
for days of war and battle?"*
JOB 38:22–23 NIV

. . . .

One of the most beautiful experiences of nature is a winter snowfall.

Snow has a distinct cleansing effect as it covers everything in a blanket of white. The sight of those big, fluffy flakes, floating down like feathers from heaven, is calming—as is the sound-deadening effect of the snow. A good snowfall muffles the noise of the surrounding world, somehow slowing the pace of our hurry-up society.

But then comes the fun. Sleds and snowmobiles, forts, snowmen, and snowballs appear. The world becomes a different place after a good snowfall.

Contemplating a "storehouse of snow" brings to mind visions of sparkling, pure white mounds of the stuff—and an awesome realization of the creative mind of God.

. . . .

*Lord, I thank You for the beauty of nature.
Help me to appreciate all that You've created for me.
I praise You for the evidences of Your power.*

Hope of the Resurrection

*"As the water of a lake dries up or a riverbed
becomes parched and dry, so he lies down and
does not rise; till the heavens are no more, people
will not awake or be roused from their sleep."*
JOB 14:11–12 NIV

. . . .

In the western Arabian Desert bordering Uz, there are scores of landlocked rivers with no outlet to the oceans. Instead, filled by brief rainstorms, they rush into myriad shallow depressions, forming inland seas. The water doesn't last. The land bakes like an oven in the desert heat, leaving behind bone-dry wadis and large, cracked salt pans.

Job noted that man's life was like these short-lived wadis and seas. You could read this desolate imagery and conclude that we live, we die, and that's it. But this verse gives an implicit hope of the resurrection: one day the heavens and the earth will indeed pass away, all things will be made new, and man will rise again.

As Job said in the next verses: "If someone dies, will they live again? All the days of my hard service I will wait for my renewal to come" (verse 14). We, too, wait to be renewed.

. . . .

*Dear God, as I realize that my physical life will end,
it's comforting to know that I shall live again.*

Fly Higher

And my temptation which was in my flesh ye despised not, nor rejected; but received me as an angel of God, even as Christ Jesus.

GALATIANS 4:14 KJV

. . . .

The English hotel was a collection of old buildings joined by pathways and separated by little lawns and gardens.

Returning late one evening, a young couple looked at the once green, grassy square, now covered by four or five inches of freshly fallen snow. They looked at each other and smiled. Without a word, and still wearing their "going out" clothes, they tiptoed onto the snow then lay down. Holding hands, then sweeping their legs and free arms through the snow, they made snow angels.

Delighted, they considered their artwork. Then the man added halos to the snow-couple.

What is it about snow angels? Is it the purity of the snow that attracts us? Or maybe it is the desire to be something better, something closer to the Lord who made the snow in the first place.

. . . .

Lord, this life weighs us down, but always, a voice inside cries out for our true nature to be released. Help us take the steps, whenever they arise, that bring us ever closer to You.

Royal Trappers and Hunters

Solomon's daily provisions were. . .ten head
of stall-fed cattle, twenty of pasture-fed cattle
and a hundred sheep and goats, as well as deer,
gazelles, roebucks and choice fowl.
1 KINGS 4:22–23 NIV

. . . .

Solomon's empire stretched from Egypt to the Euphrates. Various dignitaries visited constantly, bringing tribute. Then there were foreign ambassadors and delegations, Solomon's own royal court, and scores of Israelite nobles. Every day he had to provide huge feasts.

Israelite farmers provided the beef and mutton, but Solomon wanted to serve wild game as well, so he had a small army of hunters and trappers netting and snaring deer, gazelles, roebucks, and wild fowl to bring them to Jerusalem.

It must have been a dream job for those chosen few. Who wouldn't like to earn a living doing what he loves to do? It's great when that happens. But often, to support our families, we work at a job we're *less* than enthusiastic about, doing what we love in our spare time.

We do what we must do because we love our families—and because that's what God requires of us. If we get the dream job, too, that's just a bonus.

. . . .

God, I thank You for times that I can do what I love—
however infrequent those times are.

Real Security

Truly he is my rock and my salvation;
he is my fortress, I will never be shaken.
PSALM 62:2 NIV

. . . .

In a world that's changing faster than ever before, many are desperate for some sort of stability. Part of the attraction of the great outdoors is that sense of dependability, a feeling of absolute, unchanging permanency.

That's a pleasant idea, one we take comfort in. But it's not necessarily true. Think about it: The Grand Canyon becomes deeper and wider every year through erosion. Mount Saint Helens changed dramatically during a volcanic explosion in 1980. Earthquakes can change an area's topography in just a moment.

If you're looking for something more solid than rock, look over the canyons and beyond the mountains.

God is the one truly permanent thing in our life. Mountains and valleys will come and go, but we'll always be at the center of God's attention, the recipients of His unchanging love.

. . . .

Lord, help me remember that the things of this
world will pass away. Free me to more fully
appreciate Your unimaginable glory.

The Colorful Macaw

*"Blessed are those who are persecuted because
of righteousness, for theirs is the kingdom of
heaven. Blessed are you when people insult
you, persecute you and falsely say all kinds of
evil against you because of me."*
MATTHEW 5:10–11 NIV

. . . .

The macaw is a beautiful bird, its red, blue, yellow, white, or green feathers making it one of the most colorful creatures in the world. This amazing avian is easily seen and recognized from a long distance.

The very thing that makes the macaw such a beautiful bird, however, also makes it an easy target for predators. Killers like large cats, other birds, even human beings have a fairly easy time spotting and stalking these birds. It's tough to hide in nature when wearing such vivid colors!

As Christians, we're often easy targets in our "environment," too. The love of Jesus that shows through our lives is frequently the very thing that attracts trouble. But Jesus understands that and assures us in His Word that the kingdom of heaven belongs to us.

He knows when we have trouble. But if we stay true to the faith, we will be richly blessed.

. . . .

*Help me, Lord, always to be on my guard.
Please help me to keep You first in my mind.*

Everything Has a Purpose

There is one glory of the sun, and another
glory of the moon, and another glory of the
stars; for star differs from star in glory.
1 CORINTHIANS 15:41 ESV

. . . .

People who believe the earth came into being by chance can't fathom a God in heaven who spoke the world into existence and now sustains it. But the redeemed know better. We understand that God not only created everything, but He also keeps it in smooth running order. And everything He does has a purpose.

The sun has one kind of glory and the moon another. Individual stars have yet a different glory. Humans don't even know how many stars exist—but God knows the exact number, since He created each one uniquely.

Many people go through life trying to make sense of a supposedly random universe. But we can rest in the knowledge that God isn't fretting or trying to figure it all out. He knows exactly what He's doing.

. . . .

Lord of heaven and earth,
maker of all things, I worship You!

All in Good Time

There is an appointed time for everything.
And there is a time for every event under heaven.
ECCLESIASTES 3:1 NASB

. . . .

In the northern states, there are some clear "signs of the times."

Sap buckets hanging on the maples? It's early spring.

When the leaves on the oaks are as big as squirrels' ears, it's time to plant corn. The corn will be ready to pick two weeks after the silks first appear.

The first healthy apple that drops from the tree means it's autumn—and time to pick the ones that haven't fallen.

When *V*s of geese head south, we know winter will be here soon.

Most of us have a favorite season, and knowing it is coming helps us to get through the times we're not as fond of. But those times known only to God—they can be frustrating.

That why the writer of Ecclesiastes reminded us of God's "appointed times." We're wise to remember that He does everything perfectly—even scheduling!

. . . .

Heavenly Father, help me not to be like an impatient
child in my haste to have my way. Help me to know
that Your ways are perfect and Your timing is right.

In the Dark of Night

*"He alone stretches out the heavens and treads
on the waves of the sea. He is the Maker of
the Bear and Orion, the Pleiades and the
constellations of the south."*
JOB 9:8–9 NIV

. . . .

Those of us who live in cities—even in much smaller towns—often miss one of the greatest testimonies of God's creative power. That's because "light pollution" can obscure the breathtaking view of the countless stars He hung in the heavens.

But out in the country, far from streetlights, illuminated billboards, and twenty-four-hour gas stations, those stars have a chance to speak a great truth to our souls—a truth that the ancient Job, seeing those same stars, readily understood: God made all of them and the vast sky in which they reside.

When you get the chance to enjoy a truly dark night, take advantage of it. Let the Bear, Orion, the Pleiades—and the thousands of other stars visible to the naked eye—point you to the One who alone stretched out the heavens.

. . . .

*Creator God, Your universe is amazing. I thank You
that I'm a part of it—and that I can see You in it!*

Saving the Magnificent Animals

Bring into the boat with you a male and a female
of every kind of animal and bird, as well as a
male and a female of every reptile. . . . Store up
enough food both for yourself and for them.
GENESIS 6:19–21 CEV

. . . .

Noah's ark was a massive vessel—450 feet long by 75 feet wide by 45 feet high. God not only knew how many species would need to be saved, but how much space they'd need and how much food they'd require.

Today, due to overhunting and disruption of habitat, some of the animals Noah rescued face the danger of extinction. Many of the most beloved, magnificent species of our planet— gorillas, rhinos, tigers, and polar bears—are declining.

If God had only wanted to preserve the most "necessary" domestic animals—dogs, cats, and cattle—He could have saved Noah a great deal of trouble. But He wanted to rescue them all. This gives us a sense of God's priorities, and our responsibility as earth's stewards.

God loves people more than animals, true. But He knows that wild creatures enrich our lives, stir our imagination, and give us joy. Let's protect them, preserve their habitats, and ensure that they are here for our children's children to enjoy, as well.

. . . .

God, thank You for the amazing
diversity of animal life You have created.

Greater Than Our Disability

So Mephibosheth lived in Jerusalem,
for he ate at the king's table regularly.
Now he was lame in both feet.
2 SAMUEL 9:13 NASB

. . . .

Can a wheelchair-bound person enjoy the outdoors like those with full use of their limbs? More and more, the answer is *yes*.

Inventors with a heart for the disabled have created "wheelchairs" with motorized tank tracks; heavy-duty, four-wheeled, people-powered chairs, and snow skis fitted with seats, among other things. Physical disability shouldn't keep anyone from experiencing the outdoors.

Neither should our spiritual disabilities keep us from enjoying God. With our prominent character flaws and self-esteem issues, we may sometimes think that closeness to God is impossible. But He "invents" ways of bridging that gap, treating us as King David did the crippled grandson of his predecessor, King Saul. Mephibosheth had done nothing for David—it was only the king's kindness that brought Mephibosheth to the table.

Our king has invited us to dine with Him. God's kindness is greater than our disabilities.

. . . .

Lord, I thank You that You invite me—
with all of my disabilities—to Your table.

The Cathedral of the World

*Which made heaven, and earth, the sea, and
all that therein is: which keepeth truth for ever.*
PSALM 146:6 KJV

. . . .

The Cathedral of the Pines is in the New Hampshire countryside. Envisaged as a "cathedral without walls," this park area was set up as a permanent memorial to those who gave their lives for this country. Now it's a place of retreat and contemplation. The sense of peace there makes it a popular venue for weddings.

But there's a deeper truth implicit in the very name of the place. Humans have built some impressive cathedrals over the centuries. Many will take your breath away, but none of them will be as intricately wonderful as a single tree.

We like to have special places to worship. We feel our God deserves no less. Well, look outside. He already created the grandest, most spectacular place of worship for us. The Cathedral of the Pines is just a very small part of it.

. . . .

*Wherever we are, Lord, be it rush hour traffic, a
garden, a shop, or a park, we are in Your creation—
and we will worship You there!*

A Warning from the Papyrus Marsh

"Can papyrus grow where there is no marsh?
Can reeds flourish where there is no water?
While yet in flower and not cut down, they
wither before any other plant. Such are the
paths of all who forget God; the hope of the
godless man shall perish."

JOB 8:11–13 RSV

. . . .

The answer to this rhetorical question, as any ancient Egyptian could tell you, is *no*. Papyrus can't grow where there is no marsh, and reeds can't flourish without water. You don't even have to cut them down for them to die. They can be in full bloom, but take away the water and they wither. Their stalks will still stand, but they're rattling in the wind—dead.

That's what we're all like without the life-giving Spirit of God. We simply can't survive without the water of His Word. It's important to come to know God, to become familiar with His ways and His Word—but it's also important to *stay* close to Him.

As soon as we become distant in our hearts, we cut off our water supply. Like the papyrus reeds, we begin to wither and die. Don't let that happen to you!

. . . .

Dear Lord, help me to always stay
close to You, never to forget You.

Be on the Lookout

*Be of sober spirit, be on the alert. Your
adversary, the devil, prowls around like a
roaring lion, seeking someone to devour.*
1 PETER 5:8 NASB

. . . .

Have you ever seen a blue jay trying to crack an acorn? Not a task to wish for! Imagine slamming your beak repeatedly against a fairly hard object. And remember, the beak is attached to your head—if you're a jay.

Getting through that nutshell takes close concentration. Jays have to grip a branch and hold the acorn at the same time. Sometimes they lose control and drop the nut. That means a diligent search for it or starting over with a new one.

Beyond the nut cracking, jays pause after every two or three blows to take a sharp look around. They don't have many natural enemies, but they need to be on their guard to keep one of their own from stealing the prize just as the shell is conquered.

Few of us have physical enemies, either—but we need to look up from our work now and then to make sure we don't let pride steal the reward of our labor, or discouragement steal the joy of serving.

. . . .

*Heavenly Father, I thank You for the warnings in
Your Word. Help us to pay attention to all You
bring into our lives and to avoid the temptations
that stand ready to rob us of our reward.*

The Mind's Eye

"I am the good shepherd; I know
my sheep and my sheep know me."
JOHN 10:14 NIV

. . . .

Ever "see something" in the clouds—an elephant, a boat, Abraham Lincoln's profile?

That's because our eyes recognize patterns. In a huge crowd of people, we can recognize the one person we know because our mind remembers the pattern and spatial relationships of a face. We can see those features and know them instantly.

We might recognize a few hundred people by seeing their faces, but God recognizes every single person who's ever lived. Not only does He know us, He's concerned about us in a very personal way. He understands our struggles and celebrates our joys.

God knows us so well that He even knows how many hairs we have. Nobody on earth knows so much about another person, no matter how much he might love that person.

How much God cares for us individually is beyond the reach of our imagination.

. . . .

Lord, allow me glimpses through Your eyes, so I
can begin to appreciate how much You love me.

Longing to Know More

*But I gave no credit to their words, until I came
and mine eyes had seen; and behold, the half
of the greatness of thy wisdom was not told me:
thou exceedest the report that I heard.*
2 CHRONICLES 9:6 DARBY

. . . .

When you see beautiful photos of a place you've never visited, what goes through your mind? *Well, I've seen the pictures, so I guess that's enough.* Probably not. More likely you'd think, *This is gorgeous. I'll have to go there and see it for myself!*

Photos and documentaries of far-off places pique our interest, setting up a longing to travel. But as a picture of a hamburger doesn't quiet the rumbling in our stomach, neither do these beautiful pictures satisfy our wanderlust.

When the Queen of Sheba heard about King Solomon's greatness, she wasn't content to stop there. She had to see it for herself—and she was impressed indeed.

Luke 11:31 (KJV) tells us that "a greater than Solomon" is here. May the glory of Jesus create a longing to know Him more.

. . . .

Lord Jesus, I long to know You more.

A Sense of Peace

The LORD blesses his people with peace.
PSALM 29:11 NIV

. . . .

It's probably safe to say that few outdoors people, whatever their favorite activity, haven't described their time away from everyday life with words such as *peaceful* and *quiet*.

Sometimes we just need to get away from the hustle and busyness of the five- (or six- or seven-) day workweek. The outdoors is one place we can truly isolate ourselves from the cares of the "real" world and just enjoy some peace and relaxation.

King David understood the importance of the peace only God could give him. As the divinely appointed leader of the nation of Israel—serving through some very difficult times—David had plenty to do each and every day. But he always remembered that God was the one source of true peace in the midst of the noise and craziness life brought his way.

God wants us to understand the very same thing—and He can use our time in the outdoors to give us the inner peace we need.

. . . .

Thank You, Lord, for giving me the kind of peace only You can give. And I thank You for using my time in the outdoors to impart that peace to me.

Spirit to Spirit

*Then shall the dust return to the
earth as it was: and the spirit shall
return unto God who gave it.*
ECCLESIASTES 12:7 KJV

. . . .

It takes special equipment for humans to explore the depths of the ocean—and the deeper you want to go, the more sophisticated that equipment becomes. Simply put, human beings were not created to live in water.

In a similar sense, we've all been issued special equipment—our bodies—to live here on earth. Take an informal survey, and most people will probably tell you that we are human bodies with a spirit. In reality, we are spirits with a human body. There's quite a difference between the two views.

Our bodies are very limited, designed to last around seventy years. No matter how well we take care of ourselves, these bodies will ultimately fail. But the spirit? That's a different matter entirely.

. . . .

*Lord, help me always to remember that it's my
spirit—not this body—that's eternal. May I
connect with You from deep within.*

Calling Out Boldly

*Therefore let us draw near with confidence
to the throne of grace, so that we may receive
mercy and find grace to help in time of need.*
HEBREWS 4:16 NASB

. . . .

The exploration of caves is called spelunking. (Some have defined the term *spelunk* as "the sound of a forehead hitting a stalactite after running in terror in pitch blackness.")

Wandering about in cold, damp darkness isn't everyone's idea of fun, but it can be instructive for all of us. For example, if you've made a bad turn in a cave and can't find your way back, disregard the impulse to move and simply stay put. Shout every couple of minutes to help your partner or a rescue party locate you (and probably carry you out to treat that ugly bruise on your forehead).

It's not only in the blackness of a cave that we lose our bearings. Life can be dark, confusing, and frightening at times, but God's advice is like that of the spelunking corps: resist the impulse to run. Instead, simply rest where you are and call out to Him. God's ears are always open, and He's always ready to rescue.

. . . .

*Lord, may I draw near to You today,
calling out boldly for Your help.*

Seen from Above

He has made everything beautiful in its time.
He has also set eternity in the human heart;
yet no one can fathom what God has
done from beginning to end.
ECCLESIASTES 3:11 NIV

. . . .

Butterflies have a spectacular array of patterns and colors decorating their wings—on the top sides! But the undersides of their wings are seldom so striking. Often the patterns and colors are pale imitations; sometimes they are completely black.

Which side does the butterfly see? Does a butterfly on a stalk of grass see itself as we see it, looking down from above? Or does it see the dull, black side? Would it even understand our concept of beauty?

From time to time we might give in to self-doubt and despair, seeing only the darker sides of our personalities. But the little butterfly is a constant reminder that, no matter what we might think of ourselves, there is more to us. We are all beautiful to the One who sees us from above.

. . . .

Lord, help us realize that thoughts of inadequacy
do not originate with You—and are not true.
You are the Creator of wonders, and we are
Your most favored creation.

Avoiding Cursing the Earth

*The earth is defiled by its people; they have
disobeyed the laws, violated the statutes and
broken the everlasting covenant. Therefore a
curse consumes the earth.*

ISAIAH 24:5–6 NIV

· · · · · · ·

At times, the Israelites brought curses upon their land, and if you read Isaiah 24, you'll see there were famines caused by prolonged droughts, earthquakes, and destruction caused by foreign invasions. These were divine curses—but it was the people's disobedient, selfish choices that brought these calamities upon them.

This passage has significance for us today as well: the economic earthquakes that have shaken our society are in many ways a result of selfish decisions and unwise policies. And for centuries, we have defiled the earth by releasing pollutants into the land, the water, and the air. "Therefore a curse consumes the earth."

Our self-inflicted curses have spiritual roots in humanity's greed, selfishness, and unconcern for future generations. But there is hope: if we repent, we can stop defiling the earth and begin to undo the damage. Even if society doesn't change, we can, as individuals. God will always reward us for our obedience.

· · · · · · ·

*God, may I never contribute to
cursing the world You gave us.*

Only the Lonely

*"I am a brother of jackals,
and a companion of ostriches."*
JOB 30:29 NKJV

. . . .

Job lived in Uz, an ancient land bordering the desert, so he was familiar with jackals and ostriches, creatures that survived by eking out a meager living in an unforgiving wasteland. To Job, they epitomized living a second-rate life. And Job felt like he was one of them.

In practically the same breath, Job told God, "I cry out to You, but You do not answer me. . . . You spoil my success. . . . When I looked for good, evil came to me" (Job 30:20, 22, 26). Ever felt like that? Does it sometimes seem like God doesn't answer prayer? Think of business deals that have gone wrong, of inexplicable reverses, and of personal tragedies. Put in that context, Job's honest groans strike a chord in most of us today.

Of course, God hadn't deserted Job, no matter how Job felt at the time. And God hasn't deserted you, either—even though He allows adversity to test you. Despite all that Job suffered, he remained faithful. In the end, when God had finished the testing, the Lord restored Job's fortunes.

. . . .

*Dear God, no matter how bad I feel right now,
help me to hang in there and trust You.*

The Importance of Strength

"Do not grieve, for the joy
of the LORD is your strength."
NEHEMIAH 8:10 NIV

. . . .

What fisherman hasn't hooked into the really big one—then wondered if the knots would hold strong against that fish struggling for freedom at the end of the line?

Anglers understand the importance of using equipment strong enough for the size and type of fish they're after. They also recognize that their equipment is only as strong as the knots they use to attach their lures to their line.

There's a similar principle in our daily walk with Jesus. It's important to equip ourselves with strong faith, a firm grasp of scripture, and a consistent, abiding prayer life. But unless we tie all those things together with the simple *joy* of knowing and serving God, they won't hold firm when tests come our way.

Where does your strength come from? The power you need to live the Christian life depends on your allowing the "knot" of God's joy to dwell strongly and consistently within you.

. . . .

Lord, help me to remember that my walk
with You is only as strong as the inner
joy I allow You to place within me.

Don't Forget to Look Up

He determines the number of the
stars and calls them each by name.
PSALM 147:4 NIV

. . . .

When we're out fishing, hunting, hiking—whatever we like to do outside—it's easy to become so focused on our particular activity that we forget to look around us and see the amazing reflection of God in His creation.

The God who created all you see around has not only put those things in place, but has each one numbered and named. And still He cares for you! When King David looked out at the vast majesty of creation, he was moved to ask, "What is mankind that you are mindful of them, human beings that you care for them?" (Psalm 8:4).

When you're enjoying your favorite activities, don't forget to look up. Get a glimpse of the greatness, the creativity, and the splendor of God. Then consider the fact that this very same God thinks about you daily. . .and cares for you deeply!

. . . .

Father God, help me to see all of creation as a reflection
of who You really are and what You can really do.

Two Kinds of Climbing

*Look! The wages you failed to pay the workers who
mowed your fields are crying out against you.*
JAMES 5:4 NIV

. . . .

Many measure their lives based on profit, victory, and achievement. Others gauge their achievement by the lives they touch, the joys they share, and the people they help along the way.

Climbing—whether a mountain or the corporate ladder—can be exhausting. At the end of a business day, the weariness is both physical and emotional. Fighting corporate wars can leave us scarred and empty, without comfort in our old age.

Climbing a mountain is tiring, too, though that toll is easily overcome by a good meal, laughter with friends, and a good night's rest. The natural high and sense of accomplishment lasts for years.

Jesus Christ wants to free us from the treadmill of worldly achievement and replace it with a walk in high places—one that fills the emptiness and soothes the wounds. Will we take Him up on His offer?

. . . .

*Dear God, free me from the wars of life and put
me on Your mountain path. May I be bold,
excited, and all out for You today, Lord.*

Always Be Prepared

*Always be prepared to give an answer
to everyone who asks you to give the
reason for the hope that you have.*
1 PETER 3:15 NIV

. . . .

No matter what your outdoor activity of choice—camping, hiking, fishing—it's vital that you go into that activity prepared for anything that could come your way. Failure to do so can keep the enjoyment quotient down; sometimes it can lead to danger. Outdoor life is filled with the unexpected, which is why we need to prepare ourselves for anything and everything.

That's as true in the "real world"—where you live, work, and care for your family and friends—as it is in the outdoor realm. It's also true when it comes to using your enjoyment of the outdoors as a vehicle for sharing your faith.

Few things in life help form bonds of friendship like sharing in outdoor adventures. So when you're at the lake, the river, the mountain, or on that beautiful hiking trail, be prepared—because the person you're enjoying those things with just might need to hear about what's most important to you: the amazing, hope-inspiring love of God.

. . . .

*Remind me daily, my gracious heavenly Father, to be
prepared for whatever and whoever You send my way.*

God's Protective Boma

"Have You not made a hedge around him, around his household, and around all that he has on every side? You have blessed the work of his hands."
JOB 1:10 NKJV

. . . .

When the devil complained that God had put a "hedge" around Job, he wasn't talking about a cedar hedge. Back in Bible times, people planted hedges that doubled as deadly barbed-wire barriers—bushes with coiling, interlocking branches full of long, razor-sharp thorns.

If you've seen any old Tarzan movies, you'll remember that every time a safari camped for the night in the African wild, they cut down thorn bushes and built a *boma*, an enclosed camp, so they could sleep in safety. Even hungry lions didn't try to force their way through such a barrier.

Peter warns us that the devil is, in fact, like a roaring lion, seeking someone to devour (1 Peter 5:8), so it behooves us to seek God's protection. There was a condition to receiving God's protection: Job "feared God and shunned evil" (Job 1:1).

In Job's case—and sometimes in ours—God temporarily removed his protection to prove that Job would love Him regardless. But with that point proved, God restored the hedge.

. . . .

*Lord, help me to fear You and avoid evil,
so that I can enjoy Your protection.*

The Waves Obey God

You rule the raging of the sea;
when its waves rise, you still them.
PSALM 89:9 ESV

. . . .

Insurance companies write provisions into their policies concerning "acts of God." They're referring to weather-related damage of which the insurers are quite specific about what they will and will not cover.

We humans know inherently that weather is beyond our control. But have we considered that it's completely within God's power? He can command sea waves to rise and then be calm again.

Though He's not obligated to explain His reasoning, God has a purpose in everything He does. Perhaps His control over the sea is designed to make us marvel at His power. From our limited human perspective, ocean waves seem completely out of control. But God created them to obey Him—and they do that willingly. Each wave that crashes onto the shoreline testifies to God's power.

. . . .

Lord, I stand in awe of Your majesty and power. You
and only You have the ability to calm a raging sea.

After the Summit

Then shalt thou walk in thy way safely,
and thy foot shall not stumble.
PROVERBS 3:23 KJV

. . . .

That moment when you reach the peak of a mountain, it's like the moment when you finally "get" God. It's wonderful, but your work isn't done. Having climbed that mountain, many an inexperienced hiker thinks it will be easier on the way down. That's when maps get neglected and steps get careless. But more hikers get lost or injured on the way down from a summit than do on the way up.

In the same way your life, when you come to faith, despite what you might have expected, won't all be sunshine and roses. Oh, it will be wonderful—but you still need to watch your footing and check your direction.

Too much bother? In the elation of conquering a mountain, or finding God, it can sometimes seem so, but paying attention and walking with care is what will see you safely home in both instances.

. . . .

Lord Jesus, finding You in our hearts seems like
the ultimate achievement. . .but following in Your
footsteps will be the crowning glory of a life.

Mountain Man, Family Man

*If any one does not provide for his relatives,
and especially for his own family, he has disowned
the faith and is worse than an unbeliever.*
1 TIMOTHY 5:8 RSV

. . . .

Jedediah Strong Smith was a "mountain man," one of those hardy fur trappers who opened the unmapped American West in the 1820s. The first white man to cross the Sierra Nevada, walk into California from the American frontier, and taste the bitter waters of the Great Salt Lake, he faced danger from wolves, grizzlies, Indians, and the extreme, unforgiving conditions of the land itself. Why? As a devout Christian, Smith trapped beaver to provide an income for his needy parents.

"It is that I may be able to help [them]. . .that I face every danger," he wrote his older brother. "It is for this that I traverse the mountains covered with eternal snow. . .pass over the sandy plains in the heat of summer. . .go for days without eating. . . . Let it be the greatest pleasure that we can enjoy. . . to smooth the pillow of [our parents'] age and, as much as in us lies, take from them all cause of trouble."

. . . .

*Father, teach me the blessing of obeying Your
commandment, "Honor thy father and thy mother."*

Hearing God in the Quiet

After the fire came a gentle whisper. When Elijah
heard it, he pulled his cloak over his face and
went out and stood at the mouth of the cave.
1 KINGS 19:12–13 NIV

. . . .

It's easy sometimes to hear the spectacular sounds of nature and think of the magnificent power of God. The ear-jolting clap of thunder, the roaring of a waterfall, the relentless howl of a strong wind rushing through the trees—all these things remind us of the awesome power of God.

The Bible includes many accounts of God talking to mankind through the spectacular. He talked to Moses through a burning bush and to Job through a whirlwind. But when the deeply discouraged prophet Elijah wanted to hear from God, he had to listen past some of nature's most spectacular demonstrations of power—a powerful wind, an earthquake, then a fire.

It's an awesome thought to realize that God can speak to us in any way He sees fit. But it's also comforting to know that when we need strength and encouragement, all we need to do is listen for His gentle voice above all the noises around us.

. . . .

Thank You, Lord, for knowing when I need to hear
Your voice in a spectacular way. . .and for knowing
when I need to hear Your gentle whisper.

A Fresh Burst of Energy

So we built the wall and the whole wall
was joined together to half its height,
for the people had a mind to work.
NEHEMIAH 4:6 NASB

. . . .

It's amazing what we can accomplish when we set our mind to it. But we have to resist the urge to quit when we get tired or frustrated along the way.

Think about your experience in the outdoors. We've all been tempted to turn back at the first cramp in our side or pain in the shin. But seeing the trail marker near the end of the journey brings cheer to our heart. Glimpsing the peak gives us a spurt of energy that propels us to the top.

Our spiritual life is a long journey, filled with difficulties and reverses. But when we sense that we've reached a milestone of some sort, it's like God is encouraging us: "You can make this happen! This is doable!"

Today, let's be like Nehemiah, with "a mind to work." Between us and God, we can accomplish amazing things.

. . . .

Lord, encourage me to continue—
and keep working in my life!

Counting the Stars

And [God] brought [Abram] outside and said,
"Look toward heaven, and number the stars,
if you are able to number them." Then he said
to him, "So shall your offspring be."
GENESIS 15:5 ESV

. . . .

In 2003, a group of Australian astronomers conducted a study using two of the world's most powerful telescopes in an attempt to number the stars. They found some ten thousand galaxies and estimated that there are approximately seventy thousand million million million (or seventy sextillion) stars. The astronomers said this number was limited by the range of modern telescopes and that, in reality, the actual number of stars "could be infinite."

Step outside your house tonight and look up into the sky. Try to number the stars you can see, keeping in mind that you have only a microscopic view of the big picture. Once you're overwhelmed by the task—as Abram surely was—whisper a prayer of thanks to God for His willingness to make, and ability to keep, His promise to Abram and his descendents. Because through that promise, *you* found salvation.

. . . .

Father, I can't even fathom the number of stars—but I
thank You for keeping Your incredible promise to Abram.

The Downside of Partridge Economics

*As the partridge sitteth on eggs, and hatcheth
them not; so he that getteth riches, and not by
right, shall leave them in the midst of his days,
and at his end shall be a fool.*
JEREMIAH 17:11 KJV

. . . .

The rock partridge lives in many countries of the Middle East and southeast Europe, and is a favorite with hunters because of its stealth and swiftness in running through the underbrush. In Bible times, there was no challenge like bringing down a "mountain chicken" with a well-aimed arrow.

The partridge was cunning and often got away—but to do so it had to leave its eggs behind. Since partridges build their nests on the ground, hunters would often get the eggs. The Bible compares the partridge to a corrupt man who comes by riches unethically and warns that before his "nest eggs" hatch, he'll either be found out or die.

It's great to be a shrewd investor and to take advantage of business opportunities. But let's be sure that in all our financial dealings we're honest, never taking an unfair advantage of others.

. . . .

*God, help me to reflect Your
values in all my financial dealings.*

Fully Equipped

The Spirit of the LORD was upon him, and he
judged Israel. He went out to war, and the LORD
gave Cushan-rishathaim king of Mesopotamia into
his hand. . . . So the land had rest forty years.
JUDGES 3:10–11 ESV

. . . .

Preparing for a hike, we review and check our equipment. Soldiers heading into battle do the same thing, because the proper equipment is vital. It protects us and enables us to perform our tasks.

Israel's first judge, Othniel, undoubtedly carried all the military paraphernalia of his day—sword, shield, helmet, and more. He challenged the enemies of his people, defeated them, and brought forty years of rest to the land. In the final analysis, though, it wasn't Othniel's equipment that brought him victory—it was the Holy Spirit of God.

As believers, we have the same Spirit living in us. God provides us with that same power to fight our battles—and we can have the same results.

Let's fight the good fight today, gaining the victories that often seem elusive. Count the Spirit as your ally. Stand today and fight!

. . . .

Father, help me to realize the power of the
Holy Spirit in my life. Help me to fight and
defeat the enemies of my spiritual life.

Which Way Then?

*When the days of his ministry
were completed, he went back home.*
LUKE 1:23 HCSB

. . . .

Each year salmon, which have spent most of their life at sea, begin an amazing journey. Somehow, they return to the river where they first met the sea and begin to swim upstream.

Some salmon have been known to travel up to a thousand miles against the current, rising thousands of feet above sea level. Along the way they have to get past fishermen, waterfalls, even bears. Many never make it, but they all try. Why? They're driven by a powerful urge to get home before they spawn and die.

Fish simply follow their instincts. Humans are compelled by God's Spirit to "come home" to the Creator who made them. Sadly, many people reason their way out of His love and mercy, ending up like those salmon that perish on the journey.

Today, let's make two commitments: to be sure we're personally following God's call to come home, and that we're inviting others around us to come along.

. . . .

*Lord, please give me the strength to go
against the flow. Other forces want my
soul—but You're calling me home!*

The Things People Believe

*In the beginning God created
the heaven and the earth.*
GENESIS 1:1 KJV

. . . .

How did the universe come into being?

Well, the "Standard Scientific Model for the Creation of the Universe" says that nothing (or everything) exploded. No one knows why. It flew out in every direction at a uniform speed (which no explosion actually does). Then, amazingly, it stopped. It spent a while settling down to a uniform temperature, and then it started expanding again! Now, when scientists reckon the expansion should be slowing down, it is actually speeding up. Concepts like "dark matter," "dark energy," and "dark flow" are needed to fill holes in the model to make it work the way scientists think it should.

Men and women of faith believe God said, "Let there be light: and there was light." We get ridiculed for it sometimes. But the people who laugh tend to put their faith in the Standard Scientific Model.

Now, that's just silly, but, being nice folk, we'll try not to laugh.

. . . .

*God, when the big questions are asked, You are always
the most likely answer. Help us show a world that
doesn't want to hear. For their sake.*

The Tranquility of Nature

*What do people get for all the toil and anxious
striving with which they labor under the sun? All
their days their work is grief and pain; even at night
their minds do not rest. This too is meaningless.*
ECCLESIASTES 2:22–23 NIV

. . . .

We all deal with stress. And most of us are probably aware of the link between stress and our physical and emotional health.

God has given us many ways to help us reduce the stresses of life—it's just so easy to overlook them. Sitting on a porch swing, closing our eyes, and listening to the wind in the trees is but one. The gentle sound of rain, the chirping of birds, the ebb and flow of water against a shore, the sound of children playing, or a gentle spring breeze rippling through our hair can bring peace and tranquility into our spirits—if only we'll let them.

Maybe we can't physically enjoy those moments—but we can go there in our mind. So much of today's world is simply noise. Take some time to rest your eyes, ears, and mind. It's of the utmost value to a contented life.

. . . .

*Father, as I experience Your creation, may it lead me
into a peace-filled meditation that gives me tranquility.*

Seeking God's Blessing

He will also bless. . .the fruit of your ground, your
grain and your wine and your oil, the increase of
your herds and the young of your flock.
DEUTERONOMY 7:13 ESV

. . . .

God has set in motion a particular program regarding sowing and reaping. He expects farmers to plant their seeds, nourish the plants, and then harvest the crops, just as He requires ranchers to do the hard work of feeding, breeding, and tending their herds. But all of that is vain if God doesn't bless the work.

That's not to say that farmers and ranchers (or people in any other profession) are cursed if their work doesn't prosper. God has specific plans for each of us, and sometimes those plans involve hardships. But keeping the right perspective— one that recognizes God's right to rule in the affairs of people—should motivate us to continue the work He has called us to do, while leaving the results to Him.

When we remain faithful, the times He does choose to prosper our work become even sweeter.

. . . .

Father, I ask that You would bless
the work You've put in front of me.

Your Place in Creation

*My frame was not hidden from you when I was
made in the secret place, when I was woven together
in the depths of the earth. Your eyes saw my
unformed body; all the days ordained for me were
written in your book before one of them came to be.*
PSALM 139:15–16 NIV

. . . .

When you're outdoors enjoying the beauty and splendor of God's created world—the mountains, the rivers, the oceans, everything He made—it's only natural to wonder exactly where you fit in with everything you see.

Viewing the whole of creation—as far as that's possible for us—can make us feel small and insignificant. And while God loves humble hearts, He also wants us to understand that we have far more value, with far more importance in His eternal plans, than any of the nonhuman creation we see around us.

It's impossible for our minds to fully comprehend God's love, or to understand that far before the foundations of the world we were planned and appointed a place in His eternal story of creation.

Whether we understand it or not, it's true—and it proves just how much God loves and values each one of us.

. . . .

*Thank You, Father God, for the place to which
You appointed me in the grand scheme of creation.*

The Next Day's Journey

*"You are already clean because of
the word which I have spoken to you."*
JOHN 15:3 NKJV

. . . .

High up in a horse's saddle, things are different. We see a different perspective of our surroundings. We travel a greater distance than we would on foot.

After a long day on the trail, though, the animal will need care and grooming. We'll offer it hay and water. We'll clear its tail of ticks and tangles. We'll scour its hooves for mud and manure.

There are parallels here to our own spiritual journey. God has given us His saddle-height view of the world, helping us to see life from a loftier perspective. At His direction, we've traveled further down the road of transformation than many other people have. Through His Word, we can be filled and cleansed.

The Bible restores our faith, purifies our mind, and strengthens our resolve. Without it, we won't be ready for the next day's journey.

. . . .

Lord Jesus, speak—for Your words are life to me.

Lord of the Stone

*Now on the first day of the week Mary
Magdalene came to the tomb early,
while it was still dark, and saw that the
stone had been taken away from the tomb.*

JOHN 20:1 ESV

. . . .

Many of us who love the outdoors are accustomed to waking before the sun rises. The solitude and peacefulness to be found outside are well worth the early hour. We go forth seeking an encounter with God, knowing He'll show up.

When Mary Magdalene rose early to visit Jesus' tomb, she had no such expectations. She was simply zealous in her love for Christ and wanted to show her respects. So imagine her surprise when she saw that the stone door of the tomb had been rolled away. Mary first wept, thinking Jesus' body had been stolen—but quickly learned from angels that Jesus had risen from the dead. Soon, the One who had conquered the tomb, the stone that sealed it, and death itself, appeared to her.

As you seek God in the wilderness, go with the knowledge that He will meet you there.

. . . .

*Father, draw me to a secret place
today and show me Yourself in it.*

"The Grunion Are Running!"

God saw all that he had made,
and it was very good.
GENESIS 1:31 NIV

. . . .

There are Californians who live for the announcement, "The grunion are running!" No, it's not a new marathon; it's a unique creation event experienced over a brief period on certain southern beaches.

Don't tell any true believer that the unique silverfish called a grunion is a happenstance of nature. No! It's just one seeming "oddity" in God's grand design that He called, "very good."

For reasons known only to their Creator, the slippery little silverfish beach themselves as "couples" by the thousands. With a little dance, eggs are buried in the sand and fertilized. Later, the grunion that can avoid predators make their way to the sea their parents started from.

Like the swallows that return to Capistrano every year, into each of these seven-inch fish God has planted a compass that points toward home—the beach from whence they were born.

. . . .

Father, keep me aware of my spiritual compass; to
always remember whose I am and where I'm heading.

Do Your Part

*And he will give rain for the seed with which
you sow the ground, and bread, the produce of
the ground, which will be rich and plenteous.*
ISAIAH 30:23 ESV

. . . .

M ost Christians know that God is all-powerful.
We realize that He provides the soil and weather conditions to make crops flourish. But He could also easily plant
the seeds, irrigate them, and root out the weeds. He could
simply drop food from heaven, as on rare occasions He's chosen to do. But, generally speaking, farmers and gardeners
have to sow their seeds, care for the plants, and take in the
harvest. From there, human effort turns the raw material into
the foods we enjoy.

We are totally dependent upon God for our food—but human beings are also completely involved in the process.

That's a striking picture of the Christian life. God sup-
plies all the power. We just have to walk in it. If we don't do
our part, our spiritual lives wither and die. If we do follow
through, God grows rich and plentiful spiritual fruit into us.

. . . .

*Father, I thank You for providing all I need to
flourish spiritually—as I walk in Your ways.*

Living on the Edge

*By faith he made his home in the promised
land like a stranger in a foreign country; he
lived in tents, as did Isaac and Jacob, who were
heirs with him of the same promise.*
HEBREWS 11:9 NIV

. . . .

Most outdoors people get a rush out of tent life in the great outdoors. Weeklong fishing trips or family campouts have their difficulties and inconveniences, but they're exhilarating!

It's a different story when you live in a tent *full-time* like Abraham, Isaac, and Jacob. They dwelled in Beersheba and Beer Lahai Roi in the Negev, the arid south of Canaan. As Isaiah 30:6 says, the Negev was "a land of hardship and distress, of lions and lionesses, of adders and darting snakes."

What drove these men to pitch their tents there? They needed a toehold in Canaan and they believed God's promise—that He would give them the entire land—so they were willing to make their home in a region of "hardship and distress." What endurance. What faith.

The next time you feel ready to give up, remember the patriarchs living right on the edge, their tent pegs pounded deep into the Promised Land.

. . . .

*God, give me the faith that if I just believe and hold
on to Your promises, You'll come through for me.*

Even Trees Know the Master's Voice

Instead of the thorn shall come up the fir tree,
and instead of the brier shall come up the myrtle
tree: and it shall be to the LORD for a name,
for an everlasting sign that shall not be cut off.
ISAIAH 55:13 KJV

. . . .

How does a tree know how high it's supposed to grow? What makes the leaves appear when they do, then turn colors and fall off? Why do leaves turn up just before a storm?

When God spoke the world into existence, He placed inside each living thing a knowledge of its perfect purpose. His will for each life, whether tree, bush, animal, or person, is carefully imbedded within, though we human beings often rebel against it.

The next time you walk among trees, think about the God who gave each one its purpose. Take a moment to contemplate the complexity of creation. Each of those trees, every rock, all the blades of grass know their Creator. They recognize Him when He speaks their name across the universe.

Will we listen as He speaks to us today?

. . . .

Today, Lord, may I truly see Your creation,
the wondrous glory of Your handiwork.

Resting and Recreating. . .in Peace

"Peace be with you!"
JOHN 20:26 NIV

. . . .

Ask some people why they enjoy spending their weekends in the outdoors, and they'll tell you it's so they can enjoy a little peace and quiet.

There is something truly soothing and relaxing about being in the wild, away from the noise of home, away from the distractions life brings, away from the busyness of the everyday. These are the places where you hear the rushing of water rather than the rushing traffic, the singing of birds rather than the sounds of people arguing over a parking spot, the sound of nature as God created it rather than the sounds of human "civilization." These are the places where you can be alone with your thoughts and with your God. . .in total, uninterrupted peace.

A lot of men and women spend a lot of time in the outdoors without truly knowing what they're looking for. But for those who spend that time with God, they know that they are looking for one thing: peace—the peace only God can give them.

. . . .

Thank You, God, for giving me peace—Your peace!
Thank You, too, for giving me a natural setting
in which I can fully enjoy that peace.

In the Full Light of Day

The path of the righteous is like the morning sun,
shining ever brighter till the full light of day.
PROVERBS 4:18 NIV

. . . .

A couple was hiking and camping in a wilderness area. Rising early one morning, they packed their camp by lantern and hiked a length of trail by flashlight to a scenic overlook. Upon arriving, they dropped their packs and sat on a large rock, huddling together for warmth.

As the morning sun began to peek over the mountains, it slowly painted the valley below in blues and greens and the sky above in breathtaking reds and purples. But only when the sun was fully up and shining brightly could they see, far below them, the riverside trail they'd be taking that day.

That's a good picture of our lives. We spend a lot of time living and working in the dark—or by the limited light of our own wisdom. It's only when we let the light of God's Word shine on our lives that we can see where our true path lies.

. . . .

Creator God, help me to see the path You
have set for me by the light of Your Word.

Ancient Landmark

*Do not move an ancient boundary
stone set up by your ancestors.*
PROVERBS 22:28 NIV

. . . .

Two children cut over the hills in a direction they'd never hiked before.

They walked through overgrown fields that had once been pasture, clambered over toppled stone walls, and crawled under rusted barbed wire. They followed a grassy roadbed past the moss-covered stone foundation of a long-gone house. A tree was growing where the kitchen might have been.

Then they saw the barn—a strange, abandoned, haunting sight—built into the hillside at the edge of a wild glade. No roof. No siding. A rotting thick plank floor. Massive hand-hewn beams, rising white and skeletal against the backdrop of the emerald forest. Farm implements—antiques of cast iron and wood, older than any they had ever seen—lay inside.

It was an ancient landmark untouched by anything but time, a boundary at the intersection of the present and past. Did anyone still tell stories of the generations that had lived and loved here?

At last, the children walked back the way they'd come—changed somehow, and challenged by things they'd seen but didn't know.

. . . .

*Father, give me ears to hear the wisdom of my elders, the
lessons of days gone past, Your truths that never change.*

Mudball

*For we are his workmanship, created in Christ
Jesus for good works, which God prepared
beforehand so that we would walk in them.*
EPHESIANS 2:10 NASB

. . . .

For decades, nearly all professional baseballs have been prepared with Blackburne's Rubbing Mud, taken from a secret location in the Delaware River.

In baseball's earlier years, various leagues tried a number of things to deal with shiny, slippery new balls—mud from the playing field, ash, shoe polish, even tobacco juice! Nothing worked quite right. Then Lena Blackburne, a coach and former player, discovered the special mud formula. Today, every baseball is rubbed down with this important goo before each game.

God often seems to prepare His people in the same way. We like to put on a shiny, clean appearance for others, but God has a way of stripping us of all such pretense. Many Christians have gone through messes (been dragged through the mud) before they are just right for the Lord's purposes.

Have you had a fairly easy life, free of major troubles? God can use you. Have you experienced terrible problems—even to the point you considered your life a total mess? God can *especially* use you!

. . . .

*Lord, please help me to walk in the
good works You've prepared for me.*

A God Who Creates and Sustains

*"I say to you, unless a grain of wheat falls
into the ground and dies, it remains alone;
but if it dies, it produces much grain."*
JOHN 12:24 NKJV

. . . .

Have you ever considered the spectacle of nature as it undergoes its annual cycle of birth, life, and death. . .then repeats the very same process the very same way the following year?

Consider, for example, the stone fly. Fly fishermen know that each spring, the stone fly nymph crawls onto dry land, sheds its skin, mates. . .then deposits its eggs back into the river and dies. The process ensures another generation of stone flies, but also provides food for the birds and fish that live near the river—not to mention a great season of fly-fishing!

These things don't happen by chance. The same God who set all things in motion works year-round to sustain them, to bring them back to exactly where they need to be at exactly the right time.

If God cares that much for stone flies, think how much He cares for you!

. . . .

*Thank You, God, for sustaining Your creation,
for keeping all things moving and growing
as they have from the very beginning.*

Don't Lose Your Grip!

Therefore, let him who thinks he
stands take heed that he does not fall.
1 CORINTHIANS 10:12 NASB

. . . .

In the 1545 book *Toxophilus*, Roger Ascham presented what he saw as the essential points of archery: standing, nocking, drawing, holding, and loosing. We would call Ascham's "holding" *aiming*.

Many things have to be done well in directing an arrow to the mark. Our results are best when the essentials become habit.

But it's still easy to miss. The archer only needs to stop aiming before loosing, or to stop holding before he is satisfied with his aim. Changing his stance at the moment of loosing will also result in an errant shot.

The Hebrew and Greek words translated *sin* both literally mean "to miss the mark." It's easy for us to miss the mark if we let our eyes stray from the goal—or if we fail to stand for God's truth. If our aim is perfect but we relax our hold at the moment of temptation, we will miss God's mark.

But when it becomes a habit to obey God, we will rarely miss the mark!

. . . .

Father in heaven, I thank You for warning us against
letting our attention wander amid temptations.

Weighing In

*I will not be mastered by anything. . . . The body. . .
is. . .meant. . .for the Lord. . . . Do you not know
that your bodies are members of Christ himself?*
1 CORINTHIANS 6:12–13, 15 NIV

. . . .

Those Corinthian Christians had problems! Besides their sexual issues, undisciplined eating and drinking were apparently taking a toll on their position in the body of Christ.

The apostle Paul was concerned for the Corinthians' physical needs as well as their spiritual growth. His advice was—and is—for those whose various appetites have sidetracked their relationship with God.

Yes, it's possible for our physical eating to interfere with our spiritual health. Maybe we're carrying too many pounds and presenting a poor image of Christ to the world. Or maybe we're obsessed with our bodies and overlooking who we are spiritually.

If you have a daily appointment with the bathroom scale, remember that the race will be won by those with an honest, balanced perspective on health. God's people acknowledge a need for divine intervention in matters physical as well as spiritual.

. . . .

*Father, You call my body a temple of the Holy Spirit—
so please give me the willpower to care for it with
the diligence I care for my house or car.*

The Master Artist

"You alone are the LORD. You made the heavens,
even the highest heavens, and all their starry
host, the earth and all that is on it, the seas and
all that is in them. You give life to everything,
and the multitudes of heaven worship you."
NEHEMIAH 9:6 NIV

. . . .

Driving through the Ozark hills south toward the Boston Mountains can be an awe-inspiring trip. At times, the angle of the highway is such that you feel you might drive right into the heavens. The richness of the blue sky, the brilliance of the sun, the bulk of the mountains, and the beauty of the scenery provide a breathtaking panorama, better than any painting you've ever seen in a museum.

God, the Master Artist, has unveiled a work that gives a slight glimpse into the majesty of His entire creation. When you think of this planet traveling 67,000 miles an hour around a sun 93 million miles away—all of it traveling some 500,000 miles an hour around only one of the billions of galaxies—how can that be anything other than a spiritual experience?

. . . .

Father, You created everything we see either by
Your own hand or the hands of Your creation.
How easily You can handle my problems!

Learning in the Jungle

Let us go, we pray thee, unto Jordan, and take
thence every man a beam, and let us make us a
place there, where we may dwell.
2 KINGS 6:2 KJV

. . . .

The floodplain of the Jordan River was miles wide in places, a forbidding region of thick forests, choked undergrowth, and swamps. It was also infested with wild beasts such as lions. Small wonder that it was practically unexplored until the nineteenth century.

Now, some one hundred young men had gathered around the prophet Elisha to learn from him, but the place where they were meeting was too small. To escape the crowds and find enough wood to build a large dwelling, they entered the Jordan River valley.

It may seem exciting to have studied under the prophet Elisha in the jungles of the Jordan—but it was probably stifling hot, full of mosquitoes, and constantly prowled by wild beasts.

If these men were willing to endure all that, shouldn't we be ready to miss an hour of sleep or entertainment to learn more about God, or drive across town to attend a prayer meeting?

. . . .

God, please help me to get away from
it all at times to learn more about You.

April Showers

*"I will make them and the places surrounding
my hill a blessing. I will send down showers in
season; there will be showers of blessing."*
EZEKIEL 34:26 NIV

. . . .

Droughts are tough on farmers and others who make a living outside—and also on those of us who simply enjoy the outdoors. Lack of rain can dry up a fisherman's favorite streams and lakes, and white-water rafters know that prolonged drought removes some of the thrill of floating down their favorite river. Drought can even interfere with camping and hiking, as authorities in some areas are forced to curtail those activities out of concern for fires.

Knowing this, we who love the outdoors should view rain as a gift—sometimes a very timely gift—from our Father in heaven.

If you're ever tempted to complain when a little rain dampens your outdoor activity, just remember that rain, too, is a gift from God—and that it's absolutely essential to allowing you to enjoy your time in the outdoors.

. . . .

*Father God, I thank You for sending the
rains that make it possible for me to
enjoy my favorite outdoor activities.*

Do as I Do

As you know, like a father with his own children,
we encouraged, comforted, and implored each
one of you to walk worthy of God.
1 THESSALONIANS 2:11–12 HCSB

. . . .

Many animals live by instinct, but some act based on their training in the pack.

Lions teach their cubs to hunt in the field. Monkeys learn to make certain calls to warn others of approaching predators, their on-the-job training clarifying which sounds are the right ones.

In a similar way, God has given us wisdom that we can share with others. We have storehouses of experiences—both good and bad—that will help younger men and women succeed in life.

During Bible times, the apostle Paul shared his wisdom the same way animals pass their teachings on—by example. Let's make "Do as I do" our rule rather than just "Do as I say."

. . . .

Lord, please give me Your strength today
so that younger men and women can
see what a godly life looks like.

Ingenuity and Improvisation

*Jesus saith unto him, I am the way, the truth, and
the life: no man cometh unto the Father, but by me.*
JOHN 14:6 KJV

. . . .

Few of us pursue the brand of adventure embraced by television's "Survivorman." Carrying his own cameras, Les Stroud spends seven days in a hostile wilderness, without food, shelter, fresh water, or tools, relying on his own ingenuity and improvisation to live.

But Stroud's experience pales in comparison with that of James Lovell, Jack Swigert, and Fred Haise, astronauts of the Apollo 13 mission. On April 13, 1970, an explosion aboard their moon-bound spacecraft critically limited power, heat, and water, some two hundred thousand miles from home. The ingenuity and improvisation of the NASA team, both aboard the crippled craft and at Houston's mission control, averted a horrifying disaster.

Human beings take pride in our ability to adapt and adjust, to find ways of overcoming tough situations. But on the biggest challenge of all, bridging the gap between our sinful selves and the perfect, holy God, we're completely powerless. Only Jesus can do that, no matter how much ingenuity and improvisation we try to bring to bear.

Just accept the life He offers!

. . . .

*Jesus, Savior, may I rely completely on
Your strength and goodness—never my own.*

Signs of Life and Growth

*I went down to the grove of nut trees to look at
the new growth in the valley, to see if the vines
had budded or the pomegranates were in bloom.*
SONG OF SOLOMON 6:11 NIV

. . . .

Those of us with grapevines in our backyards understand the feeling of happy anticipation that Solomon describes in this verse. But, we might ask, why would the ruler of an empire stretching from Egypt to the Euphrates have been excited by the sight of mere grapes beginning to bud?

For the same reason that we today, busy as we are with high-level, pressing projects and important accomplishments, enjoy seeing the first carrots appear in our garden or the first tiny grapes bud in our arbor. Not only are they a promise of good things to come, but it's relaxing and therapeutic just to look at them.

Said the beloved of Solomon's love story, "Let us go *early* to the vineyards to see if the vines have budded" (Song of Solomon 7:12, emphasis added). It's good for your soul.

. . . .

*Lord, remind me to take time out from
my busy schedule to enjoy the simple
pleasures You've placed in my life.*

Choosing Your Battles

A prudent man sees evil and hides himself,
the naive proceed and pay the penalty.
PROVERBS 27:12 NASB

. . . .

It would be a naive hiker indeed who, seeing a bear cub near the trail, would not stop in his tracks. Coming between a cub and its mother is an invitation to be attacked tooth and claw—the attraction of that "cute baby bear" is not worth risking the consequences.

Experienced observers know that getting too close to the young of many animals will bring a vigorous response from the mothers. In the case of certain birds, as with the grouse hen, the mother will flee from her chicks, acting as if she's unable to fly, in hopes of luring pursuers after her. When she's drawn a potential predator far enough away, she'll end the charade and take wing to save herself.

A prudent hiker sees a bear and gets out of the way. A prudent grouse sees danger and runs the other way. A prudent Christian sees evil and hides.

Let's not be naive and "pay the penalty."

. . . .

Father God, please give me wisdom to avoid
things that would harm me or others—
to know Your paths and follow them.

Step Out from Under

*I consider thy heavens, the work of thy fingers, the
moon and the stars, which thou hast ordained.*
PSALM 8:3 KJV

. . . .

Lie on your back on a boat in the middle of the ocean—at
night! You may see them in seconds but it probably won't
take more than a couple of minutes. Shooting stars! A few
minutes later you might see them again. And again!

These tiny meteorites are burning streaks through our atmosphere all the time! But, to those of us who live inland,
with plenty of light pollution in the air, shooting stars are a
rare treat. We just don't see them because of how, or where,
we live.

Taking the walk of faith is like stepping out from under
the pollution that covers an "ordinary" life. That's when we
see better, see clearer, and see life for the basket of wonders it
really is.

. . . .

*Jesus, Savior, where we live is important only in so
much as we need to live in You. How we live should be
by following You. In doing so we pray You will show us
glory greater even than the sky on the clearest of nights.*

New Life from a Stump

*There shall come forth a shoot from the stump of
Jesse, and a branch shall grow out of his roots.*
ISAIAH 11:1 RSV

. . . .

In Isaiah's day, the Assyrians ravaged Judah, and David's
kingdom—which had filled the land like a great tree—was
decimated. Then the Babylonians invaded, carried off the
people, and deported the last of the line of David (the son of
Jesse) to Babylon.

When the Jews were finally allowed to return to Judah,
all that remained of their royal house was a chopped-down
stump. Yet just as a new shoot can spring up from a felled tree,
God promised that a branch, the Son of David, would one day
rise and that "the Branch of the LORD will be beautiful and
glorious" (Isaiah 4:2 NIV). Jesus fulfilled this prophecy.

This shoot-from-a-stump principle can work for us, too.
When our relationships, hopes, and prosperity have been
chopped down by adversity—when all that's left of our calling in life is a stump, a mere reminder of the good we once
enjoyed—God can cause new life to spring forth.

. . . .

*God, no matter how difficult things are,
help me never to give up hope that You can renew me.*

Open Our Eyes

For as the heavens are higher than the earth,
so are my ways higher than your ways,
and my thoughts than your thoughts.
ISAIAH 55:9 KJV

. . . .

Hiking a wooded trail is energizing and relaxing at the same time. And coming into a large meadow or open field can be truly exhilarating, as we see the breadth of nature spread out before us.

The grass, flowers, trees, sky, birds, and butterflies stand out immediately. But what we don't always realize is that we're viewing an ecosystem teeming with life—in the air, on the ground, and under the surface. Not just plants, birds, and butterflies, but thousands of species of insects, fungi, and other life forms fill the outdoors.

If we could strip away everything that hinders our view, we'd be amazed at the scope of life God has created. His creative genius is beyond our comprehension. We could study biology for a lifetime and only scratch the surface of God's world.

He is worthy of our praise!

. . . .

Father, I take so much for granted. Slow me
down to study Your creation—to praise
and thank You for all You have made.

Safe during a Windstorm

*Thou hast been a strength to the poor, a
strength to the needy in his distress, a refuge
from the storm. . .when the blast of the terrible
ones is as a storm against the wall.*

ISAIAH 25:4 KJV

. . . .

The Israelites were accustomed to the east wind that blew
in from the Arabian Desert, but there were times when it
was especially hot or destructive.

When a windstorm broke in all its fury, hissing with dust
and sand, Israelites took refuge in their houses. There, they listened to the blast of the wind against their walls and thanked
God that they were safe. Isaiah praised God for being "a refuge from the storm," a wall that protected the poor and needy
from the wrath of enemies and oppressors.

Few of us live near a desert and know the relief that people
feel when they safely ride out a sandstorm. But each of us has
experienced the Lord's protection when the winds of adversity
have howled around us.

Trust God that He can and will be there for you again
when you need Him most.

. . . .

*Lord, please be a protective wall, shielding
me and my family from the storm's blast.*

Build to Last

If the work which any man has built on the
foundation survives, he will receive a reward.
1 CORINTHIANS 3:14 RSV

. . . .

A thin, well-trodden path runs along the river. Long ago, it had been a railroad bed, but it is now a footpath for hunters, fishermen, and children at play. Trees are plentiful, including both hard and soft woods.

Many years before, in that same place, an old man named Eddie thought some tall, thin birches would make a good fence. He cut some down and established a fine-looking perimeter for his little acre.

It wasn't long before Eddie's fence fell apart. White birch rots quickly if not finished or seasoned.

Another man named Joseph cut down some sizeable cherry trees and hauled them to the sawmill. With the planks and boards he got back, he built a two-story garage with a workshop. That was ninety years ago—and the building still stands. Cherry is an excellent wood that, when finished, makes superb furniture. . .or a long-lasting garage.

What materials are we using in our spiritual "buildings"?

. . . .

Father, I want what I build to last. May I build
with good material, on Your sure foundation.

Showers of Blessings

"But I say to you, love your enemies. . .that you
may be sons of your Father in heaven; for He
makes His sun rise on the evil and on the good,
and sends rain on the just and on the unjust."
MATTHEW 5:44–45 NKJV

. . . .

It's natural to hate someone who has gone out of their way to make themselves your enemy and wrong you. If someone insults you—or you *feel* that they have—it's hard to love them. So why did Jesus say we are to love such people?

Jesus explained that God sends the sun to warm and light the way of evil people as well as good people. He sends rain to water the crops of both the just and the unjust. God doesn't differentiate because He loves both the lovely and the unlovely—and He asks us to do the same.

God *will* eventually judge the wicked. As Hebrews 6 says, although God is now sending rain on everyone, the day is coming when those who bear "useful herbs" will be blessed and those who bear "thorns and briars" will be cursed.

In the meantime, we are to show kindness to all people— just as God Himself is now doing.

. . . .

God, help me to love my enemies
just like You love them.

Streamside Thoughts of God

The heavens declare the glory of God;
the skies proclaim the work of his hands.
PSALM 19:1 NIV

. . . .

Those who approach fly-fishing with passion know that a day on their favorite waters can be the very definition of the word *solitude*. It's a time when anglers spend time alone with their own thoughts. . .and alone with God.

Some of the most intimate encounters with God recorded in the Bible took place in a wilderness setting. Moses received his calling there, and a battered and defeated Elijah took encouragement and strength far away from civilization. And Jesus Himself understood the importance of "getting away" so He could remain in perfect harmony with His Father in heaven.

Someone once observed, "Some go to church and think about fishing; others go fishing and think about God." While a day of fly-fishing should never take the place of regular fellowship and worship at church, it is certainly a great setting for a closer time of communion with your heavenly Father.

. . . .

I thank You, Father, for making me an active part
of one of Your houses of worship. And I thank You,
too, that I can spend quality time with You—You
alone—at some of my favorite fishing holes.

Which Way to Choose?

*Altogether, Enoch lived 365 years. Enoch
walked faithfully with God; then he was no
more, because God took him away.*
GENESIS 5:23–24 NIV

. . . .

In a particular city park, you'll find an area where hiking trails diffuse into a small network of interconnected paths with a single entry point and a single exit. Standing at the entry point, trying to determine which path to take, is confusing—even when you realize they all end in the same place.

The Christian life is a lot like that, as we're faced with choices—both small and large—every day. In each year of our lives, we stand at the beginning with only a vague idea of the countless decisions that lie ahead of us.

Enoch chose to walk closely with God every day of his 365 years. For the next 365 days of your life, which pathway will you select? Take the challenge to walk closer with God every day. He'll never disappoint you.

Choosing to put God first will make all the other choices of life easier.

. . . .

*Father, help me to choose You each and every day.
I want to travel the right path.*

Hidden Treasure

I have hidden your word in my heart
that I might not sin against you.
PSALM 119:11 NIV

. . . .

Rumors of hidden treasure have crisscrossed the world for a long, long time. The "Frenchman's gold," Blackbeard's hidden pirate treasure, the lost Aztec gold. . .such stories have captured the public's attention for centuries.

Some have devoted their lives (and other people's fortunes) to searching for these treasures. Whether they succeed or not, a new crop of treasure hunters inevitably appears to pick up the chase. The prospect of finding a hidden treasure is always alluring.

The Bible teaches that Christians have other kinds of treasure to pursue. Hidden gold may be scattered around the globe, but we do well to hide the treasure of God's word in our hearts. And then there's the treasure we store up now for heaven, as the Gospels mention.

It would be a thrill to find a long-hidden stash of gold. But let's never forget what is most important. What God offers is infinitely more valuable than any hidden treasure.

. . . .

Lord, grant me the sense to remember what
is truly important as I daily walk with You.

Basic Life Lessons

*"But ask the animals, and they will teach you,
or the birds in the sky, and they will tell you. . .
or let the fish in the sea inform you."*
JOB 12:7–8 NIV

. . . .

This verse is not saying that we, like Hollywood's Dr. Doolittle, can literally talk with animals. Job's counselors had been lecturing him on the *basics* of cause and effect, insisting that suffering often means that God is punishing humanity for sin. "Who does not know all these things?" Job asked (Job 12:3). Then he pointed them to *other* basics: look to the animals and "they will teach you" that sometimes the innocent suffer while the cruel triumph.

Men and women are not brute beasts caught up in a mere survival of the fittest—the grace of God intervenes constantly in our lives. But, as living beings, we too are subject to the influences of a sin-spoiled world, and suffer as a result. Even innocent fawns are maimed in accidents. Even trees die of disease.

We should live righteous lives, but there's no guarantee that doing so will spare us from being touched by the pain and suffering of this world.

. . . .

*God, help me to love and trust You,
even when You allow me to suffer.*

Signs of the Times

*"You know how to interpret the appearance of
the earth and the sky. How is it that you don't
know how to interpret this present time?"*
LUKE 12:56 NIV

. . . .

Whether it is true or not, every boater knows the saying:
"Red sky at night, sailors' delight; red sky in morning,
sailors take warning." We instinctively know to pay attention
to the signs of nature to see what is happening around us and
to anticipate what might lie ahead for us.

Jesus used the same illustration to communicate a spiritual truth: there are signs everywhere that God is at work
among us. Our job is to make sure we are paying attention to
them. God's hand can be found in the beauty of a sunset as
well as in the joy of playing with our kids. It can be sensed in
the circumstances surrounding an important decision or in
the godly counsel we receive from a friend.

As you go about your daily life and work, are you oblivious to the signs of God at work around you? He is always
working for His people, and we should give Him praise for
what He is doing (John 5:17).

. . . .

*Loving Father, help me to see what You are
doing around me—and to give You praise.*

A Step in Faith

Thy word is a lamp unto my feet,
and a light unto my path.

PSALM 119:105 KJV

. . . .

A hiker caught in the hills after nightfall will tell you there's nothing like the darkness of the countryside on a cloudy night. Without the benefit of street lighting, the moon, or the stars, it can be difficult to see one's own hand in front of one's face.

On the great "hike" of life, we can blunder into a similar plight. Souls strayed from Christ can feel that same smothering darkness, spiritually speaking.

Out on the trail, a flashlight—along with a map and a compass—makes it possible for us to walk for miles and arrive at our destination, regardless of the time of day. In the Christian life, we have a map and compass in God's holy Bible. And, as for a flashlight, well. . .would Jesus Christ, the Light of the world, do?

. . . .

Lord, I can't always see where I'm going.
Please help me to keep faith as I step into the
unknown. Bring me safely home at journey's end.

It Was—and Is—"Good"

*God made the wild animals according to their
kinds, the livestock according to their kinds, and all
the creatures that move along the ground according
to their kinds. And God saw that it was good.*

GENESIS 1:25 NIV

. . . .

Our times in the outdoors often present us with some great opportunities to stop and consider the word *good*.

When a fisherman tells you that the fishing is good, that usually means he caught a lot of fish. When a hunter says the hunting was good, that means that at least a few other hunters in the party bagged the birds or animals they were pursuing. And when a hiker talks about a good day of hiking, it usually means that nice weather brought an enjoyable day of getting close to the beauty of nature.

When God looked out over His finished creation, He observed that it was "good." Good to look at, good to listen to, good to enjoy as it went about its business of growing and reproducing, just as He designed it to do.

And, of course, it was good for His crown jewel of creation—humanity—to enjoy in every way.

. . . .

*Creator God, I thank You for Your goodness.
And I thank You that everything You
created for me to enjoy is itself also good.*

Death in the Pot

*Then they served it to the men to eat. Now it
happened, as they were eating the stew, that
they cried out and said, "Man of God, there is
death in the pot!" And they could not eat it.*

2 KINGS 4:40 NKJV

. . . .

Preparing for a day of wilderness activity, most of us fill our packs with food we're familiar with—sandwiches, trail mix, energy bars loaded with carbs. Unless you're a trained survivalist, you probably don't want to rely on the food available at your outdoor destination.

During a famine in Elisha's day, fellow prophets gathered a variety of plants, herbs, and gourds from the nearby fields. But they "did not know what they were" (verse 39). One swallow told them they weren't in Mama's kitchen anymore.

When we're accustomed to good food, the bad stuff just doesn't cut it. That's true of spiritual food, too. If we fill up on the "good home cooking" of scripture, we'll be able to detect when there is "death in the pot" in a world that rejects our God.

. . . .

*Lord, please fill me with Your goodness,
so I might reject the bitter taste of this world's fare.*

That You Care for Me

LORD, *what are human beings that you care for
them, mere mortals that you think of them?*
PSALM 144:3 NIV

. . . .

The biblical Sea of Galilee is known by locals as the Sea of Genneseret or Lake Kinneret. It's located in the Galilee region, the north of Israel, fed by underground streams and the famous Jordan River, which cuts through the sea, north to south.

In ages past, God knew that civilization would follow the trail of water—and He placed Genneseret strategically to provide for people. Christ performed miracles and preached to thousands along its shore.

The God who knew you before you were even conceived planned similar places for you to stop and partake of His living water, as you hike the trail of your life.

Choose the path prepared by the Creator, long before mankind walked on earth. Along its way He has placed people to encourage, assist, and teach you His ways. God thought of you, cared for you, and provided for your every need.

. . . .

*God, keep me today in Your loving care, that I might
walk the path that leads to places of Your living water.*

Obedience Brings Success

The ants are not a strong people, but they
prepare their food in the summer.
PROVERBS 30:25 NASB

. . . .

A nts have something going for them that we don't: they lack an inclination toward selfishness! Their teamwork can be seen all over the outdoors.

In some climates, ants make their nests and tunnels entirely underground. But in areas where clay soils drain poorly, they build hills of leaf stems, the needles of evergreen trees, and sand. They carry each grain of sand from wherever they find it on their travels.

The hill makes a nest and tunnel system that is well above pools that form during rain. It also sheds the drops that fall on its domed top. As weather permits, these industrious creatures enlarge and maintain their hill. Long-established hills often are overspread by moss or grasses until only their shape gives them away.

Wherever they live, ants cooperate to gather their food when it's available. They seem to function as if the entire colony were controlled by one mind.

What a picture for us as believers, to work together as if we are controlled by one mind—the mind of Christ!

. . . .

Great God, we know You would have us do all things
diligently as unto You. Help us to be of one mind,
knowing the blessing of accomplishing Your work.

No Theme Park Adventure Here

*"I will wipe from the face of the earth the
human race I have created. . . ." But Noah
found favor in the eyes of the LORD.*
GENESIS 6:7–8 NIV

. . . .

Talk about adventure: the first time people embark on a white-water rapids ride with a bunch of kids, how many vow it to be their last? "Too much water!" many declare.

Of course, it was a million times worse for those surviving the true-life water adventure of Hurricane Katrina. Perched on a tree limb, an elderly resident of New Orleans' fourth ward was heard singing the old spiritual, "My, Didn't It Rain?" followed by a catchy hip-hop rendition of the scripture, " 'But Noah found favor in the eyes of the Lord,' and he was spared!"

Finding favor—approval—in God's sight is something to be desired. Just as those little kids may have looked to you as their brave leader on an amusement park ride, so God wants us to look to Him before, as well as during, our times of testing.

. . . .

*What do Your eyes see when they look at me, Father?
Give me the spiritual as well as the emotional
desire to be a strength to those around me.*

With God, Every Day's a Great Day

Why, my soul, are you downcast? Why so
disturbed within me? Put your hope in God,
for I will yet praise him, my Savior and my God.
PSALM 42:5 NIV

. . . .

Even the best fishermen understand the frustration of getting "skunked" on a favorite lake, river, or stream. There are just some days when the fish aren't biting—and nothing the fisherman tries will change that fact.

How would you respond if all your planning and effort for a fishing trip yielded zero result, at least in terms of the number of fish you caught? With disappointment? With discouragement? By labeling your trip a failure?

The great American poet Henry David Thoreau once wrote, "Many go fishing all their lives without knowing that it is not fish they are after." Obviously, catching fish always makes a day of fishing better. But the Christian who enjoys fishing knows the actual catch is the icing on the cake—of spending a day on the water with their loving Creator.

. . . .

Thank You, Father, that even my worst day
fishing can be a great day—because I get to
spend it with family, friends. . .and You!

The Pack

"The eunuch should not say, 'Look, I am like a
dried-up tree.'" For this is what the Lord *says:*
"For the eunuchs who observe my Sabbaths
and choose what pleases me and are faithful
to my covenant, I will set up within my temple
and my walls a monument that will be better
than sons and daughters."
Isaiah 56:3–5 net

. . . .

In a wolf pack, no male except for the leader is sexually active. As young male wolves grow up, they face a decision: they can stay with the pack, helping to hunt and contributing to the pack's well-being—or they can go off on their own.

Young people today face similar choices. Do they abandon God, go off on their own, wander through life alone? Or should they serve their extended families, their churches, their communities, remaining faithful even when it doesn't make sense to trust God?

For young people who want to be married or become parents, Isaiah 56 may seem absurd. What monument could possibly be as good as children? But God always delivers on His promises.

If you're single today, stay the course. If you're married, find a single brother or sister to encourage.

. . . .

Life doesn't always make sense, Lord. Please give
me faith even when I can't understand Your plan.

Jesus Calms the Storm

*Jesus was in the stern, sleeping on a cushion. The
disciples woke him and said to him, "Teacher, don't
you care if we drown?" He got up, rebuked the
wind and said to the waves, "Quiet! Be still!" Then
the wind died down and it was completely calm.*

MARK 4:38–39 NIV

. . . .

Viewing a large body of water can be an awesome experience. Some resemble a huge bowl of gelatin, without
a single ripple to mar the placid surface. Others rage like an
angry beast seeking to destroy.

One time, the apostles—many of them experienced
sailors—were terrified in a storm at sea. All the while, Jesus
slept. Don't our lives occasionally seem like that? Things get
rough and we wonder if Jesus is sleeping. We want Him to
wake up and calm our storms immediately. Otherwise, we
fear we'll go down with the ship.

Modern ships are watertight if all the hatches and portals
are securely sealed. Our faith is lot like a ship: Watertight, it
protects us from the storm. But with holes in our faith, we risk
sinking.

. . . .

*Lord Jesus, help me to realize my ship
can't sink as long as You're in it with me.*

Intelligent Designer behind Creation

"Is it your wisdom that sets the hawk soaring,
spreading its wings toward the south? Does the eagle
fly up when you say so, to build its nest in the heights?"
JOB 39:26–27 CJB

. . . .

Sometimes we need to be reminded who is in charge. With all our scientific advances, our ability to engineer genetically and clone living beings, we get to thinking we're pretty hot. The end of such conceit is to think that we don't need God—that we are, in fact, nearly gods ourselves.

Scientists may be able to clone a hawk or an eagle, but all they're really doing is tinkering with an elaborate, astonishingly complex system already in place—a living being created by a Designer whose "understanding is infinite" (Psalm 147:5 KJV).

Only the infinitely intelligent Creator could design the DNA of the hawk so that it would instinctively soar on high thermals and engineer eagles' genes so that thousands of generations of these magnificent birds would build their nests in lofty treetops and mountain crags. Don't ever forget that!

. . . .

Lord, help me to remember that my
wisdom is limited, Yours infinite.

Purposeful Bonding

Peter said to him, "Master, it is good for us
to be here. Let us put up three shelters—one
for you, one for Moses and one for Elijah."
(He did not know what he was saying.)
LUKE 9:33 NIV

. . . .

Do you belong to a group? If not at church, perhaps in a hobby group or sports league?

What is it that makes us feel so comfortable with "the group"? Some of us find our bonding in bowling, others in hunting, yet others in cooking. We anticipate those nights with friends.

Simon Peter felt an unusual bond with James, John, and Jesus on the Mount of Transfiguration. As a matter of fact, that bonding included Moses and Elijah, too. Seemingly, Peter wanted to stay there on the mountain, building shrines for their special group.

But Jesus felt otherwise. From that mountaintop experience, He turned His face resolutely toward Jerusalem and the suffering that awaited Him there. The bonding experience was fine, but it was for a purpose—Jesus had a mission to fulfill.

Time was short. There was work to be done.

. . . .

Father, let me enjoy the comradeship of my special
group, but may it always be with a worthy purpose.

Hidden Paradise

*It is God's privilege to conceal things
and the king's privilege to discover them.*
PROVERBS 25:2 NLT

. . . .

Seeking adventure, a teenager followed the creek through the valley, rather than the well-worn trail along the curved ridge. A century and a half earlier, a coal-hauling gravity railroad had run that ridge without a locomotive, descending on its own momentum, hauled up steep grades by metal cables and a stationary steam engine. Little remained of that bygone era—only some rotted ties, tangled loops of ancient cable, an occasional rusted rail spike.

And a tunnel, big enough to walk into, the creek running through it. Wide steps of flat stone lay dark and damp on the tunnel floor. High walls of stone supported massive slabs laid across the top, forming an aqueduct beneath the trail where the train once ran. Downstream, water cascaded into a small grotto surrounded by tall trees. Remarkable and haunting, this bit of history clothed in nature's camouflage. The boy named it Hidden Paradise.

He was fifteen then. Now fifty-five, he lives two hundred miles away but occasionally drives the distance for the hike. As he walks with his children's children to Hidden Paradise, new memories are laid up for the generations to come.

. . . .

*Father, may I find what You have hidden—
and share those things with others around me.*

When the Kayak Rolls

Then he said to them all, "If anyone wants to become my follower, he must deny himself, take up his cross daily, and follow me."
LUKE 9:23 NET

. . . .

When we've rolled a kayak—it's upside down in the rapids with our head hitting rocks and our lungs bursting—everything in our flesh wants to claw our way upward toward the surface. But this is precisely the *wrong* move.

To escape, we bend against the body's impulses, lean forward, and pull the release handle on the kayak skirt. Just a little tug pops the seal, allowing water to rush in and air to bubble out, carrying our body upward with it.

Life is sometimes like the rocky rapids, as we're carried away, upside down, in the rush. Denying our fleshly nature and cravings is the most unnatural thing in the world. Indeed, the world says it is foolishness. But that's what Jesus commands of us. It's the only way to live.

. . . .

Oh, Lord who created the rapids of life, show us how to be Your followers by denying ourselves and taking up Your cross. Help us to understand what this means with each new dawn.

A Tale of Two Waterfalls

*Then they that gladly received [Peter's] word
were baptized: and the same day there were
added unto them about three thousand souls.*
ACTS 2:41 KJV

. . . .

Straddling the border of the United States and Canada, Niagara Falls is North America's most famous cataract. Millions have visited the thundering attraction, some thirty-six hundred feet in width and 160 feet high.

Few but locals know of the Dundee Falls in northeast Ohio. In a peaceful wood, a small stream trickles over a rock ledge to a pool some twenty feet below. It's tame and quiet, nothing like the mighty Niagara.

So which is better? That's a subjective question. Both were created by God, and each has undoubtedly pointed people to Him. The two waterfalls are just different—much the way people are.

In the early church, the mighty, thundering Peter once pointed three thousand souls to Jesus. But those nameless individuals—the "tame and quiet" bunch—formed the backbone of the church we're part of today.

If you're not a Peter, don't think you're unimportant. Not every waterfall can be a Niagara. But every one of us has a special, God-given job to do.

. . . .

*Father God, please show me exactly who I am in
Your plans—then help me to be the best I can be.*

A Skillful Hunter

Esau was a skillful hunter, a man of the field;
but Jacob was a mild man, dwelling in tents.
GENESIS 25:27 NKJV

. . . .

Esau was the most famous hunter in the Bible. While his brother, Jacob, was content to stay close to home, busy overseeing the camp, Esau loved to roam the wild country. He lived for the thrill of the chase. He was probably *supposed* to be overseeing the herdsmen, but he was the boss's son and the herds were fine. . .so what was to stop him from the occasional hunting trip?

Esau was set to inherit the bulk of his father's vast flocks and herds, but he traded it all for one bowl of stew. His priorities were completely out of whack. That doesn't take away from the fact that the Bible calls Esau "a skillful hunter." Unfortunately, he was out perfecting his hunting skills when he perhaps should have been shepherding.

Esau would've made a top "big game guide." He could have taught us all a thing or two about tracking and hunting. But when it comes to priorities—putting a value on the family business and keeping the camp going—that's where we have to look to Jacob.

. . . .

God, help me to keep my passion for
the outdoors in the proper perspective.

How Close Can You Get?

*Can a man scoop a flame into his lap
and not have his clothes catch on fire?*
PROVERBS 6:27 NLT

. . . .

Imagine yourself golfing a beautiful course on the coast. You unleashed a long drive, but your ball has rolled toward the edge of a cliff, overlooking a steep drop to the rocky ocean below.

The rest of your foursome, concerned over your well-being, urges you to take the drop and the extra stroke—but you think you can play the ball where it lies. The very picture of confidence, you work your way closer and closer to the ledge. . . .

Maybe golf isn't your game. But we can play a dangerous lie in the realm of our marriages. What about that attractive coworker at the office—the one who always has a few moments and a bright smile for you? Ever find yourself taking the long way to the coffeepot so you can stop by to see that person "just for a minute"?

How close do you want to get to the edge? How near can you come to the flame without being burned? Better to "take the drop" and stay out of danger.

. . . .

*Lord, give me the wisdom—and the will—
to stay away from the edge.*

On Rappel!

Now faith is being sure of what we hope for,
being convinced of what we do not see.
HEBREWS 11:1 NET

. . . .

The overhanging cliff at Whitesides Mountain, North Carolina, is 720 feet straight down. When you're hanging on a rope halfway down, it's too late to check the knot. The only thing you can do is have faith in the person who tied the knot. And the person who sewed the rappelling harness. And the person who ran the machine that made the rope. . .

Stuck in midair, we can't see any of those people or be sure of their skill. Sometimes, we're convinced the knot won't hold—and we're going to die. But to panic is to die; having faith is the only way to live. All we can do is hold on to the rope.

The Old Testament prophets couldn't see their Messiah, but they believed. Two thousand years later, we can't see our Messiah directly, either. Thomas required proof, but Jesus said, "Blessed are the people who have not seen and yet have believed" (John 20:29).

. . . .

Creator of the mountains, grant us the faith to hold on to
Your rope when we can't see what's holding us up in life!

Safeguarding Our Gains

*"Behold, I am coming quickly! Hold fast what
you have, that no one may take your crown."*
REVELATION 3:11 NKJV

....

In some places, campers need to take extraordinary care to
safeguard their food from hungry wildlife.

A park ranger has showed visitors photos of the aftermath
of a bear's attempt to get food from a parked car. Windows
were smashed and seats ripped, the food containers thor-
oughly ransacked. You can just imagine a full-bellied bear
whistling happily through the woods.

Campers are advised to store their food in tight containers, even to elevate them by a rope tied to a branch. And since
the leftovers attract beasts, too, several parks use specially designed waste containers to keep the wildlife out. It's all about
protecting what's inside.

Let's protect what we have inside spiritually. We've all seen
how the "predators" of life get inside us to ransack our peace.
Look ahead at your day's itinerary, then say a prayer for God
to guard your heart and the treasure within.

May nobody take our crown.

....

*Lord, I see how today's events can leave me
weak—so give me strength to stand for You.*

Shark Cage

"Be strong and of good courage; do not be
afraid, nor be dismayed, for the LORD your
God is with you wherever you go."
JOSHUA 1:9 NKJV

. . . .

If you ever have the privilege of visiting Australia's Great Barrier Reef, you'll see that it's full of examples of God's creation.

Shark encounters are common in the reef, usually with gray nurse sharks that pose no threat to swimmers. Since they're well fed from the abundance of fish in the area, they pay little attention to humans. For more adventure, though, you can go farther out into the ocean where the great white sharks concentrate. But you'll want to be in a shark cage.

From the safety of the cage, you can see these magnificent creatures up close—and realize just how fearsome they are. Your safety depends on those metal bars surrounding you—without them, you'd be in trouble.

We live in a world full of trouble, and there are plenty of "sharks" just waiting to attack and eat us alive. In God's presence, though, we can know that we'll always be protected from harm.

. . . .

Lord, I thank You for watching over me and
protecting me from the predators of this world.

What Kind of Soil Are You?

And he spake many things unto them in parables,
saying, Behold, a sower went forth to sow.
MATTHEW 13:3 KJV

. . . .

In the cool of a brilliant spring morning, a man went out to tend his recently planted garden. He drank in the sweet, earthy smell of the soil, and noticed some seeds beginning to sprout. A few leapt up out of the soil. Others were just breaking into the light. Weeds were already trying to choke some others. Remembering the parable of the soils, the man thought of his own heart, asking, *Which one of these am I?*

Which one are you? In certain seasons of our lives we resemble the seed sown on the side of the road. We're consumed by the cares of this world, without time for God. Sometimes we feel a strong surge in our faith, only to quickly run dry like the seed sown on shallow, rocky ground. Yet other times, we're surrounded by the "thorns" of people or attitudes that choke our faith.

Today, it's worth examining ourselves to know which of Jesus' soils best describes us. Dig deep—and make whatever changes are necessary to your mental, emotional, and spiritual health.

. . . .

Lord, please tend the soil of my heart,
making me productive for You.

In Deep Water

*"He reached down from heaven and rescued
me; he drew me out of deep waters."*
2 SAMUEL 22:17 NLT

. . . .

There is nothing as refreshing as a mountain stream, as nature filters and chills the water in ways unequaled by any bottling process.

Down from the peaks and into the valleys the streams gather, providing joy for the senses of sight, hearing, taste, and touch. Often, the water is so clear it seems that those polished pebbles on the creek bed lie just beneath the surface. But if you put a hand in, you might discover you can hardly reach the bottom!

God's love is like a mountain stream, flowing down to us from on high. Its purity makes it refreshing, and its purity takes us by surprise.

If you didn't mind getting your shirt wet, you could probably reach the pebbles in a mountain stream. But, no matter how hard you try, you will never reach the bottom of God's love.

. . . .

*Father, there are many in this world who think they've
sunk so low they're beyond love. Please use me as
Your instrument to draw them back up again.*

Inspired by Trees

Abraham planted a tamarisk tree in Beer-
sheba, and called there on the name of the
LORD, the Everlasting God.
GENESIS 21:33 RSV

. . . .

When Abraham pitched his tents near the great oak of Moreh, he built an altar and worshipped God. Again, when he moved to Hebron, he built an altar to God near the majestic oaks of Mamre (Genesis 12:6–7; 13:18). It wasn't just that Abraham enjoyed the shade. Like so many of us, he was inspired by God's creation.

There were very few trees in the arid south, so when Abraham moved to Beersheba, he *planted* a tree—one tamarisk to be exact, a small tree that thrives in arid regions. Then, after planting that tree, Abraham called on the name of the Lord.

Take a walk through a park or a forest and you'll recognize an age-old truth: there is something about trees that inspires our spirits and stirs a longing in us to worship the Creator. Perhaps it's because trees rise peacefully toward heaven, unmoved by the things that vex and concern us. Perhaps it's because, with their leaves rustling in the slightest breeze, they remind us to commune with God's Spirit.

. . . .

Thank You, God, for creating trees to
help turn my thoughts toward You.

Striving for Peace

The wolf shall dwell with the lamb, and the
leopard shall lie down with the young goat,
and the calf and the lion and the fattened calf
together; and a little child shall lead them.
ISAIAH 11:6 ESV

. . . .

When playing recreational sports, we often use phrases like "going to war" and terms like "enemies." And in some small sense, both are accurate descriptions. Giving anything less than 100 percent harms our testimony. But seeing opponents as enemies can also lead to disrespect—and clouded emotions that can spill onto the field of play.

Isaiah spoke of a future time when the wolf would dwell with the lamb, the leopard would lie down with the young goat, the calf, the lion, and the fattened calf—all of which is against their original nature. But the coming Christ-child that Isaiah prophesied would one day change their nature and bring peace to situations in which savagery once reigned.

How might you be able to change the tone of the recreational sports you play? Can you simply "dwell" with your opponents in a competitive but respectful way? How different would your team or league be if you were to speak highly of opponents before, during, and after a competition?

. . . .

Lord, help me to model Your peace
every time I step onto the field of play.

God Speaks through the Everyday

*The desert and the parched land will be glad;
the wilderness will rejoice and blossom. Like
the crocus, it will burst into bloom; it will
rejoice greatly and shout for joy.*
ISAIAH 35:1–2 NIV

. . . .

When you're outdoors enjoying your favorite activities, do you ever take time to listen to God? It's not a bad idea, because God often has a way of using what we understand to teach us things we haven't yet grasped.

From the beginning of time, God has used what His people were most familiar with to illustrate His love for them. Jesus continued that heavenly tradition when He described everyday, "outdoor" things the people of His time could understand—the birds of the air, the lilies and grass of the field—to teach them not to worry (Matthew 6:25–34).

As someone who enjoys the time outdoors, listen for God's voice as you participate in your favorite outdoor activity. It just might be that He'll use something as commonplace as a bird, a flower, or a field of grass to lovingly speak His truth to you.

. . . .

*Lord, I thank You for giving me what we call "nature"
to help me to understand so many other of Your gifts—
physical, emotional, and spiritual alike.*

Outdoor Stewardship

"The earth is the Lord's, and everything in it."
1 CORINTHIANS 10:26 NIV

. . . .

Most people, when using someone else's stuff—say a car, camping equipment, or anything else that belongs to that person—treat those things with special care, probably far greater care than we treat our own things.

But what about the outdoors itself? The Bible teaches that the earth we enjoy, including the outdoors, belongs to God—and that He's given it to us to treat with an attitude of respect and stewardship. That means we should feel free to *use* all God has given us to enjoy, but never to *misuse* it.

We are all free as people who love the outdoors—fishermen, hunters, hikers, campers, mountain bikers—to enjoy God's creation. But let's never forget that the outdoors we enjoy belongs to God Himself. . .and that we should treat it with the respect due to His "stuff."

. . . .

Loving Father, help me always to remember that
all creation belongs to You—and that I should treat
it with an attitude of stewardship, not ownership.

"Is That A.M. or P.M.?"

"Wake up, sleeper, rise from the dead,
and Christ will shine on you."
EPHESIANS 5:14 NIV

. . . .

When a group pledges to meet at a certain morning hour to fish, they meet. You can set your watch by it.

Those who fish understand the pulse-quickening joy of a good cast; the anticipation of that first nibble; the electric shock of a strike followed by the whirring of a reel.

For someone who fishes, it's no problem to rise at 4:30 a.m. But do we have quite the same excitement about the 7:30 alarm on Sunday morning? Some days, it's much easier to sleep.

The apostle Paul had sleepers in his day. When preaching in Ephesus, a listener sitting on a windowsill dropped off to sleep then fell to his death. You can read the whole story in Acts 20:7–11.

Think about it: how many of us can sit all day in a boat, with a ninety-eight-degree sun beating down, waiting for just one bite, while we struggle to listen to a thirty-five-minute sermon?

. . . .

Father, I can get passionate about things that
really capture my heart. Please don't let me
sleep through Your good opportunities ahead.

Pure Magic

*"Tell them this: 'These gods, who did not make
the heavens and the earth, will perish from the
earth and from under the heavens.'"*
JEREMIAH 10:11 NIV

. . . .

Though it's not "magic" in the supernatural sense, a good illusionist can make things magical in appearance. The creative illusionist can make the impossible appear real. Sometimes the hand really is quicker than the eye, and we can be fooled by seeing the unexpected. When performed with good showmanship, such tricks can be really entertaining.

Jesus made unexpected things happen, too—but they weren't illusions. He healed people of severe illness. He walked on water. He raised the dead back to life! People were mystified by the miracles of Jesus.

We know, though, that Jesus is God—and He can do anything. Look around at creation, which John 1:3 tells us came through Jesus, and we begin to sense the Lord's glory. He created all things out of nothing—and that's no illusion.

. . . .

*May I always be amazed as I recognize
Your incredible creation, Lord.*

Courage to Go Forward

"See, the LORD your God has placed the land
before you; go up, take possession, as the LORD,
the God of your fathers, has spoken to you. Do
not fear or be dismayed."
DEUTERONOMY 1:21 NASB

. . . .

There's a great big world out there. But few of us want to travel far from our first-world jobs, medical facilities, and entertainment for very long. For many of us, the "great unknown" can keep us at home.

The Israelites of Moses' day were much the same. Moving into the unknown Promised Land, they actually begged to return to Egypt—the land of their slavery. But they had clothing, jewelry, and manna, all provided miraculously by their God. Moses told them not to worry about entering the new land, his confidence flowing from the knowledge that God had been with them all along.

When we face something new—a place we've never been before, a job switch, a changing relationship—let's remember all the times God has been with us, and go forward with courage.

. . . .

Lord, I've seen Your hand in my life—
and that helps me face new challenges today.

Down by the Riverside

*They are like trees that grow beside a stream,
that bear fruit at the right time, and whose
leaves do not dry up. They succeed in
everything they do.*
PSALM 1:3 GNT

. . . .

Viewing the valley below, you can see clearly where the river runs—its path is lined with trees. Farmers have planted orchards in the land adjacent to the river. Farther up the valley, the trees and lush greenery fade, giving way to just a few scattered trees and dry brown grasses. The effect of the water is clear: Being close to it makes life more abundant. Distance makes life much harder.

Unlike those trees, we can choose where we're "planted"— either close to God or far away. The psalm writer tells us that choosing to walk in the path of the righteous makes us like a tree planted near the river. There we find life-giving water that feeds our soul and causes us to grow tall and full in the Lord. We'll become a green tree bearing good fruit.

Where do you want to be planted? Which way will you choose to walk today?

. . . .

*Lord, help me to choose You today, to walk in the path
of righteousness and bear the fruit of Your love.*

Serious Fishing

"Let down your nets for a catch."
LUKE 5:4 NKJV

. . . .

Fishing was the earliest enterprise that Europeans under-took along the northeastern shoreline of the New World. Fishing was also a major source of sustenance to the Indians of New England.

Rhode Island founder Roger Williams noted that his Indian neighbors were excellent fishers who carefully watched the seasons for changes of weather and movements of local fish. "Frequently they lay their naked bodies many a cold night on the cold shore [around] a fire or two or three sticks," he wrote, "and oft in the night search their nets; and sometimes go in and stay longer in frozen water."

Are we, as "fishers of men" (Matthew 4:19 KJV), as committed to our catch? Do we lie awake at night in prayer? Do we go into the cold waters of the world around us to haul in the souls of men? Whether we are gifted evangelists or not, do we see fishing for men as an essential part of our life's work?

. . . .

Father, help me to do the work of an evangelist—
to be ready always to give an answer for
the hope that is within me.

Dreams and Visions

"Your sons and daughters will prophesy,
your old men will dream dreams,
your young men will see visions."
JOEL 2:28 NIV (SEE ALSO ACTS 2:17)

. . . .

Had a vision lately?"

So read an advertisement in Sunday newspapers across the country. "Join men around the world for the adventure of a lifetime." A day later another ad appeared: "Enlightenment group forming for visionary men." The small print noted, "A nominal fee of $50 per cassette lecture, for a total of six lectures."

Who can say what that fly-by-night visionary had to offer? But prophecies, dreams, and visions are a biblical reality according to the prophet Joel. He was looking beyond his Old Testament times, even beyond the Messiah's coming, toward a specific event that would unite earthly people with God's Holy Spirit.

That event was the Day of Pentecost, recorded in Acts 2. Inspiration and revelation came upon Christian believers that very day. And God's Spirit provides us with the same today.

No need to purchase cassette lectures!

. . . .

Father, make me sensitive to Your Holy Spirit.
May my dreams, visions, and words be acceptable to You.

A Day in the Park

*"So do not fear, for I am with you; do not
be dismayed, for I am your God. I will
strengthen you and help you; I will uphold
you with my righteous right hand."*
ISAIAH 41:10 NIV

. . . .

On a sunny day in the park, a father held his young daughter upside down. The girl squealed and laughed with delight as her daddy swung her by the ankles, back and forth over the ground. It never occurred to the child that she could possibly be dropped on her head!

Children often express total faith in their parents, believing that as long as they're in their mothers' or fathers' hands, they'll be safe. Kids will enjoy their dads' hair-raising "airplane rides" without the least hesitation—as the girl in the park yelled when her father finally lowered her safely to the ground, "Again! Again!"

Imagine how much more we could enjoy our lives if we could simply realize that we are in our heavenly Father's hands. There should be no fear of any accidental drops, as long as our Lord has us in His grip. Our Father holds us securely. . .and He will not let us fall.

. . . .

*Lord, forgive me for sometimes forgetting
that I am in Your safe and loving hands.*

Learning Patience Streamside

*Being strengthened with all power according
to his glorious might so that you may have
great endurance and patience. . .*
COLOSSIANS 1:11 NIV

. . . .

The nineteenth-century fly-fishing expert Francis Francis once wrote, "The one great ingredient in successful fly-fishing is patience."

An accurate observation, to be sure, if not incredibly obvious to most fishermen.

A person needn't be a sage fly-fishing veteran to know that patience is the one virtue most needed for success. Anyone who has spent any amount of time casting flies—even the *right* fly in the *right* spots—knows there were days when the difference between failure and success was patience in continuing to present the fly known to be the ticket for that day.

The apostle Paul pointed out that living a life pleasing to God—a life of faith—requires endurance and patience. Those are two virtues God Himself gives us, both through the empowerment of the Holy Spirit and by allowing us to go through times that test and strengthen that patience.

Can you think of a better time to have that patience tested, strengthened, and refined than when you're enjoying some quiet, relaxing time outdoors?

. . . .

*Lord, I thank You for teaching me the virtue of
patience—and for doing it while I enjoy my
time at my favorite fly-fishing stream.*

Wilderness Funeral

Endure afflictions, do the work of an evangelist.
2 TIMOTHY 4:5 NKJV

. . . .

On a stormy May day in 1823, with boats anchored midstream in the Missouri River, American trappers splashed ashore for trade with the Ree Indians. Negotiations ended early, though, when the Americans refused to sell guns to the tribe.

At dusk, the shore party went warily off to sleep—until midnight, when a terrifying howl arose. The Rees were killing one of the trappers! The Americans armed themselves and waited for dawn.

At sunup, the Rees attacked with their British flintlocks, killing or wounding many of the Americans, forcing survivors to swim to their boats some ninety feet out. Some made it, some were killed trying. Others, wounded, sank beneath the cold waters.

Downriver, at a defensible island, survivors held an impromptu burial service. Jedediah Strong Smith—a courageous young Christian who would one day become famous for his wilderness exploits—stepped forward to pray in "the first recorded act of public worship in South Dakota," as commemorated in a mural in the South Dakota state capitol.

How can we show our faith in public today?

. . . .

Father, may I always step forward for You,
no matter when, no matter where.

The Center of It All

From heaven the LORD looks
down and sees all mankind.
PSALM 33:13 NIV

. . . .

From the middle of an ocean, we get an unusual perspective. Beyond sight of land, the horizon is a straight line between sea and sky—turn a complete circle and the line goes with you. If the sea is calm, the horizon often seems higher, giving us the effect of being at the bottom of a shallow saucer, or perhaps at the focal point of a lens.

It can be a lonely experience, or it can make us feel like the world revolves around us, like we are the center of it all. Strangely, both feelings are true.

In a world of seven billion people, it is possible to be entirely alone, both physically and emotionally. Yet each one of us is the focus of God's attention. In His infinite power and love, He sees nothing more important in the universe than individual human beings.

That's a sobering thought when we're contemplating a tough moral choice. But it's an incredibly comforting thought when we're far from a safe harbor.

. . . .

Father God, You see the faults I hide from the world.
Please help me to deal with them, so I might be
more the person You would have me be.

Escaping to a Mountain

*In the LORD I take refuge. How then can you
say to me: "Flee like a bird to your mountain"?*
PSALM 11:1 NIV

. . . .

Birds often build their nests in high trees or in the clefts of cliffs in the mountains. When attacked, they'll flee to their refuge.

When some of David's worried advisors warned that a conspiracy of enemies was building and that he should retreat to some wilderness stronghold, David insisted that he would take refuge in the Lord. In Psalm 18:2, David said, "The LORD is my rock, my fortress. . .my God is my rock, in whom I take refuge." David would flee like a bird to his mountain—only his rock fortress was spiritual. He would stay right where he was, trusting God to protect him.

When we know we're doing God's will—when we are right where we should be—we can trust God to protect us. We're not easily scared off. We may waver and be tempted to retreat to some "safer" place, but if we know that God is with us, the best course of action is to stand our ground.

. . . .

*God, help me take refuge in You. May I never
fear either enemies or the storms of life.*

Do Not Waver

*The one who doubts is like a wave of the sea
that is driven and tossed by the wind.*
JAMES 1:6 ESV

. . . .

The outfielder raced forward with the crack of the bat. Then, suddenly, he backtracked. Quickly he adjusted again, racing toward the plate.

By the time he decided where the ball was headed, it dropped harmlessly in front of him. What should have been an easy out turned into a bases-clearing double that put his team behind.

The ballplayer had been fooled. That happens in the Christian life, too. We go back and forth, sometimes fearing that a strong stand for God is somehow overbearing. But wavering just makes us look unstable. We're tossed around like a wave in the wind.

Doubt does that to us. Today, let's make the decision today to believe completely in God and His Word. Let's take a stand and follow Jesus.

. . . .

*Father God, bolster my faith today.
Plant my feet firmly in You.*

Lessons from the Wildflowers

*"And why do you worry about clothes? See how
the flowers of the field grow. They do not labor
or spin. Yet I tell you that not even Solomon in
all his splendor was dressed like one of these."*
MATTHEW 6:28–29 NIV

. . . .

Have you ever stopped to consider the beauty and simplicity of the wildflowers—the ones that grow so peacefully on either side of hiking trails, by the river's edge, and on the mountainsides?

There's a great life lesson to learn from each and every one of those flowers, a lesson in how they grow independently of any self-effort.

Wildflowers don't exert their own energies to grow or blossom so beautifully—and they don't worry about when or how they are to bloom. They just do it, simply because that is what God designed them to do.

Next time you're out hiking, fishing, or just enjoying the beauty of nature, take a moment to notice the wildflowers. In many ways, they live a life just like the one God wants us to live: one of peace and rest in Him.

. . . .

*Thank You, Lord, for using something as commonplace
as a wildflower to teach me not to worry. Help
me instead to cast all my cares on You.*

A Small Taste of Paradise

Jesus answered him, "Truly I tell you,
today you will be with me in paradise."
LUKE 23:43 NIV

. . . .

We who enjoy the wonderful natural beauty God has given humankind sometimes refer to our favorite outdoor places as "heaven on earth."

But think for a minute about the most beautiful natural place you've ever visited, and remember that it's only a foreshadowing of the beauty we'll enjoy with our Savior in heaven.

When Jesus told the penitent criminal that he would soon see paradise, it said something very profound about what eternity will be like for those who trust and follow the Lord. Think about it: if God in the flesh—the One who created all the natural beauty we enjoy—calls a place "paradise," it must be that that place outshines even the most amazing natural scenery on earth.

We're experiencing only a small taste of "paradise."

. . . .

Lord, I thank You for the beauty of creation and the
wonder of nature as You have designed it. I thank You,
too, that the beauty I see here on earth is but a faint
copy of the paradise that awaits me in eternity.

Rise above It

Ye are of God, little children, and have
overcome them: because greater is he that
is in you, than he that is in the world.
1 JOHN 4:4 KJV

. . . .

The buzzard was beautifully camouflaged. It scanned the field from its perch—on top of a pile of fertilizer! But, despite its unattractive situation, the buzzard was still awesome. Why? Because it had focus, it knew exactly what it was about, and it was completely at home in its feathers!

We humans, from time to time, find ourselves in less than attractive situations. Sometimes we see them as reflections of our worth. We let them lessen us. Well, we shouldn't!

The buzzard may be one of the masters of the air, but we were given the world to care for. If we remember that then we know we are not here to be dragged down by our situation, we are here to rise above it.

The buzzard was magnificent regardless of what was around it. We can be, too!

. . . .

God, we know You made us for paradise. Jesus came to
lead us back to it. Everything else is a distraction from
who we really are and where we ought to be going.

Streamside Hospitality

*Do not forget to entertain strangers, for by so
doing some have unwittingly entertained angels.*
HEBREWS 13:2 NKJV

. . . .

M ost fishermen are friendly folks, easily approached even
when they're enjoying their pastime at a favorite fishing
hole. That can change, though, if you ask an obviously successful angler what kind of bait, lure, or fly is being used.

For whatever reason, some anglers are reluctant to share
their secrets of success—as if cluing in others will diminish
their own take of fish.

But it shouldn't be that way for followers of Christ, the
men Jesus commanded to fish for people, too.

The Bible commands believers to be hospitable to everyone, to give to those who have needs, and to take advantage of
every opportunity to tell others about God's love.

So when you have the opportunity to share with another
fisherman the reasons for your success, do it cheerfully. You
never know—you might just open a door to telling someone
about the love of God.

. . . .

*Lord, remind me always to treat the others
I meet with hospitality and godly love.*

Our Helper in Trouble

*God is our refuge and strength,
an ever-present help in trouble.*
PSALM 46:1 NIV

. . . .

From a campsite facing a bare rock wall, a father and his three kids began an adventure.

The climb wasn't too difficult. Each person gripped the edges of slabs and wedged fingers in cracks to make their way upward.

At the top, though, Dad had some second thoughts. Going down the same way seemed dangerous—a forty-foot fall to the broken rocks below wasn't his idea of family fun. So he prayed.

Deciding against an immediate descent, the four walked along the ridgeline. Soon, old gnarled trees gave way to a thicket of young saplings among stumps. Evidence of a logging operation meant there must be an old skid road nearby!

Dad and the kids found the safe path, descending at a comfortable walk—and praising their helper in troubles.

. . . .

*Thank You, God, for showing us the way of life—
both for our bodies and our souls.*

The Beginning of Creation

*And unto the angel of the church of the Laodiceans
write; These things saith the Amen, the faithful and
true witness, the beginning of the creation of God.*
REVELATION 3:14 KJV

. . . .

Stargazing has always been a fascinating pastime for those
on Planet Earth.

We stand in awe looking at the Milky Way. We contemplate the Big and Little Dippers, Orion's Belt, and many other constellations. We thrill to catch eclipses or shooting stars as they occur.

Since the Hubble telescope became operational in the early 1990s, we've marveled at breathtaking photographs from deep space. You can truly have a spiritual experience viewing God's handiwork in these images.

As wonderful as the Hubble telescope is, none of its combined technology and equipment can match the optics God created in the human eye. And the eye—as incredible as it is—won't be able to absorb God's magnificence when it sees "the beginning of the creation of God," our Lord Jesus Christ.

. . . .

*Father, the evidence of Your creation is phenomenal. We
can only imagine what it will be like to see You in eternity.*

God Is Faithful to His People

The remnant of Jacob shall be in the midst of
many peoples like dew from the LORD, like
showers on the grass, which delay not for a
man nor wait for the children of man.
MICAH 5:7 ESV

. . . .

Ever visited the Holy Land or a Civil War battlefield or some other place in which history was made? Generation after generation visits such places, and each person probably has a similar thought—that history unfolded in the same dust or dew they're standing in. No matter how many decades or centuries pass, the wonder of the place remains.

God's been sending dew and rain for thousands of years, and He'll continue to do so as He pleases. The prophet Micah said that the remnant of Jacob is like that moisture that quietly yet widely settles over the land. God preserves His people throughout the ages, and no matter how much one generation frets over the faith—or lack thereof—of the next, God preserves His people.

The next time you see the dew or rain, take it as a reminder of God's promise and ability to remain faithful to believers throughout the ages.

. . . .

Father, I thank You for sending so many
reminders of Your faithfulness to Your people.

God of the Storm

*The voice of the LORD twists the oaks and strips the
forests bare. And in his temple all cry, "Glory!"*
PSALM 29:9 NIV

. . . .

If you've ever hiked through the woods during a powerful
thunderstorm, you know the mixture of fear and awe that
such a storm can evoke. The thunder rattles our bones, and
we keep a watchful eye on the writhing oaks above us, hoping
they can withstand the onslaught of wind.

Such awe is no doubt a mere glimpse of the wonder that
the heavenly beings must experience every moment in the
presence of the God who made the storms. This is the God
who simply spoke the world into existence (Genesis 1), and
He sustains it by His powerful word (Hebrews 1:3). Yet even
in His greatness, He continues to care for His people, granting
them strength and peace (Psalm 29:11).

The next time you're caught outside in a storm, take a moment to praise the One who made the storm—and rest in His
great care for His creation.

. . . .

*Mighty God, I stand in awe of Your glory and might.
Help me to rest in the peace Your greatness brings.*

I Long for Your Peace

*"Blessed is the one who trusts in the LORD, whose
confidence is in him. They will be like a tree planted
by the water that sends out its roots by the stream."*
JEREMIAH 17:7–8 NIV

. . . .

We spend so much of our lives looking for something,
often ignoring the wonders right at our feet.

Take, for example, the singular beauty that God placed
in a running stream. Sitting beside a quiet brook, we begin to sense what God desired for us when He placed these
outdoor cathedrals in our midst. Rushing through life, taking scant breaks to marvel at the wonders of creation, we
miss these small miracles—and fail to receive the amazing,
soul-satisfying blessing of His quiet, confident care.

Near the brook of our lives, there's always a new spring
leaf, bursting with color, brimming with vibrancy, waiting to
fill our spirit with God's peace and joy. Take the time to experience that—a kind of divine complacency with the Master—
near the waters of your life.

Rest in God. Lean back into His arms and trust yourself
to Him.

. . . .

*Lord, please carry my heart to Your quiet
place today. May I know You better,
trust You more, and learn to rest in You.*

Strange Things in the Sea

*O LORD, how manifold are thy works! In wisdom
hast thou made them all. . . . Yonder is the
sea, great and wide, which teems with things
innumerable, living things both small and great.*
PSALM 104:24–25 RSV

. . . .

Scientists are still finding astonishing things in the
sea—"living things both small and great"—from two-
hundred-foot-long jellyfish to stubby-limbed octopi to alien
creatures making their homes near sulfuric heat vents in
the total darkness of the ocean's floor. Scientists have even
discovered shrimp residing in the Mariana Trench—nearly
seven miles down!

In the twenty-first century, dozens of new ocean species
are still being discovered every year—some of them extremely
odd, yet all of them perfectly suited to the harsh and improba-
ble environment they call home. By their very existence, these
creatures show that an intelligent Creator had to have been
involved in their existence.

God not only designed the exotic life forms that inhabit
the depths of the sea, but He designed human life, as well.
And, like these other amazing life forms, we exist to manifest
the wisdom and the glory of God.

. . . .

*Lord, as the psalmist said, how manifold are
Thy works! In wisdom You have made them all!*

Feed My Sheep

*So when they had dined, Jesus saith to Simon
Peter, Simon, son of Jonas, lovest thou me more
than these? He saith unto him, Yea, Lord; thou
knowest that I love thee. He saith unto him,
Feed my lambs.*
JOHN 21:15 KJV

. . . .

A minister on a sabbatical sat by a fire on the lakeshore.
He had risen early and caught a few trout, and now was
cooking them over the fire.

As the smoke mingled with the morning mist rising from
the lake, the man's mind recalled a memory of another early
morning on another lake, many years earlier. Peter was fishing, occupying his body while his mind raced. He had come to
the water to consider his own future after denying his friend
and Lord, Jesus.

The minister envisioned Jesus cooking fish for His disciples then speaking directly to Peter: "Feed my lambs. . . . Feed
my sheep. . . . Feed my sheep."

The man's soul suddenly filled to overflowing. Out of that
moment came a renewed conviction of his calling, a new
sense of direction, and a stronger determination to serve the
sheep in his flock.

Though we're not all "ministers," we're all in the ministry.
How can we feed Jesus' sheep today?

. . . .

Lord, what would You have me to do today?

Remember the Rain

"He draws up the drops of water, which distill as
rain to the streams; the clouds pour down their
moisture and abundant showers fall on mankind."
JOB 36:27–28 NIV

. . . .

When the condensation of water vapor in the clouds becomes so great the clouds can no longer hold it, it drops from the sky and falls to the earth as rain.

Rain means different things to different people. When blown by strong winds, heavy rains can destroy entire cities, as evidenced by recent hurricanes. Well-timed spring rains bring life to crops growing in the fields. Children love to play in the puddles left behind by a rain—but a summer storm can ruin an otherwise great day for a baseball game.

However we view the rain, we humans can't create or prevent it. Rain is just one of the many examples we see of God's majestic, almighty power. Who but the God of all creation can control the rain?

. . . .

Lord, please help me to remember Your
infinite power—in both rain and sunshine.

Know Your Limits

*But Michael, the archangel, when he disputed with
the devil and argued about the body of Moses,
did not dare pronounce against him a railing
judgment, but said, "The Lord rebuke you!"*
JUDE 9 NASB

. . . .

M any animals show an obvious reaction to the invasion of their territory—and it doesn't always look like defense.

Red squirrels protect their turf with an enthusiasm out of proportion to their size. They regularly drive off gray squirrels, which are much larger. Even human beings get an earful of their barking objections.

But sometimes, a vigorous defense leads to bigger trouble.

Consider a pigeon, gallantly dive-bombing an owl, driving the predator away from a nest. For a while, the pigeon succeeds. But when its next approach brings it too close to the interloper, the owl might roll in midair, grabbing the attacker in its talons and flying away with its prize.

There is such a thing as "quitting while you're ahead." As believers, we should be wise, measuring our ability to defend against spiritual attacks. Some enemies must be left to God.

. . . .

*Lord, teach me Your Word so I can resist temptation—
and give me the wisdom to know when to fight
and when to leave the outcome to You.*

Our Helmet

For this reason, take up the full armor of God
so that you may be able to stand your ground
on the evil day, and having done everything, to
stand. . . . And take the helmet of salvation.
EPHESIANS 6:13, 17 NET

. . . .

Yes, that outdoor safety equipment is meant to be used.
Imagine a kayaker slipping laterally against a roaring waterfall. For an instant, he hangs there, supported by his paddle against the plunging water. Then the paddle is ripped from his hands and the kayak rolls beneath the water!

A life jacket protects the kayaker's body but not his head. Surfacing after a full 360-degree roll, he sees his helmet strapped to the front of the boat and thinks, *That's a really stupid place for a helmet*, before being dragged down again into the roiling foam. Finally, he escapes downriver.

A helmet protects our brains, but it's useless until it's worn. Only when we wear all of our armor are we truly safe.

. . . .

Lord, I know You desire my salvation. I thank You
for providing me with full spiritual protection—
help me remember to wear all of it.

Ancient Agricultural Parables

*For as the soil makes the sprout come up and
a garden causes seeds to grow, so the Sovereign
LORD will make righteousness and praise
spring up before all nations.*
ISAIAH 61:11 NIV

. . . .

Salvation and our righteousness are gifts from God. They are His work in our lives. God brings them about; we simply open our hearts to receive them. As Isaiah 45:8 says beautifully, "You heavens above, rain down my righteousness. . . . Let the earth open wide, let salvation spring up, let righteousness flourish with it."

The ancient Israelites were intimately linked to the land and dependent upon the annual rains. They knew it was God who sent rain and His soil in which seeds grew, and they understood that this was true spiritually as well—it was God who showered down His righteousness, causing crops of salvation and praise to spring up in their lives.

Jesus taught similar ideas in the parable of the sower, urging us to receive God's Word "with a noble and good heart" (Luke 8:15). That's the way to really enjoy salvation!

. . . .

*God, help my heart to be open to
Your righteousness and salvation!*

God's Autograph

He is before all things,
and in him all things hold together.
COLOSSIANS 1:17 NIV

. . . .

How can you tell if a painting is by a particular artist? Well, the paints used can be analyzed, and the brushstrokes can be examined and compared. But it's altogether easier if the artist signs the work. The prouder artists are, the more likely they are to put their name to it.

Wouldn't it be wonderful if we could find God's signature somewhere on creation?

Using modern magnification techniques it is possible to see the very material that joins one cell to another. This material, these laminins, are what hold *everything* together. Being biological they can be flexible and bend, but laid out flat they form a very familiar shape, one that would surely serve as a signature for God. For the stuff that holds the whole universe together is shaped like—a cross!

. . . .

It is only human to doubt and ask for proof. But proof
is often open to dispute and misinterpretation. Lord,
if You felt inclined to indulge us with proof it would
have to be incontrovertible; it would have to be
everywhere and everything. And it is.

The Way of a Ship

Three things are too wonderful for me;
four I do not understand: the way of an
eagle in the sky, the way of a serpent on a
rock, the way of a ship on the high seas.
PROVERBS 30:18–19 ESV

. . . .

All the way back to the time of Noah, boats have played a role in God's dealings with humans.

The Lord told Noah to build an ark and to find safety in it. Jesus got into a boat to teach people gathered on the shore. And the apostle Paul used ships to carry the gospel to faraway lands.

In doing their job of transporting people and things, ships have intrigued human beings for thousands of years. Agur, writer of this proverb, called the ship's way on the sea "too wonderful for me." Ships and boats do have a certain majesty about them.

Next time you step into a fishing boat with friends or onto a cruise ship for a vacation with the family, enjoy the sights, sounds, and sensations that people have for millennia. And remember that God has been using similar vessels throughout time to advance His kingdom.

. . . .

Father, please help me to consider
eternity in everything I do.

Bring a Friend

*"In the same way your Father in heaven is not
willing that any of these little ones should perish."*
MATTHEW 18:14 NIV

. . . .

Divers often operate on what they call the "buddy system,"
in which each diver is responsible for the safety of another. Generally using no more than a third of the air in their
tanks on each dive, should something go wrong they have
enough air to get both themselves and their "buddy" back to
the surface.

Divers don't need their "buddy" to be a close friend—any
fellow diver will do. Are we willing to serve our fellow man in
the same way?

As children of God, we know He is the Father of all who
believe in His Son, Jesus Christ. So the next time you see one
of His kids—or yet-to-be kids—in trouble, put the buddy system into effect and help him come home.

. . . .

*Father God, we know You want as many people to
know You as possible—in fact, all heaven celebrates
when a person is saved. Give me the courage to invite
everyone around me to find his way home.*

Outdoor Equipment

So God created man in his own image,
in the image of God created he him;
male and female created he them.
GENESIS 1:27 KJV

. . . .

Technology keeps improving our outdoor equipment, from the mountain bikes and four-wheelers we ride to the GPS systems that tell us how to get back home.

But our most amazing equipment has always been right with us: the human body, handcrafted by God. Think of everything the body does on a "simple" hike: The legs propel the body forward, adjusting effortlessly to changes in terrain. Arms and hands provide balance and aid progress on particularly challenging trails. Eyes and ears take in the stimuli of the woods—the colors of the leaves, the sounds of the birds— and the brain analyzes that data without slowing the ongoing physical processes in the slightest.

Meanwhile, our conscious thoughts run from family to work to church to that funny movie we just saw. . .and maybe, if we're lucky, that gallon of milk we were asked to pick up on the way home.

There will never be a machine to compare with the human body!

. . . .

Thank You, Lord, for my amazing body.
May I honor You in the way I care for it.

How to Be a Blessed Hunter

*"If you come across a bird's nest beside the
road, either in a tree or on the ground, and the
mother is sitting on the young or on the eggs,
do not take the mother with the young."*
DEUTERONOMY 22:6 NIV

. . . .

Ancient Israel had hunting laws just like we do today, and for similar reasons: God knew that unregulated hunting would, over time, deplete the wild game population. So although He didn't explain the reasons for the rule, He told the Israelites to let mother birds go free.

Domestic chickens didn't yet exist in Israel, but God knew the Israelites would enjoy cooking eggs or raising wild birds for meat. He allowed that, yet told them to let the mother birds escape and take only the young, "so that it may go well with you and you may have a long life" (verse 7).

It seemed like a small rule—and many Israelites were doubtless tempted to break it—yet God promised that if they obeyed, He would see and bless them for it. Though not always specifically stated, there are blessings attached to obeying *all* God's rules—even when no one but God is watching.

. . . .

*God, please help me to obey You,
even in the "small" rules.*

Joining Creation in Praising God

*"You will go out in joy and be led forth in
peace; the mountains and hills will burst into
song before you, and all the trees of the field
will clap their hands."*

ISAIAH 55:12 NIV

. . . .

Think about this: the scenery and the sounds you enjoy in
the outdoors are a means by which God allows the whole
earth to speak praises to His name.

God created the world around us to serve as our temporal home, but He also created it to glorify Himself. It truly
serves as a beacon of praise to the entire universe. God made
all of creation itself not just for us to enjoy, but also to joyfully
praise Him.

The next time we're out in the woods, on a mountaintop,
or near a river, let's stop to soak in the view and listen to the
beautiful sounds of nature. Let's remember that God created
and sustains all those things—then join creation in praising
His wonderful name!

. . . .

*Lord, I thank You that You allow me to live in Your
joy and peace, that You allow me to join Your
creation in praising Your holy name.*

Custer's Last Fall

Pride goes before destruction,
and a haughty spirit before a fall.
PROVERBS 16:18 NKJV

....

A daredevil from his youth, George Armstrong Custer was a reckless Union cavalry commander in America's Civil War. Tough, intelligent, and arrogant, Custer was last in his class at West Point but first in the line of battle. At the head of his troops, he often galloped into the face of enemy guns. Few of his men escaped injury, and many died—but Custer's successes helped him become the nation's youngest major general at age twenty-five.

When the war ended, Custer received command of the newly created Seventh Cavalry at Fort Riley, Kansas. He spent the next ten years fighting Indians.

On June 25, 1876, on a scouting mission with his soldiers, he decided to attack an Indian village without waiting for backup. Wanting the glory, he instead found himself surrounded by two thousand Indian warriors—and his 210 soldiers were slaughtered to a man.

The lopsided battle has been called "Custer's Last Stand." The famed Sioux chief Sitting Bull, who was present at the battle but didn't fight, later said, "They say I murdered Custer. It is a lie. He was a fool who rode to his death."

Beware of pride.

....

Lord, I would learn of You.
You are meek and humble of heart.

People of Wisdom and Understanding

From Issachar, men who understood the
times and knew what Israel should do. . .
1 CHRONICLES 12:32 NIV

. . . .

If you've ever enjoyed a "guided" fishing trip—meaning a trip with an experienced, knowledgeable guide—you know how successful you can be with someone who really knows what they're doing.

Fishing guides are an amazing breed. They know how to catch fish in the best and the worst of conditions. They know what bait to use at a given time and place, and they know how to best present it to wary fish that wouldn't give a look unless it seemed just right.

At times in our lives, we all need a "guide," someone who understands exactly what's going on with us and what we need to do about it. Some of God's greatest gifts are the wise and knowledgeable friends and acquaintances He puts in our lives for just that purpose.

. . . .

Father, I thank You for putting people in my life—
even in my recreational pursuits—whom You've
blessed with wisdom and understanding.

Join the Rescue Team

*For ye were as sheep going astray; but are now
returned unto the Shepherd and Bishop of your souls.*
1 PETER 2:25 KJV

. . . .

When someone gets into trouble on the hills there will usually be a Mountain Rescue team somewhere willing to lend a hand. The members of Mountain Rescue are usually climbers themselves and almost always volunteers. Each time they go out to bring an injured climber or lost hiker back they put themselves in danger.

Why?

The most common answer is that they hope someone would do the same for them. That's probably true, but there is also something about the hard realities of the hills that remind folks we are all in this together.

With that in mind, let's look around at our own fellow travelers. Some are on the right path, others are hurt, and others are straying into danger. Let's volunteer for the Heavenly Rescue team and bring them all home safely.

. . . .

*Lord, we know You will rejoice in our safe arrival,
but we also know each soul that doesn't make it
will break Your heart. Help us help the others,
for their sake and for the love of You.*

Finding Mercy in the Shade

Now the LORD God appointed a plant and
made it come up over Jonah, that it might be
a shade over his head, to save him from his
discomfort. So Jonah was exceedingly glad
because of the plant.
JONAH 4:6 ESV

. . . .

Kill them with kindness—it's an axiom we use to encourage one another when we've been wronged. Rather than plotting revenge, we aim to win a person over by killing our own pride. It's contrary to every part of our nature, but not to God's.

After he finally obeyed God by preaching to the Ninevites, Jonah was angry with God because the entire country repented. Jonah hated the Ninevites—before their conversion, they were one of Israel's worst enemies who, in Jonah's mind, didn't deserve God's mercy. Ironically, he was about to be blessed by God's kindness in the midst of his own selfishness.

Jonah went outside the city, sat down in despair, and hoped for death. But God showed mercy and appointed a plant to grow over his head, providing shelter from the sun.

If God could forgive the wicked city of Nineveh and send blessed shade to a selfish and disobedient prophet, shouldn't we forgive those people who wrong us?

. . . .

Father, prepare my heart to show kindness
to the next person who wrongs me.

Walk in the Light

But if we walk in the light, as he is in the light,
we have fellowship with one another, and the
blood of Jesus, his Son, purifies us from all sin.
1 JOHN 1:7 NIV

. . . .

Campers can't get enough of their favorite activity. No matter how many times we've been "out there," it never gets old. There are so many things to experience and enjoy:

- Cooking freshly caught fish on an open fire—scrumptious
- Breathing fresh, open air—exhilarating
- Sitting around a campfire with family and friends—uplifting
- Lying in a sleeping bag under the moon and stars—awesome
- Listening to the symphony of nocturnal creatures—tranquil

But getting up in the wee hours, finding the flashlight dead, tripping over rocks, stubbing a toe on a tree root, or turning an ankle in a hole—that's no fun at all.

That's exactly what life is like when we're separated from the true Light, Jesus Christ. Walk in the Light!

. . . .

Lord, this world is so dark spiritually.
Please help me always to walk in the light
of Your Word so I won't stumble and fall.

Ravaged, Majestic Forests

Even the junipers and the cedars of Lebanon
gloat over you and say, "Now that you have
been laid low, no one comes to cut us down."
ISAIAH 14:8 NIV

. . . .

The towering cedar tree with its spreading branches is so majestic that it's the very symbol of Lebanon, emblazoned upon her flag. This Middle Eastern country has been famous for its cedars for millennia, its mountains once thickly cloaked with forests.

No more. Centuries of logging have left only scattered cedar groves. The toll was especially heavy when conquerors ravaged Lebanon's forests to build fleets of warships, siege towers, and palaces. The Assyrians boasted, "I have cut down its tallest cedars" (Isaiah 37:24 NIV). No wonder that after the Assyrians fell, the trees were said to rejoice.

In our time, we need wood to build our homes and furniture—but more and more Christians are realizing the need to conserve natural resources and heritage areas for future generations. We don't have to be tree huggers, but God *does* call us to consider others' needs, to be good stewards of the world He's put in our care.

. . . .

Lord, help me to do my part
in caring for Your creation.

Pilgrim's Rest

A generous person will prosper; whoever
refreshes others will be refreshed.
PROVERBS 11:25 NIV

. . . .

A long a high, winding road overlooking Pennsylvania's
Tulpehocken Valley is a sign labeled PILGER RUH, meaning "Pilgrim's Rest." Pilger Ruh is a nearby spring, named
some 265 years ago by a traveler on a missionary journey to
the Indian towns of Shamokin and Wyoming. He was Count
Nicolas Von Zinzendorf, Moravian leader and spiritual pioneer among the American Indians.

In his native Germany, Von Zinzendorf offered asylum
to a number of persecuted Christians from Moravia and Bo-
hemia, allowing them to construct homes on a corner of his
estate. This "Moravian" group grew into a remarkably zealous
and compassionate community of believers, the first Protestant group committed to taking the gospel to unreached people in other lands.

Just as Zinzendorf's hospitality refreshed many in Europe,
so this small spring on an American hillside refreshed him
and his fellow travelers on a day in 1742.

Today, you'll still find Pilgrim's Rest bubbling from that
Pennsylvania hillside. Outfitted with a handy piece of PVC
for ease of drinking, it's as pure and refreshing as it was in
Zinzendorf's day—and a beautiful reminder of our role as
Christians in a dry, thirsty world.

. . . .

Lord, let Your living water flow from me.

The Vineyard God Planted

Return to us, God Almighty! Look down from
heaven and see! Watch over this vine, the root
your right hand has planted.
PSALM 80:14–15 NIV

. . . .

A vineyard seems like the epitome of peaceful agriculture, but in Israel, grapes grew on the slopes of forested hills. As the psalmist Asaph complained, when a vineyard's stone wall was broken down, "boars from the forest ravage it, and insects from the fields feed on it" (verse 13).

In this psalm, Asaph compared the Israelites to a grapevine God had planted in Canaan. He cleared the ground and planted them, and they flourished and filled the land. Now they were being cut down and burned by enemies. Asaph begged God to resume His tender care.

Sometimes, we're a lot like the ancient Israelites. We can look back at the miraculous ways God has provided for us—in our marriages, families, jobs, finances, health—but we also see many of those good things coming under attack, perhaps falling apart. "Why?" we ask.

Let's remember that we are God's workmanship, dependent on His ongoing care. Cry out to God for His protection and blessing—and patiently wait for His answers.

. . . .

Lord, I'm Your child. Please watch over me
and help me to live the life You want me to live.

A Steady Light

*You lead humble people to do what
is right and to stay on your path.*
PSALM 25:9 CEV

. . . .

Find the Big Dipper in the night sky. The two stars at the leading edge of the "ladle" are known as pointer stars. If you draw an imaginary line from the bottom pointer through the top and keep going, the next star you'll meet is Polaris, the Pole Star.

Throughout history the Pole Star has given northern travelers their bearings. Columbus used it as he voyaged west. Marco Polo would have watched it as he ventured east.

We may feel a kinship with previous generations as we gaze upon a steady light that they, too, saw in their night sky. But our souls have a deeper kinship with the One who created Polaris and all the other stars. The motion of the universe may eventually remove Polaris from true north—but God will always be here, showing us the perfect direction in which to travel.

. . . .

*Father, fashions and trends come and go,
and ideas of the good and right vary with
the generations. Please guide me through this
confusing world on Your path, which never changes.*

Tiger Moth Technology

The thing that hath been, it is that
which shall be; and that which is done
is that which shall be done: and there
is no new thing under the sun.
ECCLESIASTES 1:9 KJV

. . . .

Have you ever watched a movie scene of aerial combat, seen the pilot's head jerk up as he hears the beeping noise that means another plane has locked its targeting radar onto him? Then the drama begins as he tries to evade the "bogey."

Modern fighter craft are more and more dependent on radar detection and devices for avoiding radar detection. It's a technology race employing the best minds in the defense industry.

It's well known that bats use radar (or sonar) to fly and hunt, but did you know that the tiger moth (one of the bat's favorite snacks) has a radar-disrupting capability?

What we spent millions of dollars over many decades developing was actually created millions of years ago and gifted to some of the humblest of God's creatures.

. . . .

The more we understand about creation, Lord,
the more we realize we have no reason to think
so very highly of ourselves. You are the Father;
we are simply the admiring children.

Blessed in the Desert

God was with the boy, and he grew.
He lived in the desert and became an archer.
GENESIS 21:20 CJB

. . . .

Abraham dearly loved his son Ishmael. When God told Abraham that another son, Isaac, would be born and would be counted as the firstborn, Abraham cried out in prayer for Ishmael. The Lord replied, "I have heard you. I have blessed him" (Genesis 17:20).

When the day came for Abraham to send Ishmael away, it grieved his heart. But, as promised, God went with the boy. The angel of the Lord miraculously supplied water for him and Ishmael grew, mastered the bow, and became a skillful hunter. He took a wife and became the father of twelve Arab princes.

No, Ishmael didn't inherit Canaan—that was the inheritance of Isaac's descendants—but he became a hunter and a herdsman who joyed in roaming the wild, open spaces of the wilderness. And he was blessed.

God has great love for the also-rans, those who seem to be rejected, and those who must settle for second place. If you stay close to God, even the desert can be a place of joy.

. . . .

God, when I feel like a runner-up in the race of life,
help me to count my blessings.

Contentment in God Alone

Now godliness with contentment is great gain.
1 TIMOTHY 6:6 NKJV

. . . .

You've probably seen the bumper sticker that says, THE WORST DAY FISHING IS STILL BETTER THAN THE BEST DAY WORKING.

Even the most skilled and experienced fly fishermen will have days when nothing they try works—when they're "skunked," going home without catching so much as a single fish. But should they consider that a "bad day of fishing"? It depends on their perspective.

Fly-fishing—like most other forms of angling—isn't always about the number of fish caught. As someone once said, "Fishing isn't always about catching fish, but about being where the fish are." And, we might add, where we can enjoy God's presence in nature.

No fly fisherman hopes for a day without catching fish. But for those who see their time on the river as an opportunity to enjoy some quiet moments with God, a day without catching fish is still worthwhile. That's what streamside contentment looks like!

. . . .

Thank You, Father, that I can be content in spending time with You—even when my time enjoying Your creation doesn't include success at my favorite fishing hole.

Seeing the Invisible in the Visible

*For since the creation of the world God's
invisible qualities—his eternal power and
divine nature—have been clearly seen, being
understood from what has been made.*
ROMANS 1:20 NIV

. . . .

Ansel Adams was a photographer best known for his black-and-white images of natural scenery in the American West, particularly California's Yosemite National Park. You don't have to look long at a collection of Adams's art to know that he loved Yosemite's natural beauty.

Just as we can learn a lot about artists or photographers—about what is really important to them—by looking at their work, we can learn a lot about God by studying the awesomeness of the world He created.

Next time you have a chance to see a towering mountain range, a pristine tract of forest, a meandering river, or any other example of nature's beauty, consider them not only as valuable natural resources God has given you to enjoy. Look at them also as reflections of the magnificence, beauty, and goodness of the One who, with just His spoken word, made them as reflections of Himself.

. . . .

*Glorious God, I thank You that though You are
invisible to finite people like me, You have given me
glimpses of Yourself through the created world.*

Remember Past Victories

*"The LORD our God handed him over to us, and
we defeated him, his sons, and his whole army."*
DEUTERONOMY 2:33 HCSB

. . . .

Imagine a family taking up kayaking on the river rapids—
they don't tackle the most dangerous waters first. (Though
Mom might tackle Dad, who came up with this whole crazy
idea.)

Wise kayakers consider the "class" of a river before entering the water. Class I waters are easily navigated, while Class
VI rapids are considered "unrunnable." Trained guides help
less-experienced boaters advance through the levels.

In the spiritual life, God also trains in stages. He often allows us to experience small trials to give us confidence in His
faithfulness. As we remember how He's helped us through, we
build up hope and trust for the next, potentially larger, trial.

To strengthen the Israelites for coming warfare, Moses reminded them of battles they'd won with the Lord's help. Today,
as we're faced with spiritual challenges, let's remind ourselves
of past victories, too—always recalling the God who guided
us through.

. . . .

*Lord, You have been my strength in the past. Now give
me strength to overcome the new challenges I face.*

Skydive!

Come near to God and he
will come near to you.
JAMES 4:8 NIV

. . . .

There's no feeling quite like exiting a soaring airplane.

When you jump from a plane moving in excess of one hundred miles per hour, your body moves forward with the plane momentarily. Then you decelerate, and the force of gravity begins pulling you straight down. That moment of deceleration is the closest a person can come to actually flying without the aid of a machine.

As a parachutist begins to plummet toward earth, everything becomes silent. Then the parachute opens, and the built-in "dog door" flaps make a faint sound. This slight noise is the only sound to be heard as the skydiver continues to descend from the clouds.

It's hard to be more alone than at this point of a dive. Though we Christians know we're never truly *alone*, since God is always with us.

Use those quiet moments—while floating to earth under a parachute or maybe when you first get into your car for the commute home—to spend with the Lord. There's nothing like being completely alone with Him.

. . . .

Lord, during my busy day, help me to
find some quiet time alone with You.

A Gift for Your Children

Hear, my children, the instruction of a father,
and give attention to know understanding.
PROVERBS 4:1 NKJV

. . . .

One day, the nineteenth-century politician and diplomat Charles Francis Adams wrote in his personal journal, "Went fishing with my son, a day wasted." The boy, however, didn't quite see it that way. That same day, Brooks Adams wrote in his journal, "Went fishing with my father today, the most glorious day of my life!"

Many parents are amazed when they learn, too often after the fact, what was really important to their children—namely, the meaningful time they spent enjoying Mom or Dad's company doing what otherwise might have seemed unimportant and forgettable.

We live in a busy world, one that can sap us of the time and energy it takes to spend meaningful time with those we love. Why not commit to spending at least some of your time outdoors connecting with those who are most important to you?

. . . .

Father, remind me daily that You desire to use all
things—even the outdoor adventures I enjoy—to
help me connect meaningfully with those I love.

Soggy-Sandaled Sovereign

And they came to him, and awoke him, saying,
Master, master, we perish. Then he arose, and
rebuked the wind and the raging of the water:
and they ceased, and there was a calm.

LUKE 8:24 KJV

. . . .

Who can control the waves? Most of us wouldn't try. But legend has it that Canute, an English king, had his throne placed by the shore. He sat there and commanded the waves not to wet his feet. Of course he got soaked.

Historians debate whether he was serious in his intent or whether he was trying to teach his courtiers a lesson in humility. Either way, shortly afterward he hung his gold crown on a crucifix and left it there to show the King of Kings was more powerful than any ordinary king.

It sounds like Canute was not as foolish as the legend makes him seem. He knew that while no earthly power—then or now—could control the waves, there once was a man who did just that.

. . . .

From time to time, Father, we get a little too full
of ourselves. Help us follow Canute's example and
hang our self-importance on Your self-sacrifice.

Always Keeping Count

*"Even the very hairs of your
head are all numbered."*
MATTHEW 10:30 NIV

. . . .

If you ever join an organized outdoor expedition, watch the leaders. Chances are, you'll see them regularly stepping aside and casting an eye on the whole group, their fingers or lips moving. They're counting.

Those leaders might know you personally, or they might be just getting to know you—but that's beside the point. Before setting out, they'll have a *number* in mind: the number of people in the group. That figure becomes an obsession of sorts, something to be searched for and found at regular intervals during the trip. It will only be forgotten when everyone is safely home again.

On a much larger level, God is also keeping track of us. But He never knows us simply as a number. As God does with the stars, He keeps an overall count while calling us each by name (Psalm 147:4).

Now that's a God you can trust.

. . . .

*Lord, it's easy to get lost in this great,
big world—at least that's what we
sometimes think. Remind me, Father, that You
call us all by name. We are always safe with You.*

Uphill Battle

*And when they came to the place that is called
The Skull, there they crucified him, and the
criminals, one on his right and one on his left.*
LUKE 23:33 ESV

. . . .

A family was hiking up a steep hill, heading toward a place on the river called "Water Slide." It was fun for the children, okay for the parents, and sheer agony for the grandfather. His knees were on the verge of buckling and his lungs felt like they were going to explode. Often, he had to sit down to rest.

"Come on, Grandpa, you gotta see this place," his eight-year-old grandson yelled from somewhere ahead. *This is just too hard,* the older man thought. *Even to share the gospel with my grandson.*

Then he thought of another hike, of sorts—one Jesus had taken. It was much harder than this one, and it happened so talks like the man had planned with his grandson could take place. Jesus sacrificed everything for us, enduring far more than the physical stress of the crucifixion.

After a few moments of rest and prayer, Grandpa found the hill wasn't so steep after all.

. . . .

*Lord Jesus, help me to remember that Your love for me
cost You far more than anything could ever cost me.*

Grandeur of God's Creation

Who has measured the waters in the hollow of His hand, and marked off the heavens by the span, and calculated the dust of the earth by the measure, and weighed the mountains in a balance and the hills in a pair of scales?
ISAIAH 40:12 NASB

. . . .

Focused on the pressing responsibilities of life, it's easy to forget the infinite greatness of God. That's why He tells us to meditate on what He's said. Sometimes, it's easier to do that outdoors.

A change of scenery can broaden our perspective on life, unveiling the unmistakable evidence of God's power and wisdom. At the seashore, the ocean's vast, curving horizon displays the enormity of God's creation. The plains offer a similar though unique testimony, humbling us with the Lord's greatness. And looking down from a mountaintop has caused many believers to breathe out the classic hymn lyrics, "How great Thou art!"

Even Jesus took time to retreat for rest to the mountains—so why shouldn't we?

The One who created all things wants us to recognize His greatness and praise Him for it. Our peace and confidence grow in proportion to our understanding of God's power.

. . . .

Great and mighty God, what peaceful confidence I can enjoy in You. I praise You for Your power and the love You show by telling me of Yourself.

Hide and Go Seek

Where can I go from your Spirit?
Where can I flee from your presence?
PSALM 139:7 NIV

. . . .

The little boy next door has a problem—he sucks his thumb. But he thinks he's solved his problem by going down to the basement because "God can't see me down there." There are a roof and two floors between him and God.

Do we occasionally think like that?

Psalm 139 has been credited to David, something of an outdoorsman himself. What if he'd figuratively turned his adventurous spirit loose and played a one-sided game of hide-and-seek with God? Would it have been possible to climb to the highest point of Mt. Everest to escape the Lord?

Or if he could have donned scuba gear and dived seven miles down into the Pacific Ocean's Marianas Trench, would he have outdistanced God?

What if it were possible to switch off the millions of heavenly bodies and snuff out every lamp on earth—would David have been out of God's sight?

Good news! The answer to all three "what ifs" is a resounding "no!" God knows you better than you know yourself—and He loves you completely.

. . . .

Father, I'm never out of Your sight because
of where I am; You are there, too.

The Reality of Heaven

*However, as it is written: "What no eye has
seen, what no ear has heard, and what no
human mind has conceived"—the things God
has prepared for those who love him.*
1 CORINTHIANS 2:9 NIV

. . . .

Vacations take planning. Many of us pore over brochures or Internet sites, trying to decide exactly where we want to go. Finally, we narrow our choice down to that one spot that creates the most excitement—say, for example, the Grand Canyon.

When the big day arrives, we take to the road with great anticipation. At first the miles pass quickly. . .but before long, the trip seems to slow. All this "fun" actually becomes tiring.

We check the map a hundred times to verify our route. The road goes up and down, curving to the left, then the right. We stop to eat and rest then try to make up for lost time. But deep down, we know we're getting closer with every mile, and the initial excitement returns.

At last we arrive and impatiently make our way to the rim where the view immediately takes our breath away. It's more than the pictures revealed—more than we ever imagined.

Multiply that excitement by a zillion times for a preview of heaven.

. . . .

*Father, I know that when I see You and all You've
prepared for me, it'll take my breath away.*

Where Water Never Ceases

"Does the snow of Lebanon leave the crags of Sirion? Do the mountain waters run dry, the cold flowing streams? But my people have forgotten me."
JEREMIAH 18:14–15 ESV

. . . .

We often focus on the beauty of the outdoors, and justifiably so. God's creation is clearly something to marvel over. But His creation is also practical.

Sirion, also known as Mount Hermon, could experience snow on its top during summer. In Bible times, as the snow melted it ran down the mountain, providing an abundance of water for drinking or planting crops. It was an ideal environment, a place where the waters didn't run dry. No right thinking person would want to walk away from such a place.

So why do we do that with God? Though He provides for our every need, we often stray from Him. We leave His mountain in search of even more—only to find out that other places are in decay, void of living water.

Today, listen for God's call to remain on His mountain, basking in His excellent provision.

. . . .

Father, I am prone to wander. I thank You for reminding me that You always provide for my needs.

Take the Plunge

*The angel showed me a river that was crystal
clear, and its waters gave life.*
REVELATION 22:1 CEV

. . . .

A hot summer day at a park in the mountains wouldn't be
complete without a dip in the river.

Cool, clear water runs in this river, and the swimming
hole is deep enough for diving. Just back from a long, dusty
hike, you resist the urge to jump in with your gear. But now,
changed into swimming suits, you behold the water, looking
more inviting than food. . .and you jump. Breaking the surface, your whole body feels chilled, refreshed, and strangely
cleansed. Pushing off the rocky bottom to come back up for
air, you feel marvelously alive.

Diving into a relationship with God can be like that. Covered with the dust, sweat, and grime of a day in the world,
dive deeply into time with your Creator and Savior. Bring
your cares, problems, and concerns to Jesus in quiet prayer.
Lay them at His feet and immerse yourself in His love.

. . . .

*Lord, today I want to immerse myself
in You fully, deeply, and completely.*

Statesmanship and Confidence

Three things are stately in their stride,
four of stately gait—the lion, mightiest of
beasts. . .the greyhound, the billy-goat and
the king when his army is with him.
PROVERBS 30:29–31 CJB

. . . .

Some animals seem to exude confidence. They are "stately in their stride," meaning they walk around as if they own the place. The lion is fully aware of his power and the wide berth the other animals give him. The greyhound knows that he is pure speed. The billy goat is ready to lower his head and take on just about anybody.

Humans are different. A pro wrestler swaggering around, boasting loudly, is not "stately"—and is quite likely to be hit from behind by a folding chair. What *is* statesmanlike, however, is a king sure of his authority, with all the might of his army to back him up.

As Christians, we are strong when we are confident that God is with us, protecting us and fighting for us. Evil may arise, but we aren't afraid. The economy may be shaken, but we don't panic. Rumors and bad news may cross our doorstep, but we aren't troubled.

Now that's confidence.

. . . .

God, help me to trust that You are with me,
ready to fight on my behalf.

Stay with It

*And let us not be weary in well doing: for in
due season we shall reap, if we faint not.*
GALATIANS 6:9 KJV

. . . .

Hikers, bikers, and swimmers do well to remember this commonsense idea: Going out is always easier than coming back.

While you might feel fine on the first leg of the journey, the doubling back may leave you weary, blistered, and cramped—possibly even in danger. But if you travel too far on the way out, you can't just quit—especially if you're swimming. Somehow, you've got to find the reserves to keep moving, heading for home, like the hummingbird that flies, nonstop, over the Gulf of Mexico on its annual migration.

There's a parallel here to the Christian life. The apostle Paul encouraged us to "not be weary in well doing," to keep moving forward whatever the difficulties. We might be tired when we're done, but there is a reward—the "reaping" we enjoy "in due season."

So don't faint. Stay with it!

. . . .

*Lord, I get tired on this journey. Help me to "not be
weary in well doing" and never faint along the way.*

Drinking from Blessed Springs

*"The wild animals honor me, the jackals
and the owls, because I provide water in the
wilderness and streams in the wasteland, to
give drink to my people, my chosen."*
ISAIAH 43:20 NIV

. . . .

There were very few springs and streams in the desolate Sinai Desert, and when the children of Israel wandered there for forty years, God created new water sources to meet their needs. Twice He caused water to burst out of a rock. Once he made bitter water drinkable.

When the Israelites moved on and settled in Canaan, these new springs and streams were still there in the desert. The Israelites no longer needed them, but they provided welcome refreshment for desert creatures. Animals such as jackals and owls had little consciousness of God, but their constant, contented satisfaction brought honor to Him.

Often when God sends refreshment and unexpected blessings into our lives, others are blessed, too. When God gives us outstanding gifts or abilities or allows us to experience an unexpected windfall, they are to benefit not only us, but others as well—even the jackals and owls and other "rejects of society."

. . . .

*God, I thank You for the refreshment You
give me, refreshment that blesses others, also.*

In the Echo of the Most High

Their voice goes out into all the earth, their
words to the ends of the world.
PSALM 19:4 NIV

. . . .

Shout at the edge of the Grand Canyon, and your voice echoes on and on. God's voice is that way, too, reverberating over creation, calling us to turn our faces toward Him.

Life comes at us hard these days. The stresses of our daily experience make us old before our time. But if we stop and listen, we can hear God speaking to us. We can find refreshment and vitality in the wonders of His world.

God is calling to us from the "canyon rim" of life. His arms beckon us in the warm sunshine of His love. We are never far from Him, never out of His sight, never away from His protection.

Listen for His voice, and shout back to Him. In the echo of the Most High is peace and safety.

. . . .

Lord God, may I hear Your voice echoing
throughout Your creation today. Show me
Yourself in Your Word and Your world.

Thriving in the Storm

Suddenly a furious storm came up on
the lake, so that the waves swept over
the boat. But Jesus was sleeping.
MATTHEW 8:24 NIV

. . . .

What outdoors person hasn't, at one time or another, been stuck in the middle of a good old-fashioned rainstorm? We often remember those storms with laughter, recalling how helpless we felt as the water pelted down. Sometimes, however, those storms remind us of the dangers of outdoor life.

Jesus faced the latter kind of storm, the likes of which His disciples—at least four of whom were experienced fishermen—had apparently never seen before. As the rain and wind pounded their boat, they longed for Jesus to do something before they died in the middle of the lake. Jesus, on the other hand, was sleeping soundly.

Jesus could rest like that because He knew that God's plan for Him didn't include dying in a freak storm. What a picture of peace and assurance He provides!

No matter what kind of storm we face, we can rest, just like Jesus did, in the assurance that God knows what's going on—and that He's working to use that storm for our benefit and His glory.

. . . .

Father, I thank You for reminding me that You
are with me through even the worst of storms.

A Mindful Creator

When I consider your heavens, the work of your
fingers, the moon and the stars, which you have set
in place, what is mankind that you are mindful of
them, human beings that you care for them?
PSALM 8:3–4 NIV

. . . .

One of the best parts of camping is sitting out in the fresh air, just looking up and enjoying the beauty of the night sky. Away from city lights, you can see more stars than some people know exist—and if you're out at the right time of year, you can try counting the "shooting stars" during the Perseid meteor shower, an annual display of celestial fireworks that people have been watching since the time of Christ.

Even more wondrous than the night sky, however, is contemplating the love of the God who made it all.

It's difficult to fully comprehend how the God who simply spoke our cosmos into existence could have the time or the inclination to think about us. But He does—and for that reason we can enjoy both the wonders of creation and the love of our Creator.

. . . .

My Creator—and my heavenly Father—I can't
begin to express my joy and gratitude and
amazement that You made such an awesome
universe. . .yet Your thoughts are on me!

The Trash, the Trees, and the Truth

*Religion that God our Father accepts as pure
and faultless is this: to look after orphans and
widows in their distress and to keep oneself
from being polluted by the world.*
JAMES 1:27 NIV

. . . .

The television news reporter stood by a lake as she discussed the problem of pollution. People had apparently visited the lake to fish, swim, and enjoy the beauty of the water. As they left, though, their trash remained in the water and on the shore. The problem had been growing as thoughtless people failed to clean up after themselves.

Before long, the pollution made the whole area seem dirty. The water was less clear. The shore was less pleasant. The entire lake just felt tainted.

A sad story? Absolutely. And it can happen in our own lives when we are careless enough to allow "pollution" to occur. Just as a little bit of garbage contaminates a large recreational area, a little bit of sin can make our whole lives a mess.

. . . .

*Lord, I need to control my thoughts and actions.
May I never allow sin to pollute my personal world.*

Alone with God

*"I know every bird of the mountains, and
everything that moves in the field is Mine."*
PSALM 50:11 NASB

. . . .

In the busyness of life, sometimes we desperately need to be
alone with our Maker.

Many have found that a walk to some wooded spot—a
place that others rarely visit—helps. Even if we lack a fully
defined prayer to God, the time is well spent just sitting and
saying, "Lord, I'm here."

While you commune quietly with God, a curious bird
may hop nearby to investigate this new thing in his world.
Squirrels and chipmunks may frolic nearby, as well, checking
out the big creature in their territory.

Since God knows—and owns—every bird and beast, realize that He may have sent these visitors to remind you of His
own presence. Even the creatures say, "Lord, I'm here."

. . . .

*Lord, Your wisdom is glorious in the least of Your
creation. I thank You for the confidence that comes from
the knowledge that wherever I am, You are there, too!*

The Lake of Death

*Then Death and Hades were thrown into the
lake of fire. This is the second death—the lake
of fire. If anyone's name was not found written
in the book of life, that person was thrown into
the lake of fire.*
REVELATION 20:14–15 NET

. . . .

Badwater, the heart of California's Death Valley, is North America's lowest elevation at 282 feet below sea level. It is also one of the world's hottest locations. Though it appears to be a dry lake bed, hikers quickly discover that the surface is only a crust covering thick mud below.

Badwater can be a very dangerous place. An ultramarathoner challenging the elements sat down to rest within sight of his truck—and died when his dehydrated body was unable to reach the water inside the vehicle.

That's a picture of our spiritual lives. Satan wants us to think we can make it on our own—that we don't need a Savior. But the heat of temptation and the gooey muck of sin can overwhelm us, with disastrous results. Only Jesus sees us through.

. . . .

*God, I realize I can't hike through life by myself. I thank
You for Your grace that brings me through the dangers
of sin, and writes my name in Your book of life.*

The Leader Beside You

So Christ was once offered to bear the sins of many;
and unto them that look for him shall he appear
the second time without sin unto salvation.
HEBREWS 9:28 KJV

. . . .

If you go on an organized hike you might notice the group leader usually has the biggest backpack. They aren't showing off when they hoist that megapack and stroll alongside you. It will hold all their own gear, plus an emergency kit for every conceivable difficulty *you* might experience. It might seem light, but that's because they aren't thinking about it; they (if they are any good at their job) will be totally focused on you and your fellow hikers. If problems arise, they want to spot them early and be able to deal with them then and there.

What a comfort it is to know someone who has all the answers is focused on you and your problems.

Am I still talking about hiking leaders? What do you think?

. . . .

Jesus, You became human to know our faults,
were betrayed to know our despair, and died to
know our deepest fears. You have walked the trail
and come back for us. You are the Guide.

The Art of Fishing

*As Jesus was walking beside the Sea of Galilee, he
saw two brothers, Simon called Peter and his brother
Andrew. They were casting a net into the lake, for
they were fishermen. "Come, follow me," Jesus said,
"and I will send you out to fish for people."*
MATTHEW 4:18–19 NIV

. . . .

An old-timer, while fly-fishing in southwest Missouri's
Gasconade River, was asked how to catch fish. His response? The fisherman needs to act like a bug.

Then he demonstrated. The angler dropped a fly in the middle of a small circle of water ringed by leaves and debris, saying that when a bug falls from a tree into the water, it lies stunned for a few seconds before kicking a leg or flicking a wing. If he correctly imitated the bug, he said, there would be a fish waiting to grab the fly.

When the old fisherman gently jerked the line, the fly was immediately swallowed by a large black perch, which he handily whisked into a waiting net.

Is there a lesson here for us as "fishers of men"?

. . . .

*Lord, help me to present the gospel in such a way as to
attract men to You. Please make me a fisher of men.*

Bearing Up

Thou shalt guide me with thy counsel,
and afterward receive me to glory.
PSALM 73:24 KJV

. . . .

Following a compass bearing is relatively easy, once you know how.

Take a line of sight at the required angle and try to find a clear point in the distance, matching your direction of travel. Walk to that point and take another bearing, continuing the process until you reach your destination.

Open ground is easy to travel, but it's a different game walking through woods, where there are no distant markers. To hold the compass and doggedly follow its arrow doesn't really work, as trees, rocks, and other obstacles force you to deviate from the true direction. All those little turns add up—and you might come out of the woods a mile off course.

God's laws are a lot like a compass. They tell us exactly where we need to go, but sometimes we convince ourselves that bending a rule here or there won't make any difference. The reality is that all those little infractions add up to a lot of trouble.

To reach our destination safely, we need to walk on God's bearing, not our own. After all, He can see above the trees!

. . . .

Father, I think I know a lot—but You know everything.
Teach me humility, and guide me safely home.

Thirsty for God

As the deer pants for the water brooks,
so pants my soul for You, O God. My soul
thirsts for God, for the living God.
PSALM 42:1–2 NKJV

. . . .

Three kinds of deer once lived in Israel—the red deer, the spotted fallow deer, and the roe deer. None of them roam Israel's wilds anymore, but they once were a common sight in her forests and wilderness. As the sun beat down all day, deer became very thirsty. Flowing brooks were few and far between, and the deer knew exactly where they were.

David recognized that he thirsted for God just like the deer that stopped grazing, compelled to seek out a brook to slake its thirst. For David, taking time to "tank up" on God was not simply an obligation or a religious duty—it was a pressing need. He could never be too busy for God.

Thousands of years have passed and we today live in just as dry and thirsty a world. While many religions and faiths promise spiritual refreshment, there is still only one true source of flowing, life-giving water—our living God.

. . . .

God, I desperately need You. Help me
to drink deeply of Your Spirit today.

Who Made All This?

*"Lift up your eyes on high, and see
who has created these things."*
ISAIAH 40:26 NKJV

. . . .

As a believer and an agnostic stood on an outcropping of rock on a high hill, the nonbeliever marveled at the natural beauty. Without thinking, he asked out loud, "Whose idea was all this?"

Without missing a beat, the believer smiled at his good friend and answered, "No one thought of it, Frank. It just happened!"

Nearly every outdoors person—hikers, campers, hunters, fishermen, and all the rest—has had those moments when he stood before a breathtaking natural scene and marveled at the beauty of it all.

When you know God and what His written Word says about Him, you have an ironclad answer to the question that stops science and human reasoning in their tracks, namely, "Who made all of this?" Nothing we see outside exists or sustains itself apart from the Creator who expressed His love for each of us by setting in motion everything we see.

. . . .

*Father, I thank You for loving me enough to create
all I see around me. Let me never forget that
these things are Your special gift to me.*

Tumbleweeds

*Make them like tumbleweed, my God, like chaff
before the wind. As fire consumes the forest or
a flame sets the mountains ablaze, so pursue
them with your tempest and terrify them with
your storm. Cover their faces with shame,
LORD, so that they will seek your name.*
PSALM 83:13–16 NIV

. . . .

On the north Texas plains, where the land is flat and the wind is strong, tumbleweeds roll. Most bushes and trees are firmly rooted below the surface—but tumbleweeds, in a stiff wind, easily break off at the ground then roll along with the breeze.

The psalmist compares God's enemies to tumbleweeds. A tumbleweed bears no fruit. Its stalk quickly dries and becomes light and brittle. It's fit for nothing except the fire.

That's the kind of tree Jesus once described. "A good tree cannot bear bad fruit, and a bad tree cannot bear good fruit. Every tree that does not bear good fruit is cut down and thrown into the fire. Thus, by their fruit you will recognize them" (Matthew 7:18–20).

What can you do today to avoid tumbleweed status?

. . . .

*Lord, please plant my roots deep within You,
helping me to bear good fruit in abundance.*

Playing the Blame Game

*Then he said, God do so to me, and more
also, if the head of Elisha the son of
Shaphat shall stand on him this day.*
2 KINGS 6:31 ASV

. . . .

Let's face it—bad things happen to good people. We drive to the campground and discover we forgot the tent. Someone falls off his horse, but there's no first-aid kit. It's a great day on the lake—until we learn someone has forgotten to top off the fuel tank.

Tempers rise. Fingers point. Words fly.

"I thought you were going to bring it!"

"Didn't you say you've done this before?"

"Off with his head!"

Maybe that last comment is a bit extreme. But it is what the king of Israel declared about the prophet Elisha when an enemy siege caused Samaria's food to run out and cannibalism ensued. The king blamed Elisha—who was clearly not at fault.

When something good goes awry, it's not time for argument and blame. Look at it as an opportunity to show compassion to others, demonstrating God's goodness through you.

. . . .

*Lord, I know there will be times when
things don't go well. Please use me to heal
bruised egos and wounded hearts.*

Rescue the Perishing

Rescue the perishing.
PROVERBS 24:11 MSG

. . . .

Summer in the outdoors was a wonder-filled world for a young boy. Otters in the river. Beavers building dams. Turtles sunning aside the lazy waters. Morning and evening, the concert of the birds. Every night, the distant grumble of the bullfrogs in the swamp.

But the boy soon found trouble in Eden. Someone had speared eels and left them rotting on the rocks. Turtles, shot, had been left along the path. Traps had been laid for beavers in the shallows of the river bank.

One day the boy found a groundhog caught in the metal teeth of a trap. He knew the animal would chew its leg off to get free—or, he thought, he could free it himself. It was risky. The animal was wary. But the boy managed, with a long stick, to open the trap and let the groundhog go.

God wants us to "rescue the weak and the needy; deliver them" (Psalm 82:4 NIV). Far more important than animals are the weak among men—the orphans, the oppressed, the aged, and the unborn. Let's do what we can to minister to their needs.

. . . .

Father, help me to set the captive free.

The Grass That Forever Grows

Therefore, my dear brothers and sisters, stand firm.
Let nothing move you. Always give yourselves fully
to the work of the Lord, because you know that
your labor in the Lord is not in vain.
1 CORINTHIANS 15:58 NIV

. . . .

No matter how well we mow the lawn, trim with the weed eater, and pull weeds from the driveway, it will all need to be done again—often very quickly.

The grass demands much of our time and attention. To keep it nice and green, it needs to be watered. Watering it, however, makes it grow faster! To maintain a good-looking lawn, we must work on it regularly. When we stop, we notice the grass (and weeds) quickly become messy and ugly.

Such is our walk with the Lord. It takes regular work—praying often, and reading His Word for guidance—to keep our lives in line. A well-manicured relationship with Him is work. But it's work far more important than our lawns!

. . . .

Lord, draw me close to Yourself. May I have the courage
and faith to regularly maintain my walk with You.

Lord of All Creation

*"Go to the sea and cast a hook and take the
first fish that comes up, and when you open its
mouth you will find a shekel. Take that and
give it to them for me and for yourself."*
MATTHEW 17:27 ESV

. . . .

Every warm Saturday (and even some that aren't so warm),
fishermen take their friends or their kids to ponds, lakes,
and rivers, hoping that this will be the day they catch "the big
one." They'll use all sorts of methods to scout the fish: firing up
electronic fish finders, asking other fishermen about the best
spots, reading websites to find out where the fish are biting.

Imagine what must have gone through Peter's mind when
Jesus told him to catch a particular fish that would contain
enough money to cover their taxes. With His statement, Jesus
made it clear that He was not only Lord over humanity, but
also of the sea and everything in it—to the point of knowing
the exact location and contents of a single fish.

The next time one of your friends or children catches a
fish, use that experience to share an important truth: the lord-
ship of Christ.

. . . .

*Lord, You are indeed over every created thing.
I am in awe of Your power!*

The Little Things

*Catch the foxes for us—the little foxes that ruin
the vineyards—for our vineyards are in bloom.*
SONG OF SOLOMON 2:15 HCSB

. . . .

A once-promising season was falling apart. The team that had gotten off to a quick start in April was slumping in August.

Back in spring training, coaches had drilled the players on the fundamentals of baseball—and through April, May, and June they made the game look easy, winning series after series. But in July, they started to go south. Little things, at first—missed cutoffs, bungled double plays. Then the problems snowballed. A series sweep turned into a losing streak, and the promising season sank beyond recovery.

When we begin to let little things go, big things will ultimately suffer. If we "forget" to pray, stop our daily time in God's Word, sleep in on Sundays, our spiritual walk will inevitably begin to falter.

Let's focus on the fundamentals. Don't let the "little foxes" throw you off your game.

. . . .

*Lord, help me to hold on tightly to You. May I
remember—and pursue—the "little things."*

Stewards of the Outdoors

*The LORD God placed the man in the Garden
of Eden to tend and watch over it.*

GENESIS 2:15 NLT

. . . .

What goes through your mind when you hear the words *conservation* and *preservation* as they apply to the outdoors?

Sadly, too many people—Christians included—don't take the idea behind those words seriously enough. Some seem to have the attitude that the world is temporal, and therefore doesn't need to be treated with great care and respect.

David wrote, "The earth is the LORD's, and everything in it" (Psalm 24:1 NIV). That biblical truth takes on a deeper meaning for those who enjoy resting and recreating in the outdoors, for the ones who realize that the resources they use for that purpose are not their own but God's.

The Lord created the mountains we climb, the trails we hike, the streams and lakes we fish, and everything else we have the privilege of using for outdoor recreation. He never intended for us to mistreat or abuse those things, but to "tend and watch over" them.

. . . .

*Lord, help me never to forget that I am a steward and
a caretaker of the outdoor resources You created.*

AAA for the Soul

*A highway will be there; it will
be called the Way of Holiness. . . .
The unclean will not journey on it.*
ISAIAH 35:8 NIV

. . . .

One of the most frequently used metaphors for life is the old saying, "Life is a journey."

It's doubtful that the prophet Isaiah was acquainted with that figure of speech, but he does use highway as a description of life seven times in his Old Testament book. But Isaiah isn't referring to just any road—his highway is a special place. It's a godly boulevard that lifts traffic above the attitudes and corruption of the world.

Isaiah's highway is for the believer with a God-given map, for those who are committed to a holy lifestyle. The highway's toll is surrender to Christ.

This highway is for those who know just where they're going. . .and exactly who is traveling with him.

. . . .

*Father, the way of holy living can be a challenging
road; please help me find a holy lifestyle.*

Back to the Garden

Give us this day our daily bread.
MATTHEW 6:11 KJV

. . . .

One of the beautiful things of the summer is the backyard garden.

Even if we've never had a garden ourselves, we might recall our parents or grandparents and their vegetable plots. There were times when community gardens prevailed, as people rented space, planted their seeds, and fed an entire family on the produce they harvested.

In modern times, we've become so used to buying things from the supermarket that we seem to think the produce grows there on the shelves. But with the rising prices of recent years, some of those things we took for granted are now much more precious. Could this be an opportunity to move back to simpler times—with more cooperation and unity among family and friends? Could that even extend to our communities?

This is a good time to remember who our source is—and trust Him totally for our daily bread.

. . . .

*Lord, You are my source for everything. May I
never fear the pressures and trials of this world.*

He Speaks from the Wilderness

*And it came to pass, when Saul was returned from
following the Philistines, that it was told him, saying,
Behold, David is in the wilderness of Engedi.*

1 SAMUEL 24:1 KJV

. . . .

Can you remember the times you felt closest to God? Do you reflect on the times His peaceful words cleared the road ahead and sharpened you for the next challenge? Have you thanked Him for the advice, courage, comfort, and wisdom He provides?π

Find time for God.

That's one of the toughest challenges facing us today—finding time to be alone with God, time to speak to Him of our hurts and our hopes. But when we get away from the "highway," seeking solitude in the "wilderness," He can clear our heads and open our hearts to hear His voice.

The highway is littered with angry, selfish, spiteful people—those who hurt others because they haven't found their own healing with God. But He's calling to us from the wilderness of our hearts.

Meet Him there.

. . . .

*Father, give me quiet moments with You,
so I might dwell in the wilderness of Your love.*

Handling Money

*When you gaze upon riches, they are gone, for
they surely make wings for themselves, and fly
off into the sky like an eagle!*
PROVERBS 23:5 NET

. . . .

The desert in the noonday sun has its own special kind of beauty. Hiking in the desert heat, much of our fatigue comes from our muscles and internal organs overheating. That condition quickly saps our energy.

A Pentagon division, the Defense Advanced Research Projects Agency, has developed an air-conditioned glove that cools blood flowing from the hand back toward the heart and lungs. The effect is real and remarkable: it vastly increases endurance and allows soldiers to hike up and down desert ridges for much longer without rest or overheating. The glove is about the size of a boxing glove, completely encasing the hand and preventing the carrying of a weapon or use of the hand for other purposes. Cost of the project: about three million dollars.

We might obtain a similar benefit by carrying a frozen bottle of water, wrapped in a clean sock. Total cost: about a buck.

. . . .

*God, please help me to be a wise
steward of the money You've given me.*

Stronger Together

*So Peter was kept in prison, but the church
was earnestly praying to God for him.*
ACTS 12:5 NIV

. . . .

Kayak instructors sometimes play a little game with learning paddlers: they "raft up."

Calling all the kayaks alongside each other, they tell the boaters to lay their paddles across their bows. As each person grips their own paddle and that of a neighbor, there's enough stability for someone to walk or crawl along the backs of all the kayaks then make their way around the fronts.

Normally, it's just a simple exercise for beginners—but if that group were to be caught in a storm, "rafting up" would provide stability and security for everyone. It might even save a life.

Church is a lot like that. In our modern society, church can take second place to a comfortable bed, household chores, or sporting events on a given Sunday. But in times of personal need or persecution, "rafting up" with fellow believers can make all the difference.

. . . .

*Father, I thank You for Your support system here
on earth. Help me to remember that even if I don't
need the help right now, I can provide some for
a brother or a sister in Christ.*

Jets and People

*Then God said, "Let the land produce vegetation
. . . . Let the water teem with living creatures. . . .
Let the land produce living creatures. . . .
Let us make mankind in our image."*
GENESIS 1:11, 20, 24, 26 NIV

. . . .

A popular speaker on creation likes to discuss the complexity of living beings. Noting that a jumbo jet has more than six million parts, not one of which can fly on its own, he makes the point that it's only when those parts are correctly assembled that a jet functions as it should, lifting tons of passengers and baggage to heights above thirty-five thousand feet. It seems a miracle of invention that such a thing can happen at all.

The greater miracle, though, is that God created *us* to function as we do. We move, communicate, and think. And we adapt—if any of our "parts" are functioning incorrectly, the rest of our body can make adjustments automatically. How many machines can do that?

A jet plane is a wonderful invention, but nothing compared to a complex, living organism. Inventive minds conceive amazing machines from the resources God has provided—but it's *only* God who can create life itself from nothing.

. . . .

*Lord, please help me to see Your fingerprints on this
world, to stand in awe of Your magnificent creation.*

Natural Reminders of God's Goodness

"I will make rivers flow on barren heights, and
springs within the valleys. I will turn the desert into
pools of water, and the parched ground into springs."
ISAIAH 41:18 NIV

. . . .

Those of us who've hunted, fished, camped, or hiked in the west American outdoors called the "high desert" know how a good rain shower can change what had been only hours before a dry and dusty land into an area teeming with the sights and sounds of natural life.

These are great moments to enjoy the beauty, the sounds, and the smells of nature. It's also a good time to remember the goodness of God.

In the Bible, rain in a dry place is often an illustration of God coming to His people to bless them, to give to them what they didn't have before, or to restore what had been lost. So if a good shower soaks you in a generally dry place, let that be a reminder of God's goodness to you.

. . . .

Father, I thank You for the natural reminders
of Your willingness to bless and to do for
me what otherwise couldn't be done.

Unequaled Treasure Is Ours

Again, the kingdom of heaven is like unto
treasure hid in a field; the which when a man
hath found, he hideth, and for joy thereof goeth
and selleth all that he hath, and buyeth that field.
MATTHEW 13:44 KJV

. . . .

Imagine a boy spending long hours hoeing weeds in a garden. It's mindless work and not much fun. After a long day in the sun, he's eager to head inside for a good meal and a night's rest.

But one day, he finds an old stone arrowhead during his hoeing. And that little discovery turns the work into a treasure hunt. Who knows what artifact might show up under the next weed?

Now the mornings bring a certain eagerness to get back to the search. The boy is even a little reluctant to leave at dinnertime.

That's the way our Christian life should be—a daily discovery of new and exciting truths about God, the greatest treasure of all. He is worth every effort we make to find Him!

. . . .

God our Father, I thank You for making me an heir
of the kingdom through Jesus, our Savior. Help me
to keep my heart fixed on the treasure of You.

A Different Kind of Fishing

"Come, follow me," Jesus said, "and I
will send you out to fish for people."
MATTHEW 4:19 NIV

. . . .

Up north in Michigan and Minnesota, where real fishing experts pursue real fish (that would be walleye and northern pike), anglers take their sport seriously. A note on a bait shop bulletin board explains it best: "If I'm not back by sundown, tell my bride-to-be and the preacher to express regrets—the walleye are biting!"

Jesus' appeal for anglers was for a different kind of fishing, of course. To fishermen who knew what fishing was all about, continuing their trade with the Lord was an invitation they couldn't turn down. Recognizing that they had been "caught" and changed by Jesus, it was now their turn to "fish."

Without the benefit of seminary or any evangelistic training, they dropped their nets and followed their new calling with an even greater passion than that with which they'd made a living. How about us?

. . . .

Jesus, give me the enthusiasm for soul-winning
that I have for my hobbies. Help me to influence
my friends and family for You!

Peaceful Meditations

*Judah and Israel dwelt in safety, from Dan even
to Beer-sheba, each man under his vine and
under his fig tree, all the days of Solomon.*
1 KINGS 4:25 RSV

. . . .

It was hot in ancient Israel, and in the heat of the day Israelites would seek out shade. Since leafy grapevines covered almost every hill and shady fig trees were common in Israel, farmers would relax under them—whether sleeping, meditating, or talking during a break from their work.

It was considered a great blessing to be able to rest peacefully in the shade. As Micah 4:4 says, in the coming age when men beat their swords into plowshares, "They shall sit every man under his vine and under his fig tree, and none shall make them afraid" (RSV).

Do you have a "vine" or a "fig tree" you enjoy sitting under, a favorite place where you can relax and meditate on God and what He's doing in your life? Maybe it's a literal grapevine covering your back porch. Maybe it's a bench beneath a tree or a rock overlooking a creek. Maybe it's your bathtub. Wherever it is, go there today.

. . . .

*God, I thank You for the time to rest beneath
my grapevine—and think about You.*

A Picture of Compassion

"Who provides for the raven its prey,
when its young ones cry to God for help,
and wander about for lack of food?"
JOB 38:41 ESV

. . . .

Ravens are intelligent birds. But they're also scavengers, symbols of evil and death in literature. They probably aren't the most popular of birds among people.

But the Bible says specifically that God provides for the ravens. And when a raven's young cries for help, it's crying out to God. If the call came to us, we might not help—we humans tend to distribute our compassion on those we see as most deserving of it. God, on the other hand, shows compassion to even the raven.

When you're out and about today, search for a raven. If you find one, don't view it as a symbol of evil and death, but rather as a picture of God's compassion.

. . . .

Father, give me a chance to offer compassion
today to someone I might normally pass by.

Delivered from Temptation

*The Lord knows how to deliver
the godly out of temptations.*
2 PETER 2:9 NKJV

. . . .

Fly fishermen know a little something about temptation. Most serious fly fishermen carry boxes and boxes of flies—of different colors, patterns, and sizes—because they know that an ordinarily wary, selective trout is likely to give into temptation and take at least one of the flies they carry with them.

Like the fly fisherman who knows what it takes to tempt a fish, our spiritual enemy, the devil, knows well what it takes to tempt us into sin. And the best fly fisherman has nothing on the devil when it comes to presentation. Satan will lay a terrible temptation in front of us, making it look harmless—but hooking us and persuading us to do things we know displease God.

The "good news" side of the story is that God knows well how to keep us from temptation. If we look to Him for strength, He's more than willing to keep us and protect us from harm.

. . . .

*Father, I thank You for using something as simple
as fly-fishing to show me Your vigilance to deliver
me from the temptations of this world.*

Carefree in Chaotic Times

Behold the fowls of the air: for they sow not,
neither do they reap, nor gather into barns;
yet your heavenly Father feedeth them.
Are ye not much better than they?
MATTHEW 6:26 KJV

. . . .

Proverbs 6:8 (NIV) tells us to consider how the ant "stores its provisions in summer and gathers its food at harvest." Ants know that winter is coming, and they work hard to gather and store to meet those future needs.

Yet Jesus knew that we would tend to be preoccupied with the future, so He advised us to focus on one day at a time. He reminded us that even though birds don't "gather" and "store," God provides for their needs. Of course, birds work hard. They need to, since some of them must eat 100 percent of their body weight each day. And parents feeding hungry chicks are constantly searching for food.

The point is this: we should work for the future but not be anxious about it. Have a long-term savings plan, yes, but focus on one day at a time. Work hard, then trust your finances—and your future—to God.

. . . .

Father, help me do what I can
today to provide for my future.

In a Tight Spot

They called to you for help and were rescued.
They trusted you and were not disappointed.
PSALM 22:5 NCV

. . . .

You're on a smooth rock face, hundreds of feet up. You need a handhold if you're going to go any farther, but there just isn't one to be found. There is a crack in the rock but very little to grip. What to do?

Here's where you call on a friend. That's the affectionate name for a piece of climbing equipment also known as a spring-loaded camming device. Slip it into a tight space and it expands, gripping the rock. Then you can attach a carabiner, slip your safety rope through it, and relax. Even if you were to fall now, your "friend" would catch you.

Wouldn't it be great to have a friend for every tight spot we find ourselves in? Of course, we do: Jesus makes a better anchor than any camming device. Let's trust our safety to our Friend and breathe a sigh of relief. He'll never let us fall.

. . . .

Lord, the things of this world all fail, myself included.
May I trust only in You to catch me when I fall.

Apples and. . .Apples

"Every tree is known by its own fruit."
LUKE 6:44 NKJV

. . . .

The sluggish swamp was a couple of acres of small islands of spongy grass and a brush-choked peninsula that poked into the black backwater. At the end of the solid ground stood a tree that promised afternoon refreshment. Mark hadn't noticed it before—hidden amid the rushes and the reeds. But now, he could see ripe red fruit even across the wide, brackish water. Apples! He couldn't wait to eat one.

Mark scrambled up a wooded hillside, climbed down into the wash, picked his way across wet tufts of thick reeds, and pushed through the undergrowth to where the tree stood.

But what a disappointment—they were crabapples, dry and bitter. Henry David Thoreau described such wild apples as "sour enough to set a squirrel's teeth on edge and make a jay scream."

We often work hard—go out of our way, even—for things that look good but don't pay off in the end. Good fruit is not a matter of what the eye sees, but the nature of the tree. In our lives, if we are branches of God's fruitful tree Jesus, we won't just "look good"—we'll bear fruit that feeds and refreshes many (see John 15:5–8).

. . . .

Lord, You are the vine, we are the branches.

Bonds of Friendship

*A man who has friends must himself
be friendly, but there is a friend who
sticks closer than a brother.*
PROVERBS 18:24 NKJV

. . . .

On a bank of central Oregon's Deschutes River, near a camping area fishermen know as "Mecca Flat," is a small tree, surrounded at its base by chicken wire. In front of the tree, a short piece of rebar holds a sign reading, "In memory of an old fishing buddy." Hanging from the post is a rusty old coffee can, which fishermen use to dip water out of the river for the tree, in memory of fishing buddies who have passed on.

During the dry season, plant life around the little tree turns brown and brittle. But, thanks to the help of its "friends," the tree itself remains green and vibrant all summer long.

Outdoor adventures give us a chance to enjoy one of God's great blessings: the bonds of friendship with others who enjoy the same activities. Each time we head outdoors, let's remember to thank God for the "partners in adventure" He's given us.

. . . .

*Thank You, Lord, for using outdoor activities
to strengthen the bonds of friendship I enjoy
with the people You've brought into my life.*

In the Stretch for God

Let us throw off everything that hinders and
the sin that so easily entangles. And let us run
with perseverance the race marked out for us,
fixing our eyes on Jesus.
HEBREWS 12:1–2 NIV

. . . .

It's obvious that whoever wrote Hebrews had an athlete in mind when he penned these inspired words. For those who are no longer (or never were) into competitive racing, let's agree that the advice applies even to trekkers and hikers like us.

As Greek athletes competed without clothing, the above phrase "throw off everything" applied especially to them. But for the rest of us, our writer adds two comforting words: "that hinder." If it's a stone in the boot, get rid of it! If your socks are causing blisters, change your socks!

If the trail is tripping you up with tree roots and stones, step around those entanglements. Or you could even remove them from the trail.

When the summit seems out of your reach, be steadfast. Keep your eyes on your goal. Suck it up, and push on.

. . . .

Father, I'm not much of a mountain climber;
but help me understand that my goal is Your
Son, Jesus. I will keep my eyes on Him.

The Light of the Moon

*God made two great lights—the greater light
to govern the day and the lesser light to govern
the night. He also made the stars.*
GENESIS 1:16 NIV

. . . .

The second largest object in the sky after the sun—the moon—has always fascinated humans. It's inspired poems, stories, songs, and movies—and has always been associated with romance.

While there are countless references to the light of the moon, the fact is that the moon does not have a light of its own. Its light is simply the reflection of the sun.

Even more interesting, the moon causes the eclipse of the sun when it passes between the sun and the earth so that the great star is partially or wholly obscured.

We Christians are a lot like the moon. We have no light of our own but are simply reflections of the light of the Son of God. We can either reflect the brilliance of His light or we can obscure His light—or hide it altogether.

. . . .

*Lord, please help me to reflect Your light to
a dark world. Don't allow me to hide or block
Your light to those who don't know You.*

Enjoying the Journey

*"When you come into the land and plant any
kind of tree for food, then you shall regard
its fruit as forbidden. Three years it shall be
forbidden to you; it must not be eaten."*
LEVITICUS 19:23 ESV

. . . .

Walking by a fruit tree, you may find that you need to watch your step. When fruit begins to appear on a tree, it soon ripens and, if not picked, falls to the ground and rots.

It's hard to imagine such a tree struggling to produce fruit, but during their first few years, nearly all of them do. Even when that first fruit appears, it's helpful to pluck the fruit as soon as possible—not to consume it, but to prepare the tree to produce more and higher quality fruit as it ages. Some experts suggest three years of this.

"Delayed gratification"—also called *waiting*—isn't a characteristic of our current culture, which wants everything fast. But, like a home-cooked meal that takes an hour or more to prepare trumps a microwave dinner that takes five minutes, waiting often produces the best results.

Are you impatient today? What can you do to better enjoy the journey?

. . . .

*Father, I thank You for reminding me to slow down
and enjoy the journey You've started me on.*

God's Zugunruhe

"Even the stork in the heavens knows her times;
and the turtledove, swallow, and crane keep the
time of their coming; but my people know not
the ordinance of the LORD."
JEREMIAH 8:7 RSV

. . . .

Every autumn—in late August or early September—storks migrate south over Israel, headed from Europe to Africa. Flocks of birds such as turtledoves, swallows, and cranes, following their own interior clocks, also migrate over Israel at the same, predictable times every year. And they come back every spring.

God has built birds' migration instincts right into their genetic makeup, but birds are also keenly sensitive to the changing of the length of the days in their habitat; they undergo physiological and physical changes and experience *Zugunruhe* (German for "migratory restlessness") in the time leading up to migration.

Jeremiah noted that while even birds took note of the changing times, were stirred by nature, and returned to Israel, the Israelites often failed to acknowledge the laws of God and "refuse[d] to return" (Jeremiah 8:5). They weren't attuned to God's Word and failed to respond when He summoned them.

Let's not be like that ourselves. Be sensitive to God's *Zugunruhe*.

. . . .

God, help me to hear Your Word
and return to You when You call me.

What Are You Fishing For?

*He said to them, "Go into all the world and
preach the gospel to all creation."*
MARK 16:15 NIV

. . . .

Have you ever thought of your outdoor adventures as a setting for service to the God who made you one of His very
own?

"Come, follow me,"—Jesus called out to Andrew and his
brother, Peter, the fisherman turned apostle who would one
day take a place of prominence in the Lord's church—"and I
will send you out to fish for people" (Mark 1:17). While God
may not call us to leave everything for full-time service, the
way He did Peter, He has called us to "preach the gospel" in
every place He puts us.

Those who have a passion for fly-fishing know their
fellow anglers are a friendly sort, the kind of people who
enjoy discussing the kind of day they're having streamside.
So when you set out on your fishing trip—or any other outdoor adventure—make sure you take with you the message
of God's love and salvation for a fellow adventurer who
might cross your path.

. . . .

*My Savior, remind me daily that You can use
everything You give me—including my time in
the outdoors—as a tool to reach others for You.*

New Spiritual Practices

*"Now the pig has a split hoof that is completely
divided, but it does not chew the cud;
it is unclean for you."*
LEVITICUS 11:7 NCV

. . . .

Have you visited another country, or even an ethnic area in your nation? As we participate in their culture, we are soon confronted with their, shall we say, "local fare." We have to eat, after all.

If you're accustomed to meat and potatoes, you'll wonder what to do with a plate of Mexico's grasshoppers, chicken feet from Asia, and brain of lamb, a specialty of an English chef. Why else have American hamburger joints sprung up at many tourist destinations around the world?

When the Israelites trekked from Egypt to Canaan, God spelled out what foods were acceptable and forbidden to them. As slaves, they had eaten whatever they were given. Now, God told them to watch what they put into their mouths.

Before we knew God, we followed the world's ways, "eating" whatever was put before us. Now, as believers, let's pay close attention to the Bible's rules of what is acceptable and forbidden. What was once normal should now be as appetizing as pigs' hooves.

. . . .

*Lord, sometimes it's hard for me to let go
of my comfortable ways. Please give me
a greater appetite for heavenly things!*

A Land God Cares For

*"It is a land the LORD your God cares for; the
eyes of the LORD your God are continually on it
from the beginning of the year to its end."*
DEUTERONOMY 11:12 NIV

. . . .

After four hundred years in Egypt, the Israelites knew
how water worked. Barring rare disruptions, the Nile
always flowed; watering crops was so easy that they merely
had to poke a dam with their foot to direct water into irriga-
tion ditches. One word described the water supply in Egypt:
dependable.

Canaan was another matter entirely. Good harvests
depended upon two brief wet seasons, the autumn and spring
rains. These could be unpredictable and required God's constant intervention. God cared for and continually watched
over the land, but as He told the Israelites, whether it rained
or not depended upon how faithfully they obeyed Him.

Does it feel sometimes that living by faith is a hassle? We
may tire of constantly praying for God to meet our needs. We
long for a steady, sure supply. But, like the Israelites of old,
we have left the dependable decadence of Egypt and live in a
more blessed land—a life where our obedience brings God's
blessings.

. . . .

*God, I depend upon You and trust
that You will supply all my needs.*

The God of Time and Seasons

Yours is the day, yours also the night; you have
established the heavenly lights and the sun.
You have fixed all the boundaries of the earth;
you have made summer and winter.
PSALM 74:16–17 ESV

. . . .

Have you ever gone camping, or maybe sat on the deck of a house, and watched as the daylight slowly faded into darkness? You heard the crickets chirping as day turned into night, felt the temperature change, and sensed that another day was gone. But with it came the hope of tomorrow.

Poets, songwriters, and essayists have long been fascinated with the changing of day into night and summer into fall. Inherently they sensed that something bigger than themselves was at work—and they drew great comfort in knowing that such beautiful order exists in the world.

As Christians, we can enjoy all the changes that God brings with time—and we know that He established each change. Be conscious about the changing of time and seasons. Note the beauty and order of each change. And thank God for it all.

. . . .

Thank You, Father, for giving us such a variety of
change to admire as one season transitions to the next.

The Hands

Make it your ambition to lead a quiet life:
You should mind your own business and
work with your hands, just as we told you.
1 THESSALONIANS 4:11 NIV

. . . .

For the most part, human hands are the same. Four fingers and a thumb, the same muscles, the same joints and ligaments.

Brilliant composers like Mozart had hands like us. Master artists like Michelangelo had hands like us. Genius inventors like Thomas Edison had hands like us. If these people could do great things with their hands, why not us?

We may not create new technologies or music or art to be long remembered, but our hands can do things that can make an eternal difference in other people's lives. Maybe our hands can hold another's hands as we talk. Maybe our hands open the door to our homes. Maybe our hands are simply for folding in prayer for others.

Whatever we find for our hands to do, let's do it with all of our heart, just as if we were doing these things for God Himself. Because we are.

. . . .

Lord, may You be eternally pleased
with the work my hands find to do.

Take Time to Enjoy Life

*I commend the enjoyment of life, because there
is nothing better for a person under the sun
than to eat and drink and be glad. Then joy
will accompany them in their toil all the
days of the life God has given them.*

ECCLESIASTES 8:15 NIV

. . . .

Ever feel a little guilty about spending time in the outdoors, relaxing and enjoying God's creation? *After all,* we might think, *isn't there something I could be doing to further my career, to better provide for my family, or to expand the kingdom of God?*

Work truly is a blessing from God, and the Bible teaches that hard work is one of the keys to even further blessing. God wants each of us to do all our work—whether it's in ministry or in the "secular" arena—as if we are doing it for Him (Colossians 3:23).

But while the Bible clearly extols the virtue of hard work, it also honors relaxation and enjoyment. So don't feel guilty when you're on an adventure—take full advantage of the time away from the work God has called you to do.

. . . .

*Father, I thank You for the work You've
given me to do. But I also thank You for
the opportunities to "unwind" and relax.*

A Dry Wadi

"But my brothers are as undependable as intermittent streams. . .that stop flowing in the dry season, and in the heat vanish from their channels."
JOB 6:15, 17 NIV

. . . .

Job lived on the western edge of the Arabian Desert, where very few streams flowed all year long. Most wadis only contained water during the rainy season—between autumn and spring—but ceased to flow during the long dry season. The waters vanished in the summer's heat, leaving behind bone-dry channels like the dusty canals of Mars.

Job complained that his brothers and friends were as undependable as wadis. They were there for him sometimes—a modest supply of friendship and encouragement—but when he *really* needed them, in the times of his deepest grief and anguish, they vanished. They had nothing to give him.

It's hard to pour out to others when we feel empty ourselves. But to take this allegory a step further, we can't just depend upon intermittent rainfall to keep water flowing in our lives. We need to be spring fed—with God as our unfailing source—so that we can always overflow onto others, even during our own dry seasons.

. . . .

*Lord, help me not to fail my brothers
and friends in their time of need.*

I Will Walk among You

"I will walk among you and be your God,
and you will be my people."
LEVITICUS 26:12 NIV

. . . .

Walking along a beach, a calm settles over us. No matter when you visit, the waves never cease. They roll on constantly, powerfully, peacefully.

Trouble is, most of us don't live by the beach. Our visits are few and far between.

Sometimes, we crave the quiet, a peaceful place to think, to plan. But our lives are so full from day to day that we can overlook the feeding of our souls. Then we think for just a second about the beach—and we're transported in our minds to that calming place of sand and surf.

Our spiritual walk is that way. Often, we're too busy to let God into our thoughts. But He's waiting patiently for our moments of recollection—and He's there. God is always there, ready to calm and guide us. It's we who miss Him.

Make some time for God today. He'll make it worth your while.

. . . .

Allow me to live in the beauty of Your peace, Lord. When
I meet You on the beaches of life, please give me peace.

Touch-Me-Nots

"The least of you will multiply into a thousand; the smallest of you will become a large nation. When the right time comes, I the Lord will quickly do this!"
ISAIAH 60:22 NET

. . . .

In the low, wet places of the woods, poison ivy abounds. Nearby, touch-me-not (or jewelweed, as it's also known), often grows. Crushed touch-me-not is a good topical first aid for insect bites and poison ivy. Leave it to God to provide help just where we are likely to need it.

Touch-me-nots can actually be great fun, since their ripe pods pop at the slightest vibration. Walk through a whole patch of touch-me-nots in a boggy meadow, and something marvelous can happen: the first touch-me-nots to burst will throw seeds farther into the patch, striking other plants. They, too, will pop at the vibration, throwing even more seeds into the meadow. Soon, seeds are flying back and forth like an uncontrolled nuclear reaction.

What a picture of God's ways! Like the tiny mustard seed that grows into a large plant, those seemingly small things of this life all have potential for greatness.

. . . .

*Father, help me to wait for Your timing and
trust Your promises! I know that when
You are ready, You will do great things.*

Equipped for the Task

You appoint darkness and it becomes night, in which all the beasts of the forest prowl about.
PSALM 104:20 NASB

. . . .

Humans aren't the only ones of God's creation who work a night shift. Bobcats, mountain lions, coyotes, foxes, raccoons, and deer find it easy to prowl by the light of the moon and stars.

God made these animals' eyes with a reflective surface behind the retina, a special feature that allows them twice the use of the available light. The light stimulates the retina going in, and again on being reflected out. That internal "mirror" is why their eyes shine greenish yellow in our headlights.

Besides the reflective advantages, the retinas of nocturnal animals give images mostly in black, white, and shades of gray, more efficient than ours in dim light.

Most of these animals don't prowl at night to avoid humans. They're just making the best use of the abilities God has given them.

Doesn't it make sense for us to use of the talents and skills God has given us, too?

. . . .

Creator God, please help me to know my abilities and use them in ways that show You as the source of all good things.

Captured by His Love

*Then they that feared the LORD spake often
one to another: and the LORD hearkened, and
heard it, and a book of remembrance was
written before him for them that feared the
LORD, and that thought upon his name.*
MALACHI 3:16 KJV

. . . .

Imagine a coworker whose interest in fishing is proudly displayed throughout his office. There's a clock with an angler dipping his rod every second. On the bulletin board are photos of your coworker in a fishing boat, holding up the latest bass, grinning—though behind each smile seem to be the words, "Hurry up and take the picture—this thing's heavy!" Sometimes he drops by your desk to share some tasty seasoned samples of his recent catches.

Like your friend, God keeps His own record of achievements. He doesn't use a digital camera, though, but a book of remembrance. In that book, God records the names of those who think on Him and respect Him. And He returns the favor!

As you read the words of Malachi, consider what a great God you have. Know that you've been captured by His love—hook, line, and sinker. You *belong* to Him.

. . . .

*Lord, I'm so happy to be Your child—
and for You to be my God.*

Sutter's Sorrow

*"Do not store up for yourselves treasures on
earth, where moths and vermin destroy,
and where thieves break in and steal."*
MATTHEW 6:19 NIV

. . . .

A penniless Swiss immigrant who came to modern-day
California in 1839, Johann Augustus Sutter became lord
of nearly 150,000 acres along the Sacramento River.

He cleared the land and planted orchards, vineyards, and
grain fields. He trapped, fished, and oversaw a herd of thirteen
thousand cattle. He built a mill, distillery, tannery, blanket
factory, and blacksmith shop. Sutter was big.

Then in January 1848, gold was discovered on Sutter's
land. Good news, right? Not really—his estate was overrun,
his crops trampled, his horses and equipment stolen, his livestock butchered for food. Sutter's workers abandoned him to
hunt gold. The government took back a huge tract of land it
had given him earlier. In 1865, a vagrant burned the Sutter
family mansion to the ground.

Sutter spent much of his remaining life petitioning the
government for reimbursement. "Thousands made their fortunes from this gold discovery produced through my industry
and energy," he wrote, "but for me it has turned out a folly."

Johann Sutter died, poor and unrequited, in 1880.

. . . .

*Lord, may I lay up treasures in heaven,
where no thief breaks in to steal.*

Training for the Top

*And Abishai, the brother of Joab, the son of
Zeruiah, was chief of the three. And he lifted up
his spear against three hundred and slew them,
and had a name among the three.*

2 SAMUEL 23:18 ASV

. . . .

With sweat-streaked muscles gleaming in the sunlight, a man crossed the finish line of his first "Iron Man" triathlon. As he slowly sank to his knees, he pumped his fist in a sign of personal victory.

He hadn't won the race, but he'd finished. The previous year he had focused almost exclusively on this moment. The dedication and sacrifice to become one of the few who could successfully complete the course had been enormous. With a finish under his belt, the goal now became to win.

What are your goals? Are you focused on becoming a top athlete, a successful business executive, a published author? Great! Go for it.

The bigger question: are you focusing the same kind of energy and dedication on becoming a man or woman of God? That's even better. Yearn for it. Train for it. Go for it.

. . . .

*Lord, help me today to focus on
becoming the best person I can be.*

Don't Badmouth!

Consider what a great forest is set on fire
by a small spark. The tongue also is a fire.
JAMES 3:5–6 NIV

. . . .

Professional firefighters have always had a certain glamour and mystique to them, especially since that terrible day of September 11, 2001. Whether in the concrete jungles of New York City or the flaming hillsides of the American West, these highly trained specialists battle destructive blazes both natural and man-made.

The biblical writer James used the idea of fire to describe the trouble our mouths can create—and it's not limited to the ladies at church.

Forest fires of hurt feelings and broken relationships are not limited to any particular group. Every time we repeat a racist or sexist remark, we have tossed a small spark into the forest. When we pass along a joke that reflects negatively on anyone—individually or as a group—we are figuratively contributing to a fierce, destructive fire.

Race, womanhood, and religion are nothing to joke about. Let's learn that for ourselves—and teach it to the people in our sphere of influence.

. . . .

Father, I want my influence to be positive. May my
words be acceptable to You.

A Fruitful Eternity

On either side of the river was the tree of life,
bearing twelve kinds of fruit, yielding its fruit
every month; and the leaves of the tree
were for the healing of the nations.
REVELATION 22:2 NASB

. . . .

Fruit trees are always planted in hope.

When we sample our first crop of peaches or cherries, placing them atop a generous scoop of vanilla ice cream, it seems that things couldn't be better. Maybe we've even had thoughts like, *If only it could always be like this!*

God hasn't told us a lot about eternity with Him. But what He has said is all good. And He's indicated we will never have an unmet need. The One who made us also gives us good things to enjoy—for a time in this life, and forever in heaven. And in eternity, we won't have to wait a year between the fruitful seasons. We'll enjoy a harvest every month.

That's the promise we have from our great and gracious Creator. He is worthy of our praise!

. . . .

Father in heaven, You've given me a desire to live
here on earth—but I say with John of Revelation,
"Even so, come, Lord Jesus."

The Feeble Folk

The rock badgers are a feeble folk,
yet they make their homes in the crags.
PROVERBS 30:26 NKJV

. . . .

Rock badgers weigh six to ten pounds and, with their short ears and tails, resemble large guinea pigs. Also called hyraxes, they are found from Israel to South Africa and, as their name implies, they live in the rocks. Rock badgers' chief predators are leopards, hyenas, and especially eagles. At the slightest sign of danger, they dart into holes in the rocks— and are safe. As Psalm 104:18 (NKJV) explains, "The cliffs are a refuge for the rock badgers."

Rock badgers recognize that their enemies are stronger than them and present a very real danger. When an eagle swoops down from the sky, rock badgers aren't so foolish as to stand their ground and prepare to fight. They recognize their limitations and seek refuge in the rocks.

We as Christians have a similar defense. The psalms state that God is our rock, our refuge, and our fortress. Like the hyrax, we are weak, but when danger is near, we can run to God who will protect us.

. . . .

God, help me to honestly admit my weaknesses,
and to run to You to protect me.

Ancient Paths

*Thus says the LORD: "Stand by the roads,
and look, and ask for the ancient paths,
where the good way is; and walk in it,
and find rest for your souls."*
JEREMIAH 6:16 ESV

. . . .

Ever hiked through some woods you'd never been in before? If so, you probably stuck to the paths that hikers before you had followed, and from which they had presumably returned home safely. There's a comfort in knowing that others have paved the way and lived to tell about it. It sets our mind at ease, allowing us to fully enjoy our surroundings.

That's the message God spoke to Israel through the prophet Jeremiah. The Lord had already set His people on a certain course many generations before—and He wanted the present generation to travel those ancient paths, too. God told them that if they would do so, they would find rest for their souls. They could have—but they refused.

How do you view the "old ways"? Do they appear archaic and boring? They probably seemed that way to the people Jeremiah spoke to as well. Don't resist the ancient paths. Walk in them and find rest.

. . . .

*Father, show me the old paths
today and help me to walk in them.*

Surrounded by Support

*Let them praise the name of the LORD, or He
commanded and they were created. . . . Beasts
and all cattle, creeping things and winged fowl.*
PSALM 148:5, 10 NASB

. . . .

G od is praised even in the behavior patterns of domestic
and wild animals.

Those who deny the existence of God might say migrating
geese fly in chevrons because it's easier that way. But how does
every gosling figure that out on its first flight with the flock?

How is it that trout, though raised on unnatural food in
a hatchery, know what to eat when they're placed in a wild
river?

Ruby-throated hummingbirds migrate across the Gulf of
Mexico each fall. The males leave Texas first, then the females.
Last, the young of the year set out across the five hundred
miles of water. All the birds fly alone, including the young,
which have never made the trip before. No GPS here!

Like the heavens, every part of God's creation praises Him.
How? In the sense of making it obvious that God made them.
We who believe God see evidence of His work at every turn.

. . . .

*How great You are, our God and Father.
Thank You for filling our lives with examples
of Your might and infinite wisdom.*

Fountain of Youth

*The Spirit and the bride say, "Come!" And let
the one who hears say, "Come!" Let the one
who is thirsty come; and let the one who wishes
take the free gift of the water of life.*
REVELATION 22:17 NIV

. . . .

For hundreds of years, people have been searching for the fabled "Fountain of Youth."

Water from this fountain, according to legend, can stop the aging process and restore youth. The Spanish explorer Juan Ponce de León was said to have discovered these waters in Florida in the sixteenth century.

Twenty-first-century minds are too "enlightened" to believe in the Fountain of Youth, but we shouldn't overlook Jesus' promise of a life-giving drink that lasts forever. He once described this living water to a Samaritan woman, telling her it could become "a spring of water welling up to eternal life" (John 4:14 NIV).

Here's a "fountain of youth" we can all find—and share with the people around us.

. . . .

*Thank You, Lord, for the invitation to come
and drink from the water of life—the eternal
refreshment that only You can offer.*

The Century

*Forgetting what is behind and straining toward
what is ahead, I press on toward the goal to
win the prize for which God has called me
heavenward in Christ Jesus.*
PHILIPPIANS 3:13–14 NIV

. . . .

Ambitious bicyclists pursue "the century," a single-day ride of a hundred miles.

Aspirants prepare with a weeks-long training program. On the big day, they pack high-energy foods like grains, nuts, and fruits, along with plenty of water for proper hydration. Anticipation soaring, they pedal off to bicycling glory.

But for many, there's a "bonk," also known as "hitting the wall." Maybe they started too fast, forgot to eat or drink soon enough, or just weren't in as good of shape as they thought they were. Somewhere along the line, the century gets tough.

That's a lot like life. No matter how strong we think we are, there's often a bonk. It might be a physical problem, a troubled relationship, a nagging temptation. . .but it's real, and it's hard.

The apostle Paul's advice? Don't stop. Keep moving—straining, even—toward Jesus, the goal of your heavenly century. You can do it!

. . . .

*Lord, when the journey gets hard,
help me to stay the course, eyes always on You.*

High above the Earth

He who sits above the circle of the earth—
for whom its inhabitants appear like
grasshoppers—stretches out the heavens like a
curtain, spreads them out like a tent to live in.
ISAIAH 40:22 CJB

. . . .

It's vital to step back once in a while to get the "big picture." We as Christians are often so focused on ourselves—our needs and wants—that we tend to think of God as being at our service. True, we are God's beloved children, and Jesus did say, "Whatever you ask for in my name, I will do" (John 14:13 CJB), but it's important to be clear on one point:

God dwells in heaven, and we inhabit the earth. Our bodies, houses, and possessions are as impermanent as moths' cocoons, but God dwells immortal among the stars. The galaxies are like a tent spread around Him. In fact, He's so vast that not even the heaven of heavens can contain Him. We are like grasshoppers in His sight.

God loves us. He is aware of our needs, He hears our prayers and promises to answer them—but He is not our servant. He is our *God*, who created us to worship Him.

. . . .

Dear Lord, help me to keep the "big picture"
in mind, remembering that You are in charge.

The Small Things Matter

*For who hath despised the day of small things?
for they shall rejoice, and shall see the plummet
in the hand of Zerubbabel with those seven;
they are the eyes of the LORD, which run to
and fro through the whole earth.*

ZECHARIAH 4:10 KJV

. . . .

The lake seemed pretty tame. The growth around it was marshy and unremarkable. The water itself was brown and lackluster. It wasn't large enough for boating or skiing. There was really nothing exciting about the place.

But a Cub Scout troop thought otherwise. The smooth, flat stones nearby were perfect for skipping across the water. Branches pulled from the bushes on the shore became battleships on the sea. The boys even conjured up schemes to capture the elusive creatures that hid among the reeds.

We can learn a lot from kids. Adults too often go through life noticing only the humdrum scenery. Sometimes, we cave in to grumbling over another "boring day." But God reminds us to pay attention to the small things—the way children do.

Today, let's ask God to open our eyes to see what He sees—at our workplace, our church, or in our home. God loves the things He's created, and He wants us to enjoy the thrill of discovering them.

. . . .

*Lord, please open my eyes to appreciate
Your small wonders around me.*

Reach and Roll

*Now what I am commanding you today is not
too difficult for you or beyond your reach.*
DEUTERONOMY 30:11 NIV

. . . .

Unless you're an experienced kayaker, the little boat might look a bit scary. The thought of capsizing—plunging into the cold, blinding rapids and desperately scrambling for the surface—is something many of us would rather not consider.

But watch a professional kayaker. No sooner does he tip over than he's up again, in a maneuver called an "Eskimo roll." It's practiced in safer waters until it becomes a habit, an instinctive reaction in more perilous moments.

Finding himself upside down, the experienced kayaker will reach out with his paddle, sweep it through the water, and quickly turn upright. How smoothly the whole thing goes depends largely on how far out he reaches.

There's a picture of the Christian life here. None of us can tell when our entire lives might flip upside down—and we risk drowning if we don't know what to do. But if we've practiced reaching out in those quieter, safer times, we'll be able to roll with the trials.

Let's reach out for Christ in the good times—and when trouble comes, we'll soon find ourselves upright again.

. . . .

*Lord Jesus, my arms are short—but Yours encircle the
world. When I reach for You, please set me right!*

Leaving a Blessing

These alone of the circumcision are my
coworkers for the kingdom of God,
and they have been a comfort to me.
COLOSSIANS 4:11 HCSB

. . . .

You can't walk in the wilds for long without gingerly stepping over the traces animals leave behind in the form of *scat*.

It's amazing how much we can learn about an animal based on what it leaves behind. The size of the scat hints at the size of the animal. The content of the scat, such as berries or hair, tells us what the animal has been eating lately.

In a spiritual sense, we all leave something everywhere we go, too. It may be a trace of anger or calm, or perhaps fear or resolve. We leave hints of respect or disdain, smiles or frowns.

Of course, we can't please everyone all the time. But let's remember that we have all of God's strength available to us, to leave a blessing behind.

. . . .

Lord, may I make a difference
in someone's life today for good.

Choose to Obey

Pride ends in humiliation,
while humility brings honor.
PROVERBS 29:23 NLT

. . . .

Imagine a group of hikers on their first visit to a national park. Their self-proclaimed leader has been given detailed directions to a campground, but he believes he can choose a better way—his own way.

In spite of many unexpected obstacles and detours on his chosen path, the guide presses on. Two hours after the group was supposed to arrive at the campground, they're still wandering in the woods. After another hour, the other hikers begin to complain, demanding that "the leader" return to the original plan. Within an hour, they arrive at their destination.

Sound familiar? We often choose to go our own way, though we know that God has already provided a much better path—His way, the best way. Why do we ignore His clear, detailed instructions in favor of our own untested ways? Is it pride? Squelch it! Turn around and go God's way.

. . . .

Father, forgive me of my pride.
Please help me to follow Your way today.

The Gift of Life-Saving Sleep

*I will both lay me down in peace, and sleep: for
thou, LORD, only makest me dwell in safety.*
PSALM 4:8 KJV

. . . .

It turns out that animals don't just hibernate through the
winter 'cause they're lazy. Who knew! Neither do they do it
because everyone else is doing it or because their folks did it
before them.

Scientists have discovered the blood of creatures that
hibernate contains a "hibernation inducement trigger." It
kicks in when daylight decreases, makes the critter gather
food, prepare a burrow, and go for a long snooze. If you inject
HIT into other animals, they will fall asleep, too.

Now people can talk about instinct, learned behavior,
and all the rest, but unless hibernating animals redesigned
their own blood, it seems like they've been given a little extra
something to see them through hard times.

Who could have done that, then?

. . . .

*Father, the gopher, the prairie dog, and the bear are
Yours, and You designed every aspect of them. You truly
are "all in all," and we will never completely understand
that this side of heaven. Until then we will have to settle
for a life of worship and constant amazement!*

Fishermen's Paradise

And the waters of the Nile will be dried up. . . .
The fishermen will mourn and lament, all who
cast hook in the Nile; and they will languish
who spread nets upon the water.
ISAIAH 19:5, 8 RSV

. . . .

For millennia, the Nile was a fisherman's paradise. Not only was the river broad and long, but in the north it fanned out into an enormous delta of meandering estuaries and side channels, rich with food to sustain a vast population of giant catfish, carp, perch, eels, tiger fish, moonfish, and more.

The Egyptians didn't just fish for food. They fished for sport, and tomb paintings show them lazily relaxing in chairs by the riverbank, hooks dangling in the water. Fishing technology has improved since those days, but modern anglers still use the same basic techniques that the ancient Egyptians used—and still love it as much.

When God spoke of a judgment where the Nile would dry up, He described the fishermen mourning and lamenting. When our favorite river or lake becomes too polluted to sustain fish, or overfishing depletes their population, we feel a distinct sense of loss, as well. After all, God ordained fishing to be one of mankind's enjoyable pastimes.

. . . .

God, I thank You for creating fish and for
the joy and relaxation that angling brings.

God's Library

*And there are also many other things which Jesus
did, the which, if they should be written every
one, I suppose that even the world itself could not
contain the books that should be written. Amen.*
JOHN 21:25 KJV

. . . .

Scientists have identified an estimated 1.8 million plant and animal species on our planet. That's a large number, but only a fraction of the total number of all species yet to be cataloged.

The number of stars in the Milky Way galaxy is estimated in the 200 million range—and that's only one of an estimated 200 billion galaxies in the universe.

Earth's closest star is our own sun—a mere 93 million miles away. Its light takes about 8.3 minutes to reach the earth. The Milky Way's most distant star is approximately 60,000 light-years away. It's hard to wrap our minds around distances like that.

The universe we inhabit is truly amazing—because our Creator God is even more so. How many books does it take to explain God and His creation? Only one—the Bible tells us everything He's deemed necessary for us to know. Someday, He'll fill in the rest of the story in person.

. . . .

*Father, I thank You for the gift of Your Son, Jesus,
whose works are beyond print. I look forward
to learning more about Him in heaven.*

Wise, Gentle Counsel

*"People listened to me expectantly, waiting in
silence for my counsel. . .my words fell gently
on their ears. They waited for me as for showers
and drank in my words as the spring rain."*
JOB 29:21–23 NIV

. . . .

Farmers in the Middle East plowed their fields in October after the autumn rains had arrived and softened the hard earth. Then they planted their wheat and barley and waited expectantly for the spring rains to arrive to water their crops.

Job had a reputation for wisdom, for speaking the right words at the right time—and men listened eagerly when he spoke. They held his counsel in high regard. Part of Job's appeal was that his "words fell gently on their ears" like refreshing showers. He showed consideration and kindness to others and didn't berate them.

We all have areas of expertise, but when others come to us for advice, do they soak in our words like spring showers? Or do they dread the lecture that accompanies our counsel, merely enduring our speech?

Let's speak the truth in love (Ephesians 4:15) and bless others both by what we say and the way we say it.

. . . .

*Father God, please give me a wise heart
and a loving tongue so that I can help others.*

The Tick

Fear hath torment.
1 JOHN 4:18 KJV

. . . .

William Wesley Van Orsdel grew up on a farm in Pennsylvania, but God called him westward to preach the gospel. Arriving in Montana on a June Sunday in 1872, he held an impromptu service at the Four Deuces Saloon. When asked his name, his "congregation" found it too big a mouthful, so they dubbed him "Brother Van." The name stuck.

In forty-seven years of ministry, Van Orsdel converted Indians, miners, farmers, drunkards, and brothel owners. He was shot at by Indians, and once mistaken for a horse thief and almost hanged. He established a hundred churches, five hospitals, an orphans' school, and Montana Wesleyan College.

Fearless in ministry, there was one thing that rattled him: *Dermacentor andersoni*, the tick that causes Rocky Mountain spotted fever. Bitten by the malignant insect at age twenty-seven, he expected to die. Though he fought his way back to health, he was ever after tick phobic.

We don't like to admit it, but we all have fears. We also have a God who promises His love, protection, and guidance.

. . . .

Whenever I am afraid, Lord,
I will trust in You (Psalm 56:3).

High-Tech Boost

*I thank Christ Jesus our Lord, who has
given me strength, that he considered me
trustworthy, appointing me to his service.*
1 TIMOTHY 1:12 NIV

. . . .

According to *Time* magazine, Michael Phelps won eight Olympic gold medals in 2008 due in part to his swimwear. Evidently the new "LZR second-skin" suits—developed with the help of NASA scientists—contribute greatly to buoyancy and muscle control. Phelps's hard work combined with a high-tech boost ensured a record-breaking Olympic performance.

For us as Christians, success also comes through hard work and our own "high-tech boost" from the Lord, who gives us the winning edge of His own strength. If a person doesn't like their lot in life, they can take an honest inventory, rectify what they can handle themselves, and depend on God for the power to carry them over the finish line.

Every Christian has access to that power. God is perfectly happy to share it.

. . . .

*Lord God, please give me Your strength for my
workaday world and my family responsibilities.
Please keep me from shortcuts and excuse making.*

He Just Said So

*And God said, "Let the land produce living
creatures according to their kinds: the livestock,
the creatures that move along the ground, and
the wild animals, each according to its kind."
And it was so.*

GENESIS 1:24 NIV

. . . .

Who of us hasn't looked at the beauty and majesty of the natural beauty and wondered just *how* God did it? How did He make the mountains, the rivers, the forests? How did He set those things in motion? How does He keep them going day after day, year after year?

Without a doubt, the beginning of all things was a spectacle too awesome for our words. But the bottom line for God is that everything we enjoy in the outdoors was simply a matter of Him *speaking* it into existence.

God willingly and gladly blessed us with everything we enjoy when we spend time in the outdoors. He gave us the rivers, the mountains, the forests. He even gave us the time and the freedom to enjoy them. How? For Him, it was just a matter of saying the word!

. . . .

*Thank You, Lord, for showing me Your awesome
power and love by simply speaking into
existence everything that I enjoy.*

GPS

A man's mind plans his way, but the Lord
directs his steps and makes them sure.
PROVERBS 16:9 AMP

. . . .

GPS—the Global Positioning System—has become an essential tool for many, whether traveling salespeople or outdoorsmen.

Before setting off, hikers can mark their location on the device, knowing it will lead back "home." Forget the days of finding a road or river and hiking for miles to figure out where you are. GPS to the rescue!

Our spiritual lives could also use a GPS unit—God's Positioning System.

Have we wandered off from our known spiritual territory? Are we stressed out over finances, fighting in our relationships, or drowning in an unexplainable funk?

If we sense that we've left the safe path, let's listen for the GPS directions—that "still small voice"—that will lead us back home.

. . . .

Lord, I'm lost right now, but I know
You will lead me from here on out.

Set Free from the Snare

"Our soul has escaped as a bird from the snare of the fowlers; the snare is broken, and we have escaped."
PSALM 124:7 NKJV

. . . .

You've had some close calls in your life—maybe even recently. There have been times when you knew beyond any doubt that it was only *God* who rescued you from the snare of the fowler.

In ancient Israel, fowlers were hunters who caught birds in snares or with nets. These skillful men would lie in wait or set a trap, and the birds never saw disaster coming. Once caught, it was the rare fowl that escaped. But some did.

Sometimes you've made mistakes and suffered the consequences. Other times, financial crises happen and, like millions of others, you're "taken in a cruel net. . .caught in a snare" (Ecclesiastes 9:12 NKJV), no fault of your own. But think of the times that God intervened and spared you from certain disaster.

Next time you go for a walk, look up to the heavens and tell God how thankful you are for His repeated mercies in your life.

. . . .

God, I thank You for the many times You've helped me escape from the snare of the fowler.

Seeing God in the Seasons

*Be glad, people of Zion, rejoice in the LORD your
God, for he has given you the autumn rains
because he is faithful. He sends you abundant
showers, both autumn and spring rains, as before.*
JOEL 2:23 NIV

. . . .

Some fly-fishermen just seem to know what fly pattern will pique the fishes' interest on a certain day or during a certain time of year. If you're that kind of fisherman yourself, you'll never lack for fishing buddies!

Even moderately experienced fly fishermen know the importance of the seasons and what they mean to the diet of the average trout. That's the only way they can travel to their favorite stream prepared to "match the hatch". . .in other words, to use the fly that most closely imitates the insects present on a given river during a given season.

One of the wonders of God's creation is the four seasons. And each of them is an example of the wisdom of God, who lovingly created the natural world for you to enjoy year-round.

. . . .

*Father God, how can I thank You for the wonders
of Your creation and what they mean to me
as someone who enjoys the outdoors?*

Time to Move On

*"Whoever does not receive you, nor heed your
words, as you go out of that house or that
city, shake the dust off your feet."*
MATTHEW 10:14 NASB

. . . .

Fox trappers like to boast of their own shrewdness in out-
thinking these wily animals. It's as if fooling foxes proves
the trapper is even more crafty.

A fox experiencing a near miss or two quickly learns that a
disturbed patch of ground may cover a trap—no matter what
attractive smells may fill the area. Trappers often take the
fox's elusiveness as a challenge, redoubling their efforts to fool
the critter. Sometimes it works, but more often, time is wasted
that could have been spent taking fur coats from less well-
informed foxes.

Sometimes it makes sense to move on—even in the realm
of our witness. We can push to convert a hard case who has
rejected the gospel, or we can give the good news of salvation
to those who have not already resisted or denied its truth.

. . . .

*I thank You, Lord, for promising that Your Word will
not fail in its purpose. And I thank You for the reminder
that my job is to spread the word, not force the results.*

City Slickers

The LORD God is my strength; He will
make my feet like deer's feet, and He
will make me walk on my high hills.
HABAKKUK 3:19 NKJV

. . . .

Several members of a church are getting together for an annual weekend of backpacking in the high wilderness. When asked if they're really ready for the adventure, they respond with bravado: "Nothing can keep us from it."

A dozen city slickers head out to parts unknown, their feet shod in new Doc Martens and their spirits in the clouds. At noon, at the base of the trail, they're digging in their backpacks for the goodies they packed. By late afternoon, it's time to find a campsite. By evening, everyone's tucked in for the night. When a coyote howls, bodies spring out of sleeping bags and nervous voices whisper, "What's that?"

Roughing it once a year won't make a pioneer out of a city slicker. In the same way, living in our own strength doesn't make for successful Christians. The Lord God is our strength, the prophet Habakkuk reminds us. Only in God will we be able to energetically and consistently walk those "high hills."

. . . .

Father, I recognize that my strength comes from You. I'm
nothing in myself—but in You, all things are possible.

Vineyards Gone Wild

*In that day every place where there used to be
a thousand vines, worth a thousand shekels of
silver, will become briers and thorns. With bow
and arrows men will come there.*
ISAIAH 7:23–24 RSV

. . . .

Israel's soil and climate is ideally suited to cultivating grapes, and in Bible times hundreds of thousands of vineyards covered its hills. Not only were the grapes delicious, but the harvest was worth a great deal of money.

When Assyrian invaders deported most of the Israelites, their abandoned vineyards were overgrown with thorns and became the lairs of leopards, hyenas, and wild boars. The people who remained had to enter vineyards bows at the ready, lest a beast ambush them.

Hunting is great sport, but no one likes to *be* hunted while picking grapes. Why did God allow such valuable real estate to fall into ruin? Because of the Israelites' sin. They were expert farmers, careful to pull out thorns and keep out wild beasts— but they sneered when God's prophets warned them to uproot sin from their hearts.

Sin still causes losses, which is why we need today to guard our hearts and minds to keep out evil thoughts.

. . . .

*God, please help me to avoid sin—
and the unnecessary losses sin brings.*

Be Still

"Be still, and know that I am God;
I will be exalted among the nations,
I will be exalted in the earth."
PSALM 46:10 NIV

. . . .

Sailing on Lake Ouachita near Hot Springs, Arkansas, is more than fun—it can be a spiritual experience.

The lake is nestled in the hills of a national forest where no homes are allowed. In autumn, when the leaves of thousands of trees display a myriad of colors, it's a photographer's delight. Lake Ouachita reveals the handiwork of God's creative mind.

Jesus Himself—the Creator of hills and trees and lakes—appeared to enjoy the water, too. He was often in a boat with His disciples. We know of one occasion when He stilled a raging storm, making the water as calm as a fishbowl.

There's just something about water—the millions of diamond-like sparkles on its surface, the gentle slapping sound against the side of a boat, the waves rising and falling rhythmically. Whether we're relaxing in an inner tube on a pond or sailing at speed with a strong wind, being on the water is a peaceful, relaxing experience.

The water is a place we can still our minds and meditate on the Lord.

. . . .

Lord, please help me to still my mind in the midst
of the storms of life. I want to know You are God.

Dinosaurs

*"Can you pull in Leviathan with a fishhook or tie down
its tongue with a rope? . . . If you lay a hand on it, you
will remember the struggle and never do it again!"*
JOB 41:1, 8 NIV

. . . .

Chicago's Field Museum is home to Sue, the Tyrannosaurus Rex.

Sue was named after the woman who discovered the great dinosaur's bones in South Dakota. Walking around the display, you quickly see how terrifying these creatures must have been. Each of Sue's legs is thirteen feet tall—and from nose to tail she was bigger than a school bus. Her teeth range from seven to twelve inches long and could easily bite through the hide of any other animal. T. rex was truly an incredible animal.

It wasn't until the nineteenth century that scientists identified dinosaurs as a special class of animals—and we might wonder what other incredible creatures are still entombed in the earth awaiting discovery.

One thing is certain: viewing the bones of a dinosaur gives us an incredible taste of God's amazing creation!

. . . .

*Lord, I thank You for the many wonders of the world
that we continue to discover. May we all remember
You as Creator when we see Your creation.*

Wisdom for All Times

*As the Scriptures say, "People are like grass;
their beauty is like a flower in the field. The
grass withers and the flower fades. But the word
of the Lord remains forever." And that word is
the Good News that was preached to you.*

1 PETER 1:24–25 NLT

. . . .

Watch fallen leaves swirl in the breeze of a cool, crisp autumn morning, and it's difficult not to think of the cycles of life.

Coming out of a summertime bursting with life and activity, we're now beginning to head indoors for a season that hints of dying. Our lives often mimic these seasons. The things of our lives—even life itself—sometimes feel so temporary.

We long to find ourselves anchored in the permanent, the eternal. And God's Word provides that place for us. Moment after moment, day after day, season after season, His Word is always there providing an anchor for our souls.

How wonderful to know that the wisdom of the ages, given by the Author of all creation, is available for those moments, days, and seasons.

. . . .

*Lord, I thank You that Your Word is there for me
at all times, reminding me of Your loving care.*

Fishing on Famous Ruins

*"I will make you like the top of a rock; you shall
be a place for spreading nets, and you shall
never be rebuilt, for I the LORD have spoken."*
EZEKIEL 26:14 NKJV

· · · · · · ·

From the coasts of southern France to China to Mexico, you can see locals, feet dangling over the edge of stone seawalls, fishing contentedly. They seem oblivious to the fact that they're sitting on some famed historical site. They probably know, but they're living in the present, enjoying the moment.

Two-thousand-five-hundred years ago the fabulously wealthy citizens of Tyre (in modern-day Lebanon) fled their coastal city for a nearby island fortress to escape the Babylonians. Years later, Alexander the Great came along, tore down the old city, dragged its stones into the sea, built a causeway to the island, and conquered it.

Today there's a fishing village on the island and, in fulfillment of Bible prophecy, they spread their nets to dry on the causeway. Tyre was once a "city of renown. . .a power on the seas" (Ezekiel 26:17 NIV), but to God the humble fishermen are more important than Tyre in all its glory. And the fishermen? They're counting their day's catch and enjoying the moment.

· · · · · · ·

*God, I thank You for bringing down the proud
and powerful while caring for the humble.*

Beauty and Death

For now we see only a reflection as in a mirror;
then we shall see face to face. Now I know in part;
then I shall know fully, even as I am fully known.
1 CORINTHIANS 13:12 NIV

. . . .

We observe much beauty on this earth. Interestingly, much of what we perceive as beauty is actually a mixture of life and death.

Since the fall of humanity in the once-perfect Garden of Eden, our earth—according to Genesis 3:17—has been cursed. When Adam and Eve sinned, death became part of our world's equation.

Think of the beauty of the autumn leaves: those colors we so enjoy indicate the decline of chlorophyll and the impending death of the leaf. Or those shooting stars that so excite us? They're actually fast-moving rocks from space, burning up in our atmosphere.

Life on earth is really a process of death. But there is good news: a new heaven and earth are coming! Someday, we'll see God's beautiful new creation through perfect new eyes, with not a hint of death anywhere.

. . . .

Lord, help me keep my vision focused on Your promise—
no eye has seen, no ear has heard, no mind has conceived
what You have prepared for those who love You.

I Love a Mystery

*Holding the mystery of the
faith with a pure conscience.*
1 TIMOTHY 3:9 NKJV

. . . .

One man has an unusual method of determining whether a work colleague needs a gospel presentation. He asks straight-out, "When did the Genesis account of creation take place?"

If he detects wavering, he informs his colleague that the first day of creation was October 23, 4004 BC, at 9:00 a.m., based on James Ussher's dating system from the 1600s.

For many believers, such a reckoning is too tidy. It takes the great mystery out of faith. Just as Genesis 1:1 assures us that God has been at the center of all creation, so too every believer who claims the name of Christ is involved in a glorious adventure—practicing faith in the mysteries of life.

Faithful Christians can have pegs upon which they hang their not-completely-understood issues. Explaining the Trinity hangs on such a peg, as does the reconciliation of science and Genesis (though we believe, "In the beginning God created. . ."). These and many others are tests of faith that no Sherlock Holmes need solve. A mind and heart open to God will simply accept many such mysteries.

. . . .

*Father, strengthen my faith to keep my
mind and heart open to Your leadings.*

Cutting Down the Forests

"You also will have the mountain country. It is a forest. . . . You will own all of it because you will force the Canaanites to leave the land even though they have powerful weapons and are strong."
JOSHUA 17:18 NCV

. . . .

When the Israelites entered Canaan, most of its central uplands and hills were covered by vast forests. Today the forests are gone, the land greatly eroded, and the climate more arid. Certainly, four thousand years of hungry goats have taken their toll, but humans armed with bronze axes were the main factor in Israel's deforestation.

God's original intent wasn't for the Israelites to cut down the mountain forests for farmland. They were instructed to conquer the Canaanites in the plains. But many Israelites—even the numerous, powerful tribes—were afraid to battle the Canaanites. So Joshua gave them the only remaining option: clear the mountain forests and live there instead. (See the full picture in Judges 1:19–35.)

When God tells us what to do, we need to have the faith to obey so we can receive His full blessing—not settle for second best, huddled up in the hills instead. The consequences of our choices and actions affect generations to come, so let's obey God.

. . . .

God, help me to conquer the Canaanites in my life—and not to settle for second best.

The Narrow Way

*"Enter through the narrow gate. For wide is
the gate and broad is the road that leads to
destruction, and many enter through it. But
small is the gate and narrow the road that
leads to life, and only a few find it."*
MATTHEW 7:13–14 NIV

． ． ． ． ． ． ．

In Kentucky's Mammoth Cave National Park, aspiring spelunkers wiggle through spaces as small as nine inches high on the "Wild Cave Tour."

But even the Historic Tour, a two-mile underground hike for the general public, features a tight squeeze. Though the cave boasts many large, open spaces—like the Mammoth Dome—the trail at one point narrows to a crack in the rock less than a foot wide. Known by the politically incorrect nickname "Fat Man's Misery," the constricted opening forces tour takers to funnel through one by one.

That's a good picture of Jesus' description of the road to eternal life. Crowds on the wide path to destruction are big and careless, unaware of what lies ahead. The faithful, meanwhile, find themselves gingerly navigating a narrow road toward true life.

Christians are an elite group, but they should never be elitist. Call over to those on the other path, and invite them to join you!

． ． ． ． ． ． ．

*Lord, please give me the boldness to
share this faith that's changed my life.*

What Is Man?

When I consider your heavens, the work of your
fingers, the moon and the stars, which you have set
in place, what is mankind that you are mindful of
them, human beings that you care for them?
PSALM 8:3–4 NIV

. . . .

E very now and then we sense it as we peer up into the starlit night: we human beings are very, *very* small.

When we, like the psalmist, take a moment to look at all the wonders of the heavens and think about just how immense this universe really is, it can overwhelm us with a sense of just how insignificant we are in and of ourselves. Humanly speaking, we are just one tiny human being living on a speck of dust at the edge of an enormous galaxy, which itself is merely one among *billions* of galaxies! Why in the world would God pay attention to us and our concerns?

But the wonderful truth is that our sovereign God is also immensely gracious to us, His creation. In fact, the God of the universe knows the very number of hairs on our head (see Matthew 10:29–31; Luke 12:6–7), and He is intimately aware of all that happens to us. Best of all, He has promised to care for us so that we are free to serve Him (see Matthew 6:25–34).

. . . .

Sovereign God, You alone are truly great. I praise You
that You, in Your loving grace, watch over me.

Get Up and Go!

*"I am still as strong today as the day Moses
sent me out; I'm just as vigorous to go
out to battle now as I was then."*
JOSHUA 14:11 NIV

. . . .

Music suddenly filled the dark room, and Ted reached over to tap the top of the alarm. For a moment he was tempted to hit the SNOOZE button. But the years of habit kicked in, and he simply turned off the alarm. There was a rustling of the covers and the sound of Ted's feet hitting the floor. Only moments later, outside, was the steady *scrunch, scrunch, scrunch* of hiking shoes on a leaf-covered trail.

Ted had taken up walking when he turned forty. Now it was his life—or at least his mornings. The exercise had taken off excess pounds, improved his health, and kept him fit. He was proud of his work and its results.

Would we work as hard on our spiritual strength and conditioning? Do you jump out of bed in the morning, eager to spend time with God, pray, and study His Word? Don't hit that snooze. Get up and go!

. . . .

Lord, please help me to run the race and finish well.

Wise Life Lessons

*He spoke about plant life, from the cedar of Lebanon
to the hyssop that grows out of walls. He also spoke
about animals and birds, reptiles and fish.*
1 KINGS 4:33 NIV

. . . .

Solomon referred to ants, bears, pigs, snakes, and dogs in the biblical books of Proverbs and Ecclesiastes. In the Song of Songs, he described several types of plants. But, for the most part, his many observations have not come down to us in the Bible. So why are we told that he investigated both flora and fauna in great detail?

For one thing, as many botanists or zoologists will tell you, humans study plant and animal life simply because it's fascinating. The complexity and balance of nature convinces many of us that an intelligent designer must have been behind it.

Another reason: as Solomon repeatedly demonstrated with his proverbs, we can draw many life lessons from plants and animals.

We may not fully understand microbiology, genetics, or other fields of science relating to nature. But taking even a few moments to reflect on creation leaves us in awe of the power and wisdom of God.

. . . .

*Thank You for Your wonderful creation,
O God, which reminds me constantly of You!*

A Better World to Come

And after a while he returned to take her, and he turned
aside to see the body of the lion, and behold, a swarm
of bees and honey were in the body of the lion.
JUDGES 14:8 AMP

. . . .

In the television show *Man vs. Wild*, adventurer Bear Grylls
will often find a torn carcass in the bushes—evidence of a
recent predator kill. Grylls and his guide once followed large
cat tracks to a small cave where bones and other evidences of
spoil littered the ground. They had discovered the lair where
the stealthy killer eats in the dark, hidden from prying eyes.

This beastly drama of fright and flight is played out every
day. Yet a time is coming when the wild animals will fight no
more. The calf and young lion will play together, and a little
child will lead them.

Some people see savagery in the world and conclude that
God is cruel. But this world is only a twisted version of God's
original creation. The One who promised with a rainbow
never again to flood the earth has also promised one day to
make a whole new world—where death and destruction have
no part.

. . . .

Lord, I look forward to the new life You've
promised in a world without hurt or harm.

The Dark

He will cover you with his feathers, and under his
wings you will find refuge; his faithfulness will
be your shield and rampart. You will not fear the
terror of night, nor the arrow that flies by day.
PSALM 91:4–5 NIV

. . . .

Okay, let's admit it: that childish fear of the dark doesn't entirely go away.

Strange noises occur in the nighttime, ones that don't seem to be there during the day. Maybe they're the sounds of nocturnal animals that are silent during the day. Maybe we hear different sounds at night because there are fewer other manmade noises to drown them out. Or maybe, when our vision is limited by the dark, our other senses become more attuned to our surroundings.

For the most part, there is nothing in the dark that is not there in the daylight. But whatever might be "out there," God is, too. And God is bigger by far than whatever may be in the dark. . .which He created, anyway.

We have nothing to fear in the dark—or in the light—when we have our hearts full of God.

. . . .

Thank You, Lord, for always surrounding
me with Your love and protection.

Rain Forest

*"Everyone who comes to me and listens to my words
and puts them into practice—I will show you what
he is like: He is like a man building a house, who
dug down deep, and laid the foundation on bedrock.
When a flood came, the river burst against that
house but could not shake it, because it had been well
built. But the person who hears and does not put my
words into practice is like a man who built a house
on the ground without a foundation. When the river
burst against that house, it collapsed immediately,
and was utterly destroyed!"*
LUKE 6:47–49 NET

. . . .

Rain forests get their name because of heavy precipitation—
and people who live in them can understand Jesus' parable
of the builders.

People in one East African village burst out laughing
when they heard this parable for the first time. They all knew
a lazy person who had not chosen a building location with
a good foundation. The rains came, and those houses were
swept away. The villagers also knew that a good foundation
stands firm against the worst weather.

It's a perfect physical picture of an important spiritual
truth. What are you building your life on?

. . . .

*Father, help me to be quiet and listen to You.
Help me put Your precepts into practice,
building my life on Your firm foundation.*

Off Balance by Design

Then I will give you rain in due season,
and the land shall yield her increase, and
the trees of the field shall yield their fruit.
LEVITICUS 26:4 KJV

. . . .

The earth was tilted to give us seasons.

Because the world doesn't sit perpendicular to the sun there are times when we catch its heat and times when we lean back and that heat passes us by. Because of that tilt and the corresponding changes in the hours of daylight, nature knows there is a time to grow, a time to give fruit, a time to fall back, and a time to begin again.

Cynics might say seasons are a coincidental by-product of that "accidental" tilt. But imagine if it wasn't arranged that way. The north and south would be permanently barren and the central belt would constantly be in flower—for a while. With no chance to recuperate, how long would it take for a permanent summer to burn everything out? It just wouldn't work that way.

So. . .the earth was tilted to give us seasons.

. . . .

Lord, we look to the small and we look to the great,
and everywhere we find Your plan!

A Trustworthy Caretaker

You care for the land and water it; you enrich it
abundantly. The streams of God are filled with water.
PSALM 65:9 NIV

. . . .

Have you ever stood at the edge of a river or stream and wondered how—day after day, month after month, year after year—the water continues to flow? There are, of course, natural and scientific explanations to the process, but for the follower of Christ, the "process" always comes back to the One who created and sustains all things.

The Bible teaches that God didn't just create the natural wonders we enjoy then stand back to let them take their own course. No, the same God who made these things works every moment to ensure their continued operation, just as He designed them.

Think for a moment about the God who is able—just by His word—to keep and sustain the rivers, lakes, and oceans we enjoy. How much easier must it be for this loving Creator to sustain *you* in every way?

. . . .

Lord, I thank You for showing me Your great
faithfulness in sustaining all You have created.
I thank You for sustaining me, too!

Haunted by Jackals

"Babylon will become a heap of ruins, haunted by jackals. She will be an object of horror and contempt, a place where no one lives."
JEREMIAH 51:37 NLT

. . . .

In Jeremiah's day Babylon was the capital of a great empire. Protected by high walls, it was the commercial hub of the world, with tens of thousands of people milling through its markets and streets. Proud of its power, Babylon oppressed God's people for profit. A few hundred years later, Babylon was "a heap of ruins. . .a place where no one lives."

In Bible times, when people abandoned a city, nature claimed the land back. Wild animals moved in, thistles grew in its palaces, and trees rose in its streets. Jeremiah prophesied: "Babylon will be inhabited by desert animals and hyenas. It will be a home for owls" (Jeremiah 50:39). And that's exactly what happened.

When a society or a nation turns from the Lord, violates His laws, and oppresses His people, God judges them. So take hope! God will deliver you from *your* enemies and oppressors. If He can bring down mighty empires, He can certainly stop mere individuals.

. . . .

Lord, help me to trust that You will deliver me from those who attack me.

Stay Focused

Then Peter got down out of the boat, walked on
the water and came toward Jesus. But when he
saw the wind, he was afraid and, beginning to
sink, cried out, "Lord, save me!"
MATTHEW 14:29–30 NIV

. . . .

A sudden storm surprised a fishing party, two miles out from the protection of the harbor. With his small boat taking on water, the captain strained to keep the harbor light in sight. That bearing lost, the group might not make it back to safety.

The stresses and distractions of life can put us in a similar "boat," spiritually speaking. Remember the apostle Peter? He faced both a physical and spiritual storm while walking on the water to Jesus. Distracted by the elements and overcome by the fear they can bring, he lost his focus and began to sink. But then he cried out to Jesus and was saved.

Where is our focus today? Keeping our eyes on Jesus will protect us from becoming overwhelmed by life. Focusing on Him keeps us from sinking into fear and sin. Only then can we truly conquer pressures that we face daily.

. . . .

Jesus, help me to keep my eyes and focus on You.
Help me to stay on top of the water and walk with You.

Chatterboxes

*"And when you pray, do not keep on babbling
like pagans, for they think they will be heard
because of their many words."*
MATTHEW 6:7 NIV

. . . .

Hiking through the October woods, our boots crunch through a red-and-orange swirl of fallen leaves. Nearby squirrels rush up the trunks of trees, hiding themselves on the back side. But then they emerge on high branches to scold us. Surrounded by the beauty of God's fall colors, they do nothing but shoot meaningless babble our way. Their "many words" have no effect, except to prompt us to smile and chuckle at them.

Let's not be like squirrels. As we see those same multi-colored leaves, let's praise God for them! He has splashed buckets of heavenly paint over the woods, allowing us to share in the glorious scenery.

The wise Solomon once said, "Much dreaming and many words are meaningless. Therefore fear God" (Ecclesiastes 5:7 NIV). Let's use our words to praise our awe-inspiring Lord.

. . . .

*Father, You are a great artist! I am struck by the
beauty of Your creation, old and yet new every
autumn. Thank You for sharing it with me.*

Grateful for God's Provision

"Now therefore, please take your weapons,
your quiver and your bow, and go out
to the field and hunt game for me."
GENESIS 27:3 NKJV

. . . .

In Old Testament times, hunting wasn't so much a means of rest and relaxation as it is today. Men hunted because they needed food for themselves and their families. They knew that a failed hunting trip could mean going hungry—and for that reason they probably thanked God for success.

In our culture, though, hunting and fishing are generally done for recreation. Most outdoorsmen and women don't hunt and fish because they *have* to, they do it because they enjoy it.

Whether a man or woman hunts or fishes for need of food, like in the old days, or simply because he or she enjoys it, there is a common aspect: God is the One who blesses each endeavor and gives success.

Whether it's hunting or fishing, white-water rafting or hiking that you enjoy, remember always to thank God. He wonderfully meets all your needs, and gives you a place to spend some of your "down" time.

. . . .

My gracious, generous Provider, I thank You
for giving me everything I need—and more—
to enjoy the life You've given me.

Beauty and Strength

And Adam said, This is now bone of my
bones, and flesh of my flesh: she shall be called
Woman, because she was taken out of Man.
GENESIS 2:23 KJV

. . . .

They upgraded the sea defenses on a stretch of coast by laying a five-foot-high line of granite boulders in front of the promenade. The spring after the "wall" was completed, some interesting colors began to appear behind the gray of the granite. Despite being doused twice a day by seawater, some wildflowers had made their home there and were blossoming

The strength of the boulders had made a safe place for beauty to flower. In their turn the flowers gave an extra purpose to those rocks. On their own the rocks weren't much. On their own in that place the flowers would never have survived. Together they make a sight worth seeing.

Maybe God had something similar in mind when He made a man then thought to Himself, "Hmmm. . . "

. . . .

It takes awesome power to make a universe—but,
God, You made a beautiful universe! We reflect
aspects of You individually, but we come closer
to completion by being together.

A Friend in Need

And when the chief Shepherd shall appear, ye shall receive a crown of glory that fadeth not away.
1 PETER 5:4 KJV

. . . .

The shepherd recalled searching for his flock in a blizzard. The sky became the same color as the ground, and soon he was lost in a "whiteout." When he found footprints, he thought they might lead him somewhere safe. When he realized they were his own footprints, he knew he was a short while away from death.

That's when he said to his dog, "Home, Peat. Home!" *At least Peat might survive,* he thought. Peat did indeed know the way home, and he walked slowly enough for the shepherd to follow him all the way.

We often rely on our own strengths for too long. What we need is someone we can count on when we are at the very end of our capabilities—and before! The lucky shepherd had Peat. You and I have Jesus!

. . . .

*Lord, You will be strength when we need strength,
peace when we need peace, and love when we need
love. All we have to do is get out of the way and
let You be everything we need.*

We're All Different

*When the boys grew up, Esau was a skillful
hunter, a man of the field, while Jacob
was a quiet man, dwelling in tents.*
GENESIS 25:27 ESV

. . . .

Those of us who are parents—or who expect to be parents someday—have aspirations for our children. As they grow up, we want to pass on the things that matter most to us. For some parents, that's often an interest in sports or the outdoors. But sometimes, kids just aren't wired the same way we are.

Look at Esau and Jacob. Esau was a skillful hunter. Jacob was a quiet man who preferred to dwell in a tent. Early on, their father, Isaac, favored Esau because he liked to eat the game Esau hunted.

With your own kids, look for their natural tendencies, then support them in those personal interests. Rather than choosing sides, involve yourself in your child's interests. Whether you're hunting, biking, or playing with Legos, you'll grow closer as a result.

. . . .

*Lord, when I'm tempted to squeeze my kids into my
own mold, remind me of Jacob and Esau. Please help
me to encourage my kids in their own interests.*

Gym Buddies?

*Dear friend, I pray that you may enjoy good
health and that all may go well with you.*
3 JOHN 2 NIV

. . . .

Don't think that Jesus and the twelve spent time on a tread-mill to keep in shape—they were walkers. In fact, there's only one reference to Jesus using another form of transportation, the colt He rode on Palm Sunday.

Among the twelve, we never read of illness. People around them were sick, dying, or dead—but not Peter and his buddies. (Though the great disciple's mother-in-law once needed healing from a dangerous fever.) Of course, the Gospel writers were primarily concerned with spiritual, as opposed to physical, well-being.

But in his later years, the apostle John recognized the blessing of good physical health in his letter to his "dear friend Gaius." Jews had long believed that well-being was a reward for obedience to God, while illness resulted from sin. By New Testament times, they were beginning to see that their own behavior affected their health.

Good health is ultimately a gift from God. But He often allows us to participate in keeping our bodies fit and strong. What can you do today to work with Him?

. . . .

*Father, my primary goal is a healthy soul—but I
know that a weak body makes spirit health harder to
maintain. Help me discipline my body for good health.*

Confidence without Fear

For by Him all things were created, both in the heavens and on earth, visible and invisible. . . . He is before all things, and in Him all things hold together.
COLOSSIANS 1:16–17 NASB

. . . .

Sometimes on a still, frosty autumn morning, the rising sun makes its presence known in an unexpected way.

In the warmth of the day's first rays, the dry leaves still hanging on mature beeches seem to change their minds. One by one, then in troops, they let go of the twigs and sail in uncertain loops and circles to the ground at the foot of the tree. The leaves on the younger trees, though, are not so easily swayed. They often hang on their branches until new leaf buds swell the next spring.

We could try to explain the physical reasons why some leaves fall and others hang on. But we who take God at His word can be confident knowing that He holds all things together within His purposes. In all the universe, every atom exists because Christ holds it together. With such a God, we need fear nothing.

. . . .

Dear God, our Father, thank You for telling us of Your power and care in our lives and Your creation.

Make the Leap

*Therefore being justified by faith, we have peace
with God through our Lord Jesus Christ.*
ROMANS 5:1 KJV

. . . .

The hardest part of learning to rappel is going over the edge of that cliff. That's when you have to lean out, backward, over the abyss. Everything you have ever been taught tells you it's a bad idea, but you have to do it or you're just sliding down a rope.

Once you get that initial positioning correct, it's surprisingly easy. You might go down in little steps the first time, but soon you'll be flying in great bounds, backward, forward, double-handed, and single-handed. It's a real buzz, and you can't believe you wasted so much time being scared!

Coming from the secular world to faith is like stepping over that cliff. There will be no shortage of people telling you it's a crazy thing to do. But once you step beyond that and get your initial positioning right (kneeling down) then the exhilaration knows no bounds, and you can't help but wonder why you didn't do it before.

. . . .

*Father, I am so glad I took that step. Help me
help others to get their "positioning" correct.*

I Love My Stuff

*For the love of money is a root of all kinds
of evil. Some people, eager for money,
have wandered from the faith and pierced
themselves with many griefs.*
1 TIMOTHY 6:10 NIV

. . . .

You can spend a bundle of money on outdoor equipment and excursions. Whether for the newest GPS technology, the coolest sport clothing, or the best-ever overseas trip, those dollars can run away faster than a startled rabbit.

The Bible never says we shouldn't spend money on our love of the outdoors. But there are some cautionary principles to remember.

Scripture warns of "the love of money" as "a root of all kinds of evil." For most of us, the love of money doesn't mean we stack and admire our coins and bills—we enjoy the *stuff* those coins and bills can buy. And when that stuff pulls us away from God. . .when we buy it to impress (or worse, *depress*) others. . .when we allow our spending to interfere with our giving to church or other people—then we have a problem.

So enjoy all the blessings God has given you—both the great outdoors and the stuff you use in them. But always beware of that creeping love of money.

. . . .

*Lord, please help me to use money and love people—
never the other way around.*

In the Valley of Trouble

I will return your vineyards, and then
Trouble Valley will become Hopeful Valley.
HOSEA 2:15 CEV

. . . .

Have you ever heard the phrase, "Jesus came to comfort the troubled and trouble the comfortable?" He did and He does. His hands reach across time and space to hold us when we most need held, and to turn us when we desperately need correction.

Many a person has climbed a hill to seek solitude from the troubles of life. In such a quiet place, above the traumas and trials below, God can do His most life-changing work. The nearness of His creation and the simple beauty of His handiwork combine to clear our minds of the troubles and concerns that slow us down and clutter our lives.

In these powerful, reflective moments, we are free to sit quietly and listen for God's voice, awaiting His promise to turn the troubled valley below us into hope.

. . . .

Lord, please free my heart from all the noise and
clutter, so I might hear Your voice in my life.

Caring for Our World

*Then the LORD God took the man and put him
in the garden of Eden to tend and keep it.*
GENESIS 2:15 NKJV

. . . .

Have you ever gone hiking in a beautiful state or national park, arrived at an isolated Eden overlooking a breathtaking vista. . .only to find Styrofoam lunch boxes, candy wrappers, and beverage cans left behind by the last hikers? A stunned question comes to mind: "If they loved this beautiful spot enough to come here, why did they trash it?"

The answer is that they really don't care. They're moved by the view of wild beauty, true, but their worldview is so self-centered that once they've enjoyed something, they don't care how they leave it. They don't have the *big picture*.

As Christians, God expects more of us.

The first commandment God gave to mankind—even before, "Be fruitful and multiply"—was to care for the earth. When God placed Adam in the paradise of Eden, it wasn't only to enjoy the garden's awesome beauty. Adam was also to "tend and keep it"—in other words, to care for it and make it even more beautiful, to preserve it for future generations.

. . . .

*Father, please help me to fulfill my
responsibility to care for Your creation.*

Outdoor Fellowship

. . .not giving up meeting together,
as some are in the habit of doing,
but encouraging one another.
HEBREWS 10:25 NIV

. . . .

It's safe to say that most people who enjoy the outdoors know that few things strengthen the bonds of friendship like hunting, fishing, hiking, and camping. While society calls times like these "bonding," the Bible refers to them as "fellowship."

Shared adventures in the woods, at the fishing hole, on the hiking trail, and at the campground are some of the best possible times to really get to know someone. Almost as enjoyable is reminiscing about adventures past—and planning for future exploits.

Some outdoor adventures are great settings for times of solitude, for prayer and "alone time" with God. But, in addition to regular get-togethers at your local church, they're also great settings for fellowship with your brothers or sisters in Christ.

. . . .

Father, thank You for giving me times of outdoor
solitude. But I thank You also for giving us the
outdoors as a setting for fellowship.

Close to Life

*And he said unto me, It is done. I am Alpha
and Omega, the beginning and the end.
I will give unto him that is athirst of the
fountain of the water of life freely.*
REVELATION 21:6 KJV

. . . .

You'll be astonished when looking up at the highest waterfall in the world.

Venezuela's Angel Falls drops 3,212 feet in total, the water generally turning to mist long before it reaches the base. It's not easy or cheap to see this amazing site, though. Hardy adventurers must fly in by plane, travel by car, then hike for an hour to view the beautiful wonder.

Many people go to great lengths to enjoy this unusual waterfall. But the greatest wonder of all is ours for the taking—God's water of life. He *wants* us to experience it, and He doesn't require a long, costly trip to obtain it. This distance between our knees and the ground is all we need to drink in the water of life.

. . . .

*Lord, I'm feeling stressed. As I return to You again,
I ask that You fill me with real life.*

With a Little Help from Our Friend

*It does not, therefore, depend on human
desire or effort, but on God's mercy.*
ROMANS 9:16 NIV

. . . .

Let's face it: we like to be in charge. We enjoy independence, and the great outdoors seems to offer us that. For hours or for days, we can revel in autonomy, depending on no one but ourselves. Our own ability determines whether we make it home safely.

Or so we like to think.

A little experience in the forest, on the sea, or up the rock face reminds us that we are really only a twisted ankle, a sudden snowstorm, or a wrong map reading away from real trouble. Who do we turn to then?

As wonderful as we like to think we are, in the end we are utterly dependent on Someone much bigger, stronger, and more impressive than ourselves. The great outdoors simply reminds us of that fact.

. . . .

*Father God, don't let me become too big
for my boots. But when I do overreach,
I thank You for being there to catch me.*

Cut Down

"Whoever sheds man's blood,
by man his blood shall be shed."
GENESIS 9:6 NKJV

. . . .

A stately old oak stood upon a hilltop within sight of the tomb of president James Buchanan. It was one in a line of many tall trees that bordered Greenwood Cemetery. But it stands there no more.

It killed a man. That wasn't the tree's fault; it was the man's. He'd been drinking. He was driving too fast when he hit the tree.

But it didn't matter how faithfully the tree had guarded the graves at its feet. Or how long it had granted shade to man and bird and beast. It killed a man.

It's a terrible thing when someone dies suddenly, violently, senselessly. But it's also a tragedy to blame the innocent. "Whoever sheds man's blood, by man his blood shall be shed," the Bible says. That's justice. But what happened to the old tree wasn't. They came with trucks, tackle, and saws—and they cut it down. It wasn't sick, damaged, or even in the way. It was just "guilty."

God, the ultimate Judge, wants us to judge as He does—fairly. We shouldn't give the guilty a pass, nor should we condemn the innocent. We honor Him by honoring His standards.

. . . .

Father, help me, when I judge, to judge justly.

It's All for You!

Come and see what God has done,
his awesome deeds for mankind!
PSALM 66:5 NIV

. . . .

Most people—Christian or not—can believe that God created the natural world they see around them. But what many, even followers of Christ, don't understand is that creation itself is an expression of God's love for humankind.

A well-known Christian leader who happens to be an avid bass fisherman once marveled, "It's amazing to me that God loved me so much that he made these slimy little creatures. . . just so I and my friends could enjoy them!"

The diversity we see in creation—the differences in the world's lands and waters, as well as the variations in the animals, birds, and fish God placed in them—is a testament to the creativity of the God we serve. But it's also a testament to the lengths God is willing to go to just to demonstrate His love for each of us.

Next time you're enjoying the outdoors—in whatever activity you choose—don't forget to personalize your gratitude for what God has created. . .just for you!

. . . .

I thank You, my Creator, for all the wonderful
work You have done on behalf of humankind—
and for me individually!

Prayer of a Shriveled Leaf

And we all do fade as a leaf; and our iniquities,
like the wind, have taken us away. And there is
none that calleth upon thy name.
ISAIAH 64:6–7 KJV

. . . .

Fall, with its swirling colors and chill air, can be a beautiful and invigorating season. Still, there's something deeply sad about a barren tree, standing dark against a gray sky. There's something lonely about a faded leaf scuttling down a dark street, driven by a biting wind.

If God is the tree, we are those leaves—and sin not only severs our connection to the life of God, it rips us loose and drives us away down empty streets. Sadly, when we reach such a state, we're usually no longer even praying for help.

Yet, even in such a desperate condition, we *can* cry out to God. In the very next verses, Isaiah prays for mercy: "Yet you, LORD, are our Father. . .do not remember our sins forever. Oh, look upon us, we pray" (Isaiah 64:8–9 NIV).

Are you in that state? Or are you still attached to the tree but about to drift away? Do you need God's presence renewed in your life? Pray. . .*now*.

. . . .

O Lord, You are our Father. . .do not remember
our sins forever. Oh, look upon us, we pray!

Start in the Dark

*For I am not ashamed of the gospel of Christ: for it
is the power of God unto salvation to every one that
believeth; to the Jew first, and also to the Greek.*
ROMANS 1:16 KJV

. . . .

Most climbers have to travel to find new, exciting routes.
They might rise before the sun, organize their kit while
their family sleeps. That's often the most dangerous part of
their day. The lure of bed will be strong, muscles get phantom
aches, fear of death gets a tighter grip on a tired mind. It's
amazing some climbers get as far as the car!

If we want to spend eternity with our family and friends
then the work has to be put in while things are still dark. The
climber's hours of doubt are washed away by the joy of being
tethered to a climbing buddy. The time spent persuading others of the truth in this life will seem as nothing when we have
them with us in the next!

. . . .

*It's one thing to be brave on a mountain, Lord.
It's another to stand by You through the mockery
of the world. Help me remember which is the
truer, more important, courage.*

Written on Stone

And thou shalt write upon the stones
all the words of this law very plainly.
DEUTERONOMY 27:8 KJV

. . . .

There's a rock between the sea and a stretch of road that has "Jesus Saves" painted on. Commenting that it had been there as long as he could remember, a man was surprised to hear his grandfather say it had been there as long as *he* could remember!

That rock, and the paint, gets battered by waves every day, so generations of anonymous believers must have kept the message fresh. They do it, not for themselves, but so passing motorists might see it and think.

The rock has three messages for us. One, (most importantly) that Jesus saves; two, that faith needs constant renewal if it is to survive; and three, that the rock was witness to creation and it will sing at the end of it all when Jesus comes back to save the very last of us.

. . . .

In walking the walk of faith and in constantly
renewing my bond with You, God grant that someone
may see and be inspired. I don't need to know about it.
It is sufficient that You know.

The Television

*For it is time to seek the LORD, until he comes
and showers his righteousness on you.*
HOSEA 10:12 NIV

. . . .

Sure, there's occasionally some good and interesting programming on television. But honestly, the TV is generally the greatest time waster ever invented.

The average American household watches more than six hours every day—just imagine what you could do with that extra time. Think of the greatest inventors, artists, and writers who ever lived, and ask what they might have produced if watching television 25 percent of their lives!

God wants us to think and to do worthwhile things with our lives. He called us to be good stewards of our time. We all have a twenty-four-hour day. If a third of that is spent sleeping, and another third at work, we have about eight free hours. If the average household watches six-plus hours of television every day, no wonder we never have time to get things done!

What could you accomplish with an additional six hours each day?

. . . .

*Lord, help me resist the urge to waste time. May I
make good use of what You have given me.*

Swimming in Healing Waters

Afterward he measured a thousand; and it
was a river that I could not pass over: for the
waters were risen, waters to swim in.
EZEKIEL 47:5 KJV

. . . .

The prophet Ezekiel had an amazing vision that one day water would gush out of the temple of God in Jerusalem and flow east to the Dead Sea. When the river poured forth from the temple, it was only ankle deep. Soon it was knee deep, then waist deep, and finally so deep that the prophet could swim in it.

At present, the waters of the Dead Sea are so salty that no fish can survive there. But in Ezekiel's vision, the waters healed the Dead Sea and made it fresh—its waters teemed with fish life. Great numbers of trees also grew on the river's banks.

This amazing river is far more than some therapeutic hot spring. It is the very "river of the water of life. . .flowing from the throne of God" with the trees of life growing on its banks (Revelation 22:1–2 NIV).

The waters are also symbolic of God's Word and the miraculous healing it can bring into our lives. The Bible is indeed "waters to swim in."

. . . .

God, I thank You for the waters of life I can
swim in to find refreshment and healing.

The Mouse Trap

The night is far spent, the day is at hand:
let us therefore cast off the works of darkness,
and let us put on the armour of light.
ROMANS 13:12 KJV

. . . .

Winter brings many changes. The temperature drops, grass stops growing, birds fly south. Mice move inside.

Mice? It may seem a strange topic for a devotional, but stick around for the point.

It's interesting to observe mice. They're extremely quick, seeming to disappear at the slightest human stirring. Mice seem to eat everything, though their favorites appear to be cheese and peanut butter. Approaching a trap, they seem to sense danger—but the draw of the bait is so strong they can't resist. There might be a lifeless mouse in another trap nearby, but more often than not a mouse will scurry past to take the bait in an active trap. But don't be too hard on the mouse—he has an excuse. He can't reason.

What about us, though? We've seen the results of those who took Satan's bait, but—far too often—we're tempted to go for the bait ourselves. And we might end up in the same state.

. . . .

Father, help me always to be on guard against
the dark works of the devil. Help me every
day to put on the armor of light.

Deep Blue Sea

There is the sea, vast and spacious,
teeming with creatures beyond number—
living things both large and small.
PSALM 104:25 NIV

. . . .

Only within the last few years have scientists been able to capture a live giant squid on camera. Occasionally, creatures thought to be long extinct are found living and thriving in the oceans. It's been suggested that there are more unknown, never-before-seen creatures living in the ocean than there are creatures we've identified. In many ways, it seems, we know more about the surface of the moon than we do the ocean floor!

God has given us a wonderful world to explore, and we marvel at His creation as we learn more and more about this planet and everything in it. Will we ever get to the point where we'll have seen everything God has made on earth? That's unlikely. His creation is far beyond our full knowledge.

That's the kind of God we serve—deeper than the oceans, more varied than the life they contain. And yet He knows each one of us intimately!

. . . .

Lord God, may I always be in awe of Your wondrous
creation—and of the love You have for me.

Slow but Sure

*"I did this as an example so that you
should do as I have done for you."*
JOHN 13:15 NCV

. . . .

One way to descend a steep, snow-covered slope is to zip up your waterproof suit and launch yourself downhill, face-first, arms by your sides. This human bobsled maneuver is called "penguin diving," and it's great fun—until someone hits a rock.

Alternatively, you could take the lead, examine the terrain, and descend slowly, kicking foot holes in the snow. Others will know your path is safe, and each time they step in your footprints, they'll compact the snow even more, making the trail safer still for the rest.

That's a good picture of Christian leadership. Go for the "cool, flashy" way, and others will probably follow you—with potentially awful results. But if you want to be a leader worthy of the name, follow Christ. It's not always the popular way, but others will see it's good—and they can follow your footsteps all the way home.

. . . .

*Jesus, the devil makes his work seem so attractive. Please
keep the true cost of the world's way always in my mind,
because Yours is the only way worth following.*

The God Who Gives. . .Joyfully

*"With my great power and outstretched arm I
made the earth and its people and the animals
that are on it, and I give it to anyone I please."*
JEREMIAH 27:5 NIV

. . . .

If you happen to have children, you know the joy parents
take in sharing all they have, everything they can, with their
kids. Parents don't give only because they're *expected* to; they
give because they want their children to have the very best.

Our heavenly Father is like that. And He demonstrated
that kind of generous love when He gave us the earth and
everything in it to enjoy.

The next time you're out enjoying a favorite outdoor
activity—especially if you're with your children—think
about how much it pleases you, an imperfect human being,
to give all you can to them. Then consider the perfect, giving
love your heavenly Father shows you every day, in every way.

. . . .

*Lord, I'm amazed that You gave me everything,
including the outdoors, to enjoy—and not
only that, but You were pleased to do so!*

He Speaks to Us Everywhere

*Bless the LORD, O my soul! O LORD my God, You
are very great; You are clothed with splendor and
majesty, covering Yourself with light as with a
cloak, stretching out heaven like a tent curtain.*
PSALM 104:1–2 NASB

. . . .

North of the forty-fifth parallel, you'll sometimes see the
night sky come alive with flashes and streaks of color
where, usually, only the stars twinkle against the dark backdrop of space. These "northern lights" are technically known
as the aurora borealis.

In North America, the most common colors are greens
and blues. Sometimes we get only a brief glimpse. At other
times, they hang motionless for a few minutes then collapse
or seem to slide away.

Auroras hold our attention as would a great waterfall,
which, occasionally, they resemble. They can present the appearance of curtains across a stage, seeming to wave slightly
as if in a light breeze.

Scientifically, we understand how particles in the solar
wind interact with Earth's atmosphere and magnetic field to
produce these shifting lights. But it's a privilege to watch God
stretch out those "tent curtains" for our enjoyment.

. . . .

*Lord God of creation, I thank You for showing us evidence
of Your power and wisdom. You are truly very great!*

An All-Knowing Guide

*Now when they had gone through Phrygia and
the region of Galatia, they were forbidden by
the Holy Spirit to preach the word in Asia.*
ACTS 16:6 NKJV

. . . .

Many people enjoy packaged tours, with expert guides overseeing all the tourists' needs.

Those guides know exactly what will make our cameras flash—and our hearts surge. They lead people to establishments that not only quench thirst but tickle palates. Packaged tours exist for those who love the cities—with their parks, museums, and nightlife—as well as the more daring tourists who prefer the frozen tundra, the African plains, or the Amazonian jungle.

In a sense, the great missionary, Paul, was on a guided tour—though he didn't know it at the time. At one point in his journeys, Paul intended to travel to Asia. But his all-knowing Guide had other plans—with incredible results.

For us as believers, our lives on this earth are also being guided, with every need provided. On this "tour," you've got the best package available!

. . . .

*Lord, please be my guide, leading me to
greater vistas than I could have dreamed.*

God's Fishermen and Hunters

"I will send for many fishermen, and they will
fish for them. Afterwards, I will send for many
hunters; and they will hunt them from every
mountain and hill and out of caves in the rocks."
JEREMIAH 16:16 CJB

. . . .

In Jeremiah's day, the Israelites had turned from God to worship idols; as a result, God judged them by allowing the Babylonians to conquer them. The Israelites fled into hiding, but God sent the invaders after them. Like expert fishermen, the Babylonians angled them out of their hiding places. Like skillful hunters, they tracked them down.

When God has your number, there's no hiding. As verse 17 says, "I see all their ways; they are not hidden from me" (CJB).

But this coin also has a happier side: when judgment is passed and God shows mercy, He is just as diligent to seek out His people wherever they are and restore them. Jesus gave a touching picture of a shepherd who went into the wilderness, searching diligently until he found and restored a single lost sheep (see Matthew 18:12–14).

It's really a good thing to be God's "prey."

. . . .

Father God, nothing I do is hidden from You—
and You know exactly where to find me.
Thank You for putting such an emphasis on me!

God Sees All

*"For His eyes are upon the ways of a man, and He
sees all his steps. There is no darkness or deep shadow
where the workers of iniquity may hide themselves."*
JOB 34:21–22 NASB

. . . .

We can spend all day in a forest and see only an occasional chickadee or squirrel. But the morning after a fresh snowfall, we'll probably see evidence of a flurry of activity.

The long strides of a deer show the path it chose in browsing from tree to tree. A straight and steady dotted line of rounded tracks means a fox was intent on reaching some destination—when the line weaves back and forth, he was looking for a meal.

There are little mysteries, too. The tiny trail of a shrew seems to stop next to the end of a protruding stick. A closer look reveals, between stick and snow, a gap just big enough for that smallest of mammals to sneak down to a protected world next to the earth.

Tracks in the snow are evidence of what we don't see—and a good metaphor for God's work in our world.

Sometimes we fret about what we can see—the evil and sin that plagues humanity. But the wickedness of humankind does not escape the eyes of God. He will deal with it in His time.

. . . .

*Lord, I thank You that no one can hide from
Your sight when doing evil—and that You will deal
with each one according to Your righteousness.*

Enjoy Today!

Do not say, "Why were the old days better than these?" For it is not wise to ask such questions.
ECCLESIASTES 7:10 NIV

. . . .

Fishermen are oftentimes the reminiscent types. They remember the first fish they caught, the biggest fish they caught, and the day when and where they caught the most fish.

Some of our best memories come from our times spent outdoors. These are the kinds of adventures we can look back on fondly, both for the success we enjoyed and for the friendships we forged.

While there is nothing inherently wrong with remembering the good times—in fact, it can be quiet enjoyable to remember past blessings from God—we should never lessen today's blessings by comparing them to what we enjoyed yesterday. . .or yesteryear.

Each day God gives us is a special blessing all its own. These are times for new experiences, new friendships, and new revelations of God's goodness. So enjoy your memories of the past, but don't allow them to cloud what God has given you *today*.

. . . .

Father, I thank You for my memories of past adventures. But never let me forget that today is a blessing all its own.

Longing for Your Love

*Descend from the crest of Amana, from the top
of Senir, the summit of Hermon, from the lions'
dens and the mountain haunts of leopards.*
SONG OF SOLOMON 4:8 NIV

. . . .

In the Song of Songs, Solomon describes his love for a beautiful woman known only as the beloved. We can only guess at her identity, but this mysterious female moved the heart of the king like none other—and his song celebrates the wonders of their marital bliss.

But for some reason, the beloved became distant toward him. To Solomon it was as though she had withdrawn to the cold mountains of Lebanon in the north, wilds which no man dared ascend because of the fierce lions and snarling leopards that lived there.

People today can identify. Whoever we are—men or women—when our loved one withdraws and the temperature in the room chills as if that person has removed to a remote mountain. We can all experience both the frustration and longing that Solomon felt.

That should also give us insight into how God feels when we, as believers, choose to be distant to Him. No one likes getting the cold shoulder—so let's keep our love warm.

. . . .

*God, help me to understand the people I love—
and please help me to understand myself.*

God's Clock

And God said, "Let there be lights in the vault
of the sky to separate the day from the night,
and let them serve as signs to mark sacred
times, and days and years."
GENESIS 1:14 NIV

. . . .

The American pioneer and founder of Rhode Island, Roger Williams, noted that his Indian neighbors "with no help of clock or watch" ordered their days by God's timepieces.

Williams wrote that the natives "were punctual in measuring their day by the sun and their night by the moon and the stars. And their lying [often] abroad in the air, and so living in the open fields, occasions even the youngest among them to be very observant of the heavenly lights."

The Indians were very punctual, and sometimes accused Williams of lying when he himself was tardy—even if he had a good excuse.

Williams wrote that, even for more primitive people, "the sun and moon. . .are the great directors of the day and night, as it pleased God to appoint in the first Creation."

Though clocks are everywhere in our world, stop to consider the sun or moon today—as a reminder of God's gift of time.

. . . .

Father, may I make the most of the time
You've given me—whether I measure it
by the sun, the moon, or my watch.

Thanksgiving Dinner

Sing and make music in your heart to the Lord,
always giving thanks to God the Father for
everything, in the name of our Lord Jesus Christ.
EPHESIANS 5:19–20 NIV

. . . .

There's little adventure in Thanksgiving dinner these days. The turkey, potatoes, stuffing, and pumpkin pie usually come from a nearby restaurant or grocery store.

But in 1621, generally acknowledged as the first such celebration in North America, Thanksgiving dinner required the men to go out hunting. "Our Governor sent four men on fowling," one colonist wrote. "They four in one day killed as much fowl as, with a little help beside, served the Company almost a week." Meanwhile, the Wampanoag Indians who joined the pilgrims "went out and killed five Deer."

And what was the big deal? In the words of the already-mentioned colonist, "that so we might after a more special manner rejoice together" over the good harvest God had provided.

Nearly four hundred years later, we do well to remember God's blessing, too. Starting today, let's make thanksgiving a staple of our diet.

. . . .

Gracious God, I thank You for all that
You've given me—both physical and spiritual.
May I always remember to give You praise.

The Cute Alligator

Do not be deceived: God cannot be mocked.
A man reaps what he sows.
GALATIANS 6:7 NIV

. . . .

Zoos often stage informative programs for children, allowing the kids to get to see exotic animals up close. Sometimes, they even get to touch or hold the creatures.

In one zoo, the keeper produced a baby alligator from a case. Boys in the audience pronounced the alligator "cool," while the girls thought it was "cute." Everyone got a chance to touch the gator as the handler held it, keeping both the kids and the animal safe. During his talk, the zookeeper informed the kids that this "cute" baby gator would someday be a ferocious fourteen-footer.

Sin's a lot like that. What begins as a small, seemingly "safe" indulgence eventually becomes much bigger than we can handle. We may think we have things under control, but in a short time, sin can grow to a dangerous size. Often, by the time we realize the danger, it is too late.

The next time temptation comes calling, think of the baby alligator.

. . . .

Lord, help me to stay pure in heart by
keeping myself away from temptation.

A Personal Expedition

We will go three days' journey into the
wilderness, and sacrifice to the LORD
our God, as he shall command us.
EXODUS 8:27 KJV

. . . .

Captain Robert Scott wanted to conquer the South Pole. Sadly, he was beaten there and none of his team made it back to base camp. Scott kept a diary that tells how his very different men behaved *in extremis*. Faced with the desolation of Antarctica and the closeness of death, the true nature of Scott's companions came to the fore.

"Each man in his way is a treasure," Scott wrote.

Modern life, for most of us, is more comfortable. There will be relatively few times when we need to be all we can be. What we need to bring out the best in us is a focus. For Scott and his men the focus was the trek to base camp. For us it is the walk to heaven.

We are on an expedition toward a God who knows our true nature. In His diary we are all treasures.

. . . .

Tribulation is for no other purpose than this, that we
might rise above it and begin to see the You that is in us.

God's Purpose Always Prevails

Many are the plans in a person's heart,
but it is the LORD's purpose that prevails.
PROVERBS 19:21 NIV

. . . .

In winter 2007, southwest Missouri suffered its worst ice storm on record. Three different storms in as many days delivered freezing rain and layers of ice that caused power lines, trees, even houses to fall. Thousands were without power for days, many for weeks.

Sounds to rival a Fourth of July celebration filled the air—the cracking, popping, and smashing of breaking limbs combined with the booms of exploding electric transformers. Crews from all over the country worked hard to trim branches, cut down damaged trees, and repair power lines. Eventually, the humans caught up.

But even nature was affected by the storm. As spring arrived, flowers and trees came to life later than usual. But they still did what flowers and trees do. Clearly, God had allowed them to adapt to the extremes of the weather, enabling them still to fulfill their purpose.

He does that for us, too.

. . . .

Lord, please help me adapt to changes, problems, and
unexpected circumstances, so that I may fulfill Your purpose.

Being Subject to the Authorities

*Remind the people to be subject to rulers
and authorities, to be obedient, to be
ready to do whatever is good.*
TITUS 3:1 NIV

. . . .

Ever found yourself annoyed at the rules, regulations, and limitations placed on you by those who manage and preserve the natural resources you enjoy? If so, think for a moment of the consequences of people ignoring those rules and doing whatever they wanted to do.

In His infinite wisdom, God commands us to subject ourselves to earthly rulers and authorities. Why? Because He knows that to do otherwise will cause us actually to lose the freedom to enjoy the gifts He's given us.

Our God is a God of order, and one of the reasons He makes us subject to earthly authorities—including those who manage our natural resources—is to maintain order, protecting and preserving that which He's given us.

. . . .

*Father, I thank You for putting authorities in place
to protect the outdoor resources I enjoy. They both
preserve Your gift and remind me of the importance
of subjecting myself to earthly authority.*

Walking Near the Edge

*For thou art my rock and my fortress; therefore
for thy name's sake lead me, and guide me.*
PSALM 31:3 KJV

. . . .

There are few experiences like walking a snow-covered mountain peak. But it comes with certain perils: sometimes the ground underfoot is treacherous.

Wind can blow snow into a ledge—called a "cornice"— that might extend over a steep drop. So climbers have found it's a good idea to tie themselves to a rock before venturing too near the edge. If there are no rocks handy, a piece of equipment known as a "deadman" (similar to the blade of a small shovel) can be driven into the snow as an anchor. Should they suddenly fall through a cornice, the deadman may well save a climber's life.

In the sinful world we live in, the ground can drop out from under our feet at any moment. But the Christian has an anchor in the most unexpected situations—a dead man who came back to life.

Tie yourself to Christ, and you can go anywhere with confidence.

. . . .

*Jesus, my Savior, guide my feet in the uncertain places of
life. Please put me on the firm ground that leads to You.*

The Moon

"May the LORD bless his land with the precious
dew from heaven above and with the deep
waters that lie below; with the best the sun
brings forth and the finest the moon can yield."
DEUTERONOMY 33:13–14 NIV

. . . .

There's just something magical about the moon. We've all stopped to appreciate its beauty on a clear night. Many of us have had a closer look at its craters through a telescope. Twelve people have even walked on its surface, bringing back soil and rock samples so we can study and learn more about the moon.

But the moon is more than just an interesting and pretty thing in the sky. It actually helps our earth to recycle itself and sustain life, through its effects on tides and ocean currents. The moon's size and placement are precisely what the earth needs.

Who but the almighty Creator of the universe could have so perfectly invented a natural satellite to orbit our planet to maintain its ability to sustain life?

. . . .

Lord, always remind me of Your care for us—
even the moon itself is proof of that!

God's Ways of Sharing

*"I have no need of a bull from your stall
or of goats from your pens, for every
animal of the forest is mine."*

PSALM 50:9–10 NIV

. . . .

Ever thought of the beauty of the outdoors as yet another way that God shares Himself with you? As His way of reminding you of His goodness, power, and generosity? As another reason to praise His name every day?

We know that God Himself is completely self-sufficient. He doesn't *need* our praise or worship or admiration.

But still, He gave us all our world and everything in it. And He did that to share with us the most wonderful thing in the entire universe—Himself.

The outdoors is just another example of God's generosity. So the next time you're enjoying your favorite activity "out there," don't forget to make Him an important part of your day. Thank Him for sharing Himself with you.

. . . .

*Heavenly Father, I thank You for Your
willingness—Your desire—to share Yourself
with me as I enjoy Your wonderful creation.*

Praise on Skis

Hast thou entered into the treasures of the snow?
or hast thou seen the treasures of the hail?
JOB 38:22 KJV

. . . .

The Nobel laureate Fridtjof Nansen may have been a little tongue in cheek when he said, "It is better to go skiing and think of God than it is to go to church and think of skiing." But he did have a point. A champion skier, skater, and an influential Arctic explorer, Nansen knew about finding God out of doors.

Church is important. It helps create a sense of community, gives people of faith somewhere to recharge their batteries, and often plays a great role in supporting the hungry and needy. And you can worship God there!

But Nansen knew God was also in the hiss of the snow under his skis, in the chill wind against his cheeks, and in the howl of the distant wolf.

So, don't neglect your church, but when you are skiing or playing football or cycling or walking the dog or. . .well, think of God while you're doing it. He made it all possible!

. . . .

Snow, ice, hail, sun, rain, desert,
woodland, sea, mountain, peace, or storm.
Lord, I praise You everywhere!

Lord of the Trees

"And all the trees of the field shall know that I,
the LORD, have brought down the high tree and
exalted the low tree, dried up the green tree
and made the dry tree flourish."
EZEKIEL 17:24 NKJV

. . . .

Over and over again, the Bible compares people to trees. For example, the righteous are said to be like a thriving, green tree planted by a river (see Psalm 1:1–3); and the king of Assyria and his kingdom were said to be a lofty, proud cedar tree, towering over the other trees of the forest (see Ezekiel 31:3–7).

Trees provide a vivid illustration of the way God works in our lives: He can chop down tall trees in the height of their glory and exalt low, humble trees by replanting them in rich soil where they will grow. He is capable of drying up the green trees—the healthy and the wealthy—by taking away their water, and He can make a dry, dying tree suddenly flourish.

The variables that affect the trees are relatively simple compared to our complex lives—but God is sovereign and capable of doing exactly what He wishes.

. . . .

God, I acknowledge that You are in charge
of my life. I acknowledge Your power,
both over the trees and over me.

Compassion on the Needy

Like fluttering birds pushed from the nest, so are
the women of Moab at the fords of the Arnon.
"Make up your mind. . .render a decision."
ISAIAH 16:2–3 NIV

. . . .

For hundreds of years the Moabites had been unfriendly neighbors—and while Israel was often trodden underfoot by world conquerors, the Moabites in their mountain highlands were usually untouched. As a result, they became complacent and conceited.

Then the Assyrians struck—the Moabite men were killed and the women were scattered. They waded into the Arnon River and begged for permission to cross over into Israel. God told the Israelites, "Let the Moabite fugitives stay with you; be their shelter from the destroyer" (Isaiah 16:4 NIV).

To God, these women were like fluttering baby birds pushed out of their safe haven—helpless nestlings that wouldn't survive long unless someone offered help and protection.

Do any evicted nestlings need your help today? Maybe it's a wayward daughter who wants to return home, or perhaps a stressed-out neighbor who needs help. Sometimes we just can't help—but usually when God tells us to "render a decision," it's compassion He desires.

. . . .

God, help me to have the heart of a protector.
Let me offer a helping hand when I can.

X Marks the Spot

So you should look for the Lord before it is too late;
you should call to him while he is near. The wicked
should stop doing wrong, and they should stop
their evil thoughts. They should return to the LORD
so he may have mercy on them. They should come
to our God, because he will freely forgive them.
ISAIAH 55:6–7 NCV

. . . .

Those who never read Robert Louis Stevenson's Treasure Island missed one of the great joys of childhood. Today's adventure novels and movies hold only a flickering candle to Jim Hawkins's adventure with a treasure map bearing a black "X."

All the evil forces of pirating, all of Long John Silver's cunning ways, failed to stop young Jim from finding his heart's desire.

You're probably familiar with another story of hidden treasure. We call it "the Bible," and the treasure, "eternal life." The Old Testament prophet Isaiah provides direction for spiritual adventurers, telling us what to do (stop doing wrong), where to go (return to the Lord), when to do it (before it is too late), and what we'll find (mercy and forgiveness).

That's better than pirate's gold any day.

. . . .

Father, I want the treasure of mercy and
forgiveness in my life, so I can give mercy
and forgiveness to those around me.

The Walnut Tree Stump

I have seen the burden God has laid
on the human race. He has made
everything beautiful in its time.
ECCLESIASTES 3:10–11 NIV

. . . .

A talented wood-carver was told about a tree stump of burl walnut. The tree had been cut down many years ago, and the landowner wanted to clear out what was left over. If the carver wanted the wood, he need only find a way to haul it off.

So several men uprooted the stump, dragging it to the wood-carver's workshop. There, the old stump was transformed into one of the finest, most beautiful carvings of a steam engine ever created.

God transforms us like that. When we seem to be at the lowest point of our lives—when we feel like an old tree stump that should be cleared away—He takes us. With His loving hands, He works us into something beautiful and worthwhile.

God never asked us to be worthy of Him. But in His love for us, He'll do wonderful things in our lives.

. . . .

Take control of my life today, Father,
and make me into what You'd like me to be.

He Came to Save

*"For the Son of Man has come
to save that which was lost."*
MATTHEW 18:11 NKJV

. . . .

Outdoor adventures have the potential to become dangerous. An unwary backpacker loses her way in the woods . . .a sudden snowstorm blinds a skier. . .an avalanche strands climbers.

When an outdoors person is in trouble, hundreds of hunters, skiers, climbers, and other hardy folks often mount a massive search-and-rescue effort. They might march in formation, looking for clues to the lost hiker's whereabouts. They'll scale steep mountain faces to rescue trapped climbers. They soar in helicopters, seeking out the lost. The effort expended is mind boggling—and greatly appreciated by those who receive the aid.

We can't even imagine the amount of help God has sent into our world. We see His hand in the homeless shelters, crisis centers, hospital visits, church outreaches, and the innumerable volunteers who mop up after natural disasters. He works through everyday people like all of us.

No matter how bad things get, God will be there with the help we need. And then He'll be happy to use us to share that help with others.

. . . .

*Lord, here are two hands—show me how I can
be part of Your network of aid to the world.*

Inheriting the Gift

There is but one God, the Father, from whom
all things came and for whom we live.
1 CORINTHIANS 8:6 NIV

. . . .

Have you had the opportunity to paddle a canoe on a mountain lake? Ever caught sight of a hawk or eagle in flight? Have you visited one of the hundreds of natural wonders, large and small, around our nation? If so, did you contemplate the beauty of the scenery? God the Creator made it for each one of us.

Millions slog through life, oblivious to the panoramic slide show God has put on for them. Our busy lifestyles often shut many of us out from the beauty all around—and we miss the One who made it all possible.

If you're going through a hard time right now. . .if you're seeking answers to questions you're afraid to ask. . .if your life is one of fatigue and disappointment, you're missing the secret. There's a gift right before your eyes, if you'll only look for it.

. . . .

Father God, please give me the courage to stop and
gaze on Your creation, so I might better appreciate You.

Facing Old Enemies

*The people of Manasseh never were able to take
over these towns—the Canaanites wouldn't
budge. But later, when the Israelites got stronger,
they put the Canaanites to forced labor.*
JOSHUA 17:12–13 MSG

. . . .

A re you set in your ways, or open to new challenges?
Some of us had a bad experience earlier in life—maybe
those swimming lessons didn't go so well, or we flopped the
first motorcycle we rode, or we resembled a whirling, careening
cartoon character the first (and last) time we tried to ski.

Now, as adults, we're physically stronger and able to face
our difficulties with a clearer mind. Want to tackle one of
those challenges again?

Millennia ago, God told the Israelites to secure the Promised Land by driving out its inhabitants. But the people didn't
think they could. It wasn't until later, when they gained more
strength, that they were able to tackle the job.

Were you daunted years ago by some spiritual task, one
that others further along the journey seemed to handle with
ease? If so, now may be a good time to revisit that challenge—
and find a new pathway of growth.

. . . .

*Lord, please help me to face my old issues
in Your strength, once and for all.*

Unexplained Phenomena

*The secret things belong unto the LORD our
God: but those things which are revealed
belong unto us and to our children for ever.*
DEUTERONOMY 29:29 KJV

. . . .

Bigfoot! The Loch Ness Monster! UFOs! The Bermuda Triangle!

Countless television programs and websites have focused on these unexplained phenomena. Great numbers of people have made these mysteries a large part of their lives. It isn't hard to find people on a never-ending quest for Bigfoot, search for the Loch Ness Monster, or pursuit of unidentified flying objects. We seem to enjoy the strange and unusual.

At first glance, there are many unexplained phenomena described in the Bible. Sick and crippled people are suddenly healed, a man comes unharmed from a den of hungry lions, men thrown into a fiery furnace aren't burned, another man walks on water. They were all "unexplained phenomena" to many of those who witnessed the events.

But these occurrences aren't really so mysterious. We know that our God works in mysterious ways. These phenomena, described in His Word, may be "unexplainable" to some—but to an all-powerful God, these miraculous events are nothing extraordinary.

Ask Him for some of that power in your life today.

. . . .

*Lord, may I forever marvel at
Your power and greatness.*

Darkness

*"Whoever follows me will
never walk in darkness."*
JOHN 8:12 NIV

. . . .

Beneath a common outcrop of Pennsylvania sandstone, a narrow hole opens into the hill. A dead-end crevice? No, it continues, a tunnel large enough to crawl into. Within a few feet, there is room to stand—but the walls are angled and narrow, and the adventurer must proceed on a tilt. Farther along, tables of high, flat rock welcome the explorer to sit for a moment. If you were to turn off your flashlight, you'd realize just what true darkness is!

In fact, you'd see absolutely nothing. The human eye needs light, even the smallest smidgeon, to see. Without that light, the total darkness becomes disorienting. The mind begins to race, and even the body struggles to maintain equilibrium. Turn on the light again, though, and normality returns.

In the spiritual realm, the mind without Jesus can only imagine ultimate reality. God's Word is light (see Psalm 119:105), shining on everything around us so that we can walk in His ways.

Let's shine that light in our world today.

. . . .

*Lord, may I reflect Your light
in everything I say and do.*

Pure Forever

Purify me with hyssop, and I shall be clean;
wash me, and I shall be whiter than snow.
PSALM 51:7 NASB

. . . .

S nowy landscapes have a pure beauty, free of the unpleasant details of other seasons. The dazzling white stuff that covers the ground hides some less appealing images of warmer seasons—muddy trails, rotting logs, and bugs lie buried out of sight.

Who isn't warmed by scenes of a snug, well-lit home blanketed in snow against the bitter winds of winter? A wisp of smoke from the chimney tells us all is well. The yard displays nothing to spoil the picture of peaceful contentment. Come spring, though, the melting snow may reveal a yard full of trash, broken toys, and weeds.

Let's be thankful that when God clothes us in the righteousness of Christ, He no longer sees our sins—we are whiter than snow in His sight. And, unlike snow, His righteousness covers us forever!

. . . .

Father, I need Your cleansing. I thank You for
providing the way for me to be clean in Your
sight, through the sacrifice of Your Son.

Have a Beat-Boredom Venture

"Let your light shine before others,
that they may see your good deeds
and glorify your Father in heaven."
MATTHEW 5:16 NIV

. . . .

I'm bored!" is a common twenty-first-century phrase. Ever say it yourself? While not worth a mouth soaping, boredom can indicate the problem of turning inward.

Why not try an "adventure in light shining"? Start by turning off the television and computer. Stand up. Walk to the front porch or apartment balcony. Take a deep breath of fresh air. Say, "Thank You, God, for this day!" Look at the house on your right, your left, and across the street. Declare, "I am going to show these neighbors that I care for them." Finally, determine how you and yours will convince those neighbors of your resolve.

No concordance of any Bible translation contains the word bored, but the scriptures are saturated with admonitions to be more concerned about others than about ourselves. Try reading these verses: Matthew 25:38–40; Luke 14:13–14; Romans 12:10.

Erase the word bored from your vocabulary—and your behavior.

. . . .

Father, strengthen my will to fight
boredom; help me live outside myself.

The Grand Canyon(s)

*Follow God's example, therefore,
as dearly loved children.*
EPHESIANS 5:1 NIV

. . . .

Whether they've been there or not, most everyone is familiar with the Grand Canyon, the massive Arizona gorge carved out by the Colorado River. It is one of the United States' oldest national parks.

But other locales claim the "Grand Canyon" name, as well. There's "the Grand Canyon of Pennsylvania," Pine Creek Gorge in the north central section of the Keystone State, and at least two places that bill themselves as "the Grand Canyon of the East": Letchworth State Park near Perry, New York, and the New River National River Gorge near Fayetteville, West Virginia.

If imitation is the sincerest form of flattery, the "real" Grand Canyon should be pleased—just as God is pleased when we imitate Him.

How can we imitate God? Read the verses following Ephesians 5:1 for a few ideas: "Walk in the way of love, just as Christ loved us and gave himself up for us as a fragrant offering and sacrifice to God. But among you there must not be even a hint of sexual immorality, or of any kind of impurity, or of greed, because these are improper for God's holy people" (Ephesians 5:2–3 NIV).

. . . .

Father, may I imitate You today in everything I do!

Made for This!

*"By this everyone will know that you are
my disciples, if you love one another."*
JOHN 13:35 NIV

. . . .

Ben is a sheepdog from a long line of sheepdogs. But he was re-homed without setting paw in a farm. As a new puppy he wasn't allowed outside. When the time was right his owner started taking him for short walks along the river. As Ben grew bigger the walks grew longer.

Then came the day when a walk took them between two farm fields. Ignoring the field of cows, Ben strained to reach the sheep field. He stood there for some time with his head through the fence looking puzzled. There was something he was supposed to be doing there!

When you and I walk past someone in need, when we omit to do something for our community, we might have a good excuse, but we still feel bad. It's the same thing.

Whether he knew it or not, Ben was made for herding sheep. Whether we agree with it or not, you and I were made to love our neighbor.

. . . .

*Lord, if I settle for comfort, fortune, or fame,
then I settle for less than my purpose.*

Drawing Strength from Others

*And I told them of the hand of my God which
was good upon me, as also of the king's words
that he had spoken unto me. And they said, Let
us rise up and build. So they strengthened their
hands for the good work.*

NEHEMIAH 2:18 ASV

. . . .

In the course of planning a trip, we might be inspired to pore over stories of our destination. And those stories might inspire us to become better people.

Think of the pioneers who crossed the mountains in spite of the terrible wind and snow or the valiant soldiers who contested the battlefield. Stories of past conquests inspire us to imitate those brave men and women who achieved so much. Somewhere, deep in all our hearts, is a desire to rise above obstacles and accomplish great things.

So it was when Nehemiah told the Israelites of God's hand upon him. Inspired by God's goodness and presence, the people strengthened their hearts to rebuild the war-ravaged wall around Jerusalem.

Let the Bible's stories inspire you. Find strength in biographies of people who were moved by God to achieve much. Imitate them—and inspire those behind you.

. . . .

*Lord, as You've worked wonderfully in the
lives of others, please work in my life, too.*

Celebrating God's Goodness

But as for me, it is good to be near God.
I have made the Sovereign LORD my refuge;
I will tell of all your deeds.
PSALM 73:28 NIV

....

In the movie *A River Runs Through It*, a Presbyterian preacher and his two sons enjoy a day of fly-fishing in which all three men catch trout from Montana's Big Blackfoot River.

"I'd say the Lord has blessed us all today," the preacher says, looking at his sons' catches. Then he pulls a trout from his creel that dwarfs the boys' fish. With a smile, he says, "It's just that He's been particularly good to me!"

There's a great blessing in acknowledging that all good things—even something as simple as a successful day of fishing—come from the hand of our very good God. It's wonderful to know that He desires to do good for those who love Him.

When we tell others of God's goodness, we set ourselves—and them—up to receive further blessings from the hand of God. His love and generosity to those who love Him know no bounds.

....

Remind me daily, Father, that You are the source
of all good things—because You Yourself are good.

A Fresh Start

"While the earth remains, seedtime and
harvest, cold and heat, summer and winter,
day and night, shall not cease."
GENESIS 8:22 ESV

. . . .

As one year winds down and another approaches, many of us evaluate the mistakes we made in the previous twelve months and make resolutions to be different in the coming year. Sometimes we follow through, sometimes we don't—but with each new year comes the chance to start fresh.

After God wiped the slate clean with the flood of Genesis, He promised never to repeat His action. And in the words of the verse above, He told humanity that He was giving us a fresh start. There would be many opportunities for other fresh starts, too. In fact, God built a fresh start into every cycle of time, weather, and seasons: seedtime and harvest, cold and heat, summer and winter, day and night.

We don't have to wait for January 1 to start over. This day—this very hour—can be one of renewal.

. . . .

Father, I thank You for giving me so many
opportunities to turn from my old ways
toward a life that pleases You.

The Way of an Eagle

[The LORD] was like an eagle building its nest
that flutters over its young. It spreads its wings
to catch them and carries them on its feathers.
DEUTERONOMY 32:11 NCV

. . . .

For the past two centuries, the eagle has been the national bird and symbol of the United States. But for millennia mankind has admired the eagle as an icon of unfettered freedom and fierceness in battle. The biblical proverb writer Agur said that one of the most awe-inspiring things he could think of was "the way an eagle flies in the sky" (Proverbs 30:19 NCV).

Though it is the epitome of power and independence of spirit, there is something even more poignant and wonderful about an eagle—how fiercely protective it is of its young. And that is how God is toward His people, those who love and obey Him.

God hovered over the Israelites in the wilderness, sheltered them, and led them on to the Promised Land. That same God lives today and hovers over you, protecting you when you stay in the shadow of His wings.

And when you stumble, God is there to lift you back up with those same wings.

. . . .

Lord, I thank You for tenderly caring for me—
and for being fiercely protective of me.

Follow the Leader

"Where you go I will go, and where you stay
I will stay. Your people will be my people and
your God my God."
RUTH 1:16 NIV

. . . .

Athletes, adventurers, and soldiers often follow their leaders through varying levels of suffering. Some leaders command obedience through fear. Others draw followers to their hardworking example. Still others earn devotion through their compassionate care for those who follow them.

In many cases, the followers would do almost anything for their leader. So athletes pull together to win championships, adventurers survive the ravages of nature, and soldiers battle enemies to ultimate victory.

What better leader could there be than our great God? Stories are told, in the Bible and throughout history, of people who committed their lives to follow Him no matter what. Many have suffered or died for their faith—and received a heavenly reward.

What experiences have helped solidify your devotion to God? What promises best express your commitment to follow Him?

. . . .

Lord, as Peter asked, "Who else shall I follow?"
You have the words of eternal life!

The Soft Whisper

*The Lord said, ". . .Look, the Lord is ready to pass
by." A very powerful wind went before the Lord,
digging into the mountain and causing landslides,
but the Lord was not in the wind. After the
windstorm there was an earthquake, but the Lord
was not in the earthquake. After the earthquake,
there was a fire, but the Lord was not in the fire.
After the fire, there was a soft whisper. When Elijah
heard it, he covered his face with his robe.*
1 KINGS 19:11–13 NET

. . . .

A popular song has many of us "dreaming of a white Christmas." Once in a while, we actually get to enjoy such a thing!

At those times, if we leave the holiday revelry and slip outside on a quiet, cold December night, our feet crunch in newly fallen snow. When we stand still, calm and silence lie over the land. And if we allow ourselves to listen carefully, we might hear the softest sound of all: the gentle whisper of falling snowflakes.

That's often how God speaks to our hearts.

. . . .

*God, it is so hard in this world of music and
advertisements just to hear Your whisper. Please
make me open to hear what You have to say.*

Roughing It

And she brought forth her firstborn son, and wrapped
him in swaddling clothes, and laid him in a manger;
because there was no room for them in the inn.
LUKE 2:7 KJV

. . . .

When it comes to campers, the "roughing it" scale varies dramatically.

Some insist on an intimate connection with nature, eschewing even a tent. A sleeping bag under the stars is quite enough for them.

Others prefer a tent covering but still lay on the ground. An air mattress seems right to some, while others like their tent to "pop up" from a trailer with pullout beds. RVers camp in what are essentially rolling hotel rooms, featuring televisions, refrigerators, and showers.

Mary, soon to deliver the baby Jesus, could only dream of a comfortable place to stay. With the Bethlehem inn declaring NO VACANCY, Mary and her husband, Joseph, ended up in a cave or stable—nobody knows for sure, just that there was an animal feeding trough handy. There, in the most humble circumstances, the Creator and King of the entire universe was born as a helpless infant.

You could say Jesus was "roughing it" on earth—dramatically so some thirty years later when He died on the cross for our sins.

And aren't you glad?

. . . .

Lord Jesus, thank You for the sacrifices
You made on my behalf.

Happy Birthday, Boss

Unto you is born. . .a Saviour.
LUKE 2:11 KJV

. . . .

Depending on your age, this scene, inspired by a 1973 *Rick O'Shay* newspaper comic, might be familiar. With thanks to cartoonist and fellow Christian Stan Lynde, here goes:

On a cold Montana Christmas Eve, Main Street was empty, except for the lonely sight of Deadeye Holloway astride his mount, ambling toward the edge of town.

Horse and rider, their breath like smoke in the subzero weather, passed the little Methodist church. The lights of the sanctuary filtered through stained glass to paint the snow-covered churchyard in a kaleidoscope of suffused colors. Strains of "Silent Night" escaped the walls and drifted heavenward like the thin tendril of wood smoke rising from the church's chimney.

Up into the hills Deadeye rode, until there was no path except the one he blazed through the windblown drifts. On a ridge that stared out over a hundred miles of Montana topography, Deadeye reined his horse and turned his eyes toward the star-spangled skies. One star stood out above the rest, dancing in the frigid heaven. *Just like over Bethlehem,* he thought.

He took off his hat and said quietly, "Happy Birthday, boss." Then he turned his horse and headed back down the mountain.

. . . .

Father, I thank You for Your Son,
the baby who was God over all!

Christopher's Christmas

*Attend to the public reading of scripture, to
preaching, to teaching. . .by so doing, you will
save both yourself and your hearers.*

1 TIMOTHY 4:13, 16 RSV

· · · · · · ·

Christopher Gist, eighteenth-century backwoodsman,
sometimes shot buffalo for breakfast. He made fires
during snowstorms to cook lunch. He chased wildcats out of
dens to obtain a dry place to sleep at night. And no matter
where Gist went, he carried a well-worn copy of the *Book of
Common Prayer.*

On December 25, 1750, Gist camped in an Indian town
on Elk's Eye Creek, near present-day Newcomerstown, Ohio.
There, on that cold Christmas Day, he read prayers to an as-
sembly of white traders and Wyandot Indians. The natives,
assuming he was a minister, begged him to "marry them after
the Christian Manner, and baptize their Children." Though
Gist could not consent to that, he told them that he hoped that
"the great King [of England] would send them proper ministers" to meet their spiritual needs.

In sharing his habit of daily devotional prayer, Gist
touched hearts and made history. His Christmas reading can
be considered the first Protestant church service west of the
Allegheny Mountains.

· · · · · · ·

*Father, wherever I find myself in Your world,
help me to take Your Word with me—
for the sake of my soul and the souls of others.*

Peace with Nature

*The baby will play safely near the hole of a
cobra. Yes, a little child will put its hand in a
nest of deadly snakes without harm. Nothing
will hurt or destroy in all my holy mountain.*
ISAIAH 11:8–9 NLT

. . . .

Snake charmers allow their infants to play in the midst of de-poisoned cobras so that when the kids grow up, they won't be afraid of deadly serpents. But we *should* have a healthy respect for venomous snakes. They are, after all, very capable of "hurting and destroying."

Nevertheless, the Bible speaks of a blessed time coming when humanity will be at peace with nature—even with deadly adders. Babies will crawl safely among poisonous snakes, and wild animals will live in harmony with people.

More importantly, since wars destroy more millions than wild animals ever have, nations will be at peace with each other and beat their weapons into farm tools.

Christ is in the process of changing our hearts now, and when His kingdom comes He will restore nature to the peaceful state it enjoyed in Eden. That is why we are told to pray, "Amen! Come, Lord Jesus!" (Revelation 22:20). Only the return of Jesus Christ will finally bring peace on earth.

. . . .

Amen! Come quickly, Lord Jesus!

Earthly Paradise. . .Made Perfect

He made known to us the mystery of his will
according to his good pleasure. . .to be put into
effect when the times reach their fulfillment—
to bring unity to all things in heaven and on
earth under Christ.
EPHESIANS 1:9–10 TNIV

. . . .

It's probably safe to say that most Christians who've enjoyed the natural beauty of God's created world have also found their thoughts directed toward heaven and eternal perfection.

We Christians can enjoy the wonders of the created world—but we also know the biblical truth that what was once perfect was thrown into chaos when sin entered the Garden of Eden.

There are wonderful promises, though, in God's written Word. One day, all things will be restored to their original state of perfection!

Imagine for a moment your very favorite places on earth—places you spend time enjoying the natural beauty God has created for you. Then imagine those places as not only pleasant, but absolutely perfect. . .just like you will one day be in Jesus Christ.

. . . .

Thank You, Father, for Your promise that one
day we will live as perfectly redeemed people—
and in eternal perfection!

The Wonderful Wind

*"The wind blows wherever it wants. Just as you
can hear the wind but can't tell where it comes
from or where it is going, so you can't explain
how people are born of the Spirit."*
JOHN 3:8 NLT

. . . .

In Hawaii, it's said, you can lean into the stiff winds at the Nuuanu Pali State Park and actually find yourself held up. Though that's a dramatic example, we see the effects of the wind around us all the time—there are gentle breezes that rustle the leaves, howling storms that rattle our windows, and frightening hurricanes that demolish whole buildings.

Jesus said God's Holy Spirit is like the wind—invisible in itself, yet showing powerful effects. What did the Spirit of God do in our lives when we were born again? Hasn't He comforted us in times of trial, helped us when we didn't know how to pray, and given us boldness when we had the opportunity to share the gospel?

And, like the Hawaiian winds, the Spirit also holds us up when we're buffeted by temptation. He even lifts us up to the throne of the Father after we have sinned, so we can confess and receive forgiveness.

. . . .

*Father, I thank You for Your Holy Spirit who lives
within me. Help me to lean on Him and His power.*

Things Unseen

By faith he left Egypt, not fearing the king's anger;
he persevered because he saw him who is invisible.
HEBREWS 11:27 NIV

. . . .

Mountain climbers know it's a good idea to tie their group together with a safety rope—as it's not unusual to walk into a whiteout.

In a blinding snowstorm, fellow climbers might be only a few feet away but impossible to see or hear. Without a safety rope, it's easy for a team member to wander off and become lost. Roped together—even if they can't see the others—climbers know their friends are nearby and heading in the same direction.

Faith is the believer's safety rope. Often, like a climber in a whiteout, we have no idea where we're going. But with our faith firmly attached to Jesus—even when we can't always "see" Him—we can be sure we're heading in the right direction.

. . . .

Lord, I don't always recognize the path You've chosen
for me—but help me to walk confidently in Your
footsteps, with faith as my safety rope.

Song of the Stars

Praise him, sun and moon,
praise him, all you shining stars.
PSALM 148:3 NIV

. . . .

When is the last time you stood alone in the night, watching the stars?

God's handiwork can be millions of miles away—yet as close as a quiet moment in the backyard. Did you ever stop to think that you are seeing the same stars that shone on King David, Christopher Columbus, and George Washington? Those stars were placed on the day God created the heavens—and still point us to our powerful Lord today.

So many of us are caught up in the rat race, searching for peace but missing some of the quiet signposts to God's presence. The night sky holds a million secrets—and waits for us to step away from this hectic world and reach for His hand.

If your life seems to be careening out of control, stop the treadmill. Pull the power cord of your existence for a while, and listen to the song of the stars. Your Creator waits on you, tonight.

. . . .

Gracious God, my Creator, please help me to stop
racing long enough to hear Your voice when
I gaze in wonder at the stars.

An Unexplored Gift

*"But seek his kingdom, and these
things will be given to you as well."*
LUKE 12:31 NIV

. . . .

You might not have heard of *shinrin yoku* but have probably enjoyed it! The Japanese term means "wood-air bathing" and refers to the uplifting feeling you get from a walk in the woods. Studies in Japan show that trees "breathe" out compounds, half of which are as yet unidentified, that have a positive effect on our mood.

So that sense of calm well-being you get under a wooded canopy is actually a gift from the trees themselves. As well as making us feel good, it has been suggested those compounds improve health, with beneficial effects being recorded in people with diabetes and other illnesses.

We haven't really begun to explore the blessing that this world is. Who knows what else is out there. It's very possible creation already has everything we could possibly need. Let's not spoil God's gift before we get to see how wonderful it really is!

. . . .

*Father, You have already provided for us abundantly.
Help us understand, care for, and, most of all, enjoy
Your all-encompassing creation.*

Author Biographies/Index

Mark Ammerman is a licensed minister, graphic designer, and award-winning author. He and his wife, Terri, are foster and adoptive parents, with four children of their own (plus two cats and a dog). They live in Lancaster, Pennsylvania. (Day 7, 41, 76, 95, 111, 129, 147, 151, 176, 182, 216, 235, 252, 270, 311, 328, 346, 358, 359)

David Barrett has worked for five years as a freelance Bible reference editor and cartographer (www.biblemapper.com). He lives in Chambersburg, Pennsylvania, with his wife, Anisea, and their four children. (Day 117, 162, 287)

Tom Blubaugh is a freelance writer. He has written nonfiction articles for business and denominational publications. He resides with his wife, Barbara, in southwest Missouri where he is currently writing fiction for young adults. (Day 23, 30, 47, 64, 84, 100, 109, 126, 160, 180, 197, 210, 222, 238, 268, 279, 283, 318, 332)

James Davis is an editor for the *Morning Sentinel* newspaper. He has written a regular gun column for the paper and articles for outdoors magazines. He lives in the woods of Maine with his wife, Susan, and has six children. (Day 14, 35, 54, 60, 98, 106, 122, 159, 167, 195, 207, 228, 250, 255, 258, 276, 303, 322, 325, 347)

Stephen Fierbaugh is a missionary with Pioneer Bible Translators. He is the author of *Celibacy Sucks, But We're Not Alone*, on long-term living as a Christian single. On a recent missions trip to East Africa, Stephen climbed Mount Kilimanjaro. (Day 4, 29, 32, 125, 130, 134, 168, 208, 214, 224, 249, 292, 297, 356)

Steve Husting is a mild webmaster by day and fearless writer by night. He loves chocolate, hiking, and making the Bible's message clear to his readers. He and his wife, Shirley, live in Southern California with their son. (Day 2, 13, 18, 20, 33, 39, 43, 57, 62, 65, 78, 87, 103, 120, 135, 145, 189, 215, 242, 251, 262, 264, 273, 290, 309, 323, 342, 344, 351, 355)

John Long is a pastor, speaker, pilot, and sport pilot flight instructor living with his wife and two puppies in central Florida. He has a PhD in theology and enjoys music, sports, and boating. (Day 71, 92, 121, 163, 203, 223, 248, 306, 343, 364)

Steve Mathisen spends days writing requirements (very short stories about software) and evenings writing stories for children. He is married and has two lovely daughters and five grandchildren. He, his wife Carol, and their cat Norman live in beautiful western Washington. (Day 10, 81, 94, 114, 133, 137, 146, 154, 165, 194, 199, 219, 253, 265, 281, 288, 296, 362)

David McLaughlan used to write whatever turned a buck, but now he writes about faith and God. It doesn't pay as well—but it does make his heart sing! He lives in bonny Scotland with Julie and a whole "clan" of children. (Day 11, 22, 24, 27, 36, 44, 49, 51, 58, 66, 75, 82, 83, 107, 118, 138, 152, 157, 170, 172, 178, 184, 185, 192, 193, 209, 211, 225, 234, 263, 266, 293, 299, 300, 304, 310, 314, 315, 320, 331, 334, 337, 350, 363, 365)

Paul M. Miller is a freelance writer residing in Prairie Village, Kansas, where he is an active churchman and supporter of the arts in greater Kansas City. He is a retired publishing company editor, playwright, Christian theater director, and the father of two adult children. (Day 15, 21, 89, 99, 123, 128, 143, 148, 196, 221, 229, 237, 254, 271, 277, 284, 302, 340, 348)

Paul Muckley serves as senior editor for nonfiction at Barbour Publishing. Under the pseudonym Paul Kent, he has written several books of Bible trivia. Paul and his wife, Laurie, have adopted three children and live in eastern Ohio. (Day 25, 55, 104, 131, 173, 201, 260, 286, 305, 329, 349, 357)

Todd Aaron Smith has fourteen books published, some of which have appeared on the Christian bestseller lists. Todd also works with a ministry for native Mayan children living in Guatemala and southern Mexico. He and his family live near Joplin, Missouri. (Day 3, 8, 17, 40, 45, 52, 61, 96, 115, 136, 144, 149, 166, 190, 206, 217, 226, 245, 259, 280, 291, 316, 319, 330, 335, 341, 345)

Ed Strauss has authored eighteen books for children, tweens, and adults, and coauthored an additional sixteen. Ed has a passion for biblical apologetics and besides writing for Barbour, has been published by Zondervan, Tyndale, Moody, and Focus on the Family. (Day 6, 12, 26, 28, 37, 38, 42, 48, 50, 56, 59, 67, 68, 73, 80, 91, 101, 105, 108, 110, 112, 116, 127, 132, 139, 153, 164, 169, 174, 181, 183, 186, 200, 202, 212, 230, 233, 240, 243, 247, 256, 261, 267, 269, 274, 278, 282, 285, 289, 295, 307, 313, 317, 324, 327, 338, 339, 354, 360)

Tracy Sumner is a veteran writer and editor in the Christian publishing field. His books include *How Did We Get the Bible?* for Barbour Publishing. Tracy lives in the beautiful Pacific Northwest. (Day 1, 5, 9, 16, 34, 46, 63, 69, 70, 72, 77, 86, 93, 97, 102, 113, 119, 124, 141, 142, 150, 155, 156, 158, 175, 177, 187, 188, 191, 204, 205, 213, 220, 227, 232, 236, 241, 246, 272, 275, 294, 298, 308, 312, 321, 326, 333, 336, 352, 361)

Lee Warren is an author, editor, and freelance writer from Omaha, Nebraska, with three books and hundreds of articles in print. He writes for Baptist Press Sports and cowrites a singles blog ("Single Purpose") for CBN.com. (Day 19, 31, 53, 74, 79, 85, 88, 90, 140, 161, 171, 179, 198, 218, 231, 239, 244, 257, 301, 353)

Scripture Index

Old Testament

Genesis
1:1—Day 83
1:4—Day 44
1:11, 20, 24, 26—Day 226
1:14—Day 328
1:16—Day 238
1:24—Day 272
1:25—Day 119
1:27—Day 173
1:31—Day 89
2:1—Day 5
2:15—Day 220, 307
2:23—Day 299
5:23–24—Day 114
6:7–8—Day 123
6:19–21—Day 56
8:22—Day 353
9:6—Day 311
15:5—Day 79
17:20—Day 186
21:20—Day 186
21:33—Day 139
25:27—Day 132, 301
27:3—Day 298

Exodus
3:2—Day 13
8:27—Day 331

Leviticus
11:7—Day 242
19:23—Day 239
26:4—Day 293
26:12—Day 248

Numbers
11:4—Day 43
Deuteronomy
1:21—Day 145
2:33—Day 189
7:13—Day 85

11:12—Day 243
22:6—Day 174
22:7—Day 174
27:8—Day 315
29:29—Day 345
30:11—Day 263
32:11—Day 354
33:13–14—Day 335

Joshua
1:9—Day 136
14:11—Day 288
17:12–13—Day 344
17:18—Day 285

Judges
3:10–11—Day 81
14:8—Day 290

Ruth
1:16—Day 355

1 Samuel
2:2—Day 33
23:14—Day 12
24:1—Day 223

2 Samuel
9:13—Day 57
16:11–12—Day 38
22:17—Day 138
22:20—Day 36
23:18—Day 253

1 Kings
4:22–23—Day 50
4:25—Day 230
4:33—Day 289
19:11–13—Day 356
19:12–13—Day 77

2 Kings
4:39—Day 120
4:40—Day 120
6:2—Day 101
6:31—Day 215

1 Chronicles
12:32—Day 177

2 Chronicles
9:6—Day 62
15:15—Day 39

Nehemiah
2:18—Day 351
4:6—Day 78
8:10—Day 69
9:6—Day 100

Job
1:1—Day 73
1:10—Day 73
6:15, 17—Day 247
8:11–13—Day 59
9:8–9—Day 55
12:3—Day 116
12:7–8—Day 116
14:11–12—Day 48
14:14—Day 48
29:21–23—Day 269
30:20, 22, 26—Day 68
30:29—Day 68
34:21–22—Day 325
36:27–28—Day 166
38:22—Day 337
38:22–23—Day 47
38:41—Day 231
39:9–11—Day 26
39:13—Day 37
39:26–27—Day 127
41:1, 8—Day 280

Psalms
1:3—Day 146
3:1—Day 18
4:8—Day 266
8:3—Day 107

8:3–4—Day 205, 287
8:4—Day 70
11:1—Day 153
12:3—Day 9
18:2—Day 153
19:1—Day 113
19:4—Day 203
20:7—Day 23
22:5—Day 234
23:2–3—Day 16
23:4—Day 20
24:1—Day 220
25:9—Day 184
29:9—Day 162
29:11—Day 63
30:5—Day 42
31:3—Day 334
33:13—Day 152
42:1–2—Day 212
42:5–6—Day 124
46:1—Day 159
46:10—Day 279
50:9–10—Day 336
50:11—Day 207
51:7—Day 347
62:2—Day 51
65:9—Day 294
66:5—Day 312
71:20—Day 4
73:24—Day 211
73:28—Day 352
74:16–17—Day 244
80:13—Day 183
80:14–15—Day 183
82:4—Day 216
83:13–16—Day 214
84:3—Day 6
89:9—Day 74
91:4–5—Day 291
104:1–2 Day 322
104:18—Day 256
104:20—Day 250
104:24–25—Day 164
104:25—Day 319
111:10—Day 40
119:11—Day 115
119:105—Day 118

124:7—Day 274
139:7—Day 196
139:13–14—Day 30
139:15–16—Day 86
144:3—Day 121
145:10–11—Day 17
146:6—Day 58
147:4—Day 70
147:5—Day 127
148:3—Day 364
148:5, 10—Day 258
150:6—Day 3

Proverbs
3:23—Day 75
4:1—Day 191
4:18—Day 94
6:8—Day 233
6:27—Day 133
11:25—Day 182
15:3—Day 24
16:9—Day 273
16:18—Day 176
17:22—Day 46
18:24—Day 236
19:21—Day 332
22:28—Day 95
23:5—Day 224
24:11—Day 216
25:2—Day 129
26:2—Day 38
27:12—Day 106
29:23—Day 265
30:18–19—Day 171
30:19—Day 354
30:25—Day 122
30:26—Day 256
30:29–31—Day 200

Ecclesiastes
1:9—Day 185
2:21–23—Day 84
3:1—Day 54
3:10–11—Day 341
3:11—Day 66
5:7—Day 297
7:10—Day 326

8:15—Day 246
9:11—Day 32
9:12—Day 274
12:7—Day 64

Song of Solomon
2:11–12—Day 42
2:15—Day 219
4:8—Day 327
6:11—Day 105
7:12—Day 105

Isaiah
4:2—Day 108
7:23–24—Day 278
11:1—Day 108
11:6—Day 140
11:8–9—Day 360
14:8—Day 181
16:2–3—Day 339
16:4—Day 339
19:5, 8—Day 267
24:5–6—Day 67
25:4—Day 110
30:6—Day 91
30:23—Day 90
32:19–20—Day 28
35:1–2—Day 141
35:8–9—Day 221
37:24—Day 181
40:8—Day 15
40:12—Day 195
40:22—Day 261
40:26—Day 213
40:31—Day 21
41:10—Day 149
41:18—Day 227
43:20—Day 202
45:8—Day 169
45:18—Day 34
55:6–7—Day 340
55:9—Day 109
55:12—Day 175
55:13—Day 92
56:3–5—Day 125
60:22—Day 249
61:11—Day 169

64:6–7—Day 313
64:8–9—Day 313

Jeremiah
6:16—Day 257
8:5—Day 240
8:7—Day 240
10:11—Day 144
10:12—Day 8
16:16—Day 324
16:17—Day 324
17:7–8—Day 163
17:11—Day 80
18:14–15—Day 198
27:5—Day 321
50:39—Day 295
51:37—Day 295

Ezekiel
17:24—Day 338
26:14—Day 282
26:17—Day 282
34:26—Day 102
47:5—Day 317

Hosea
2:15—Day 306
10:12—Day 316

Joel
2:23—Day 275
2:28—Day 148

Jonah
4:6—Day 179

Micah
4:4—Day 230
5:7—Day 161

Habakkuk
3:19—Day 277

Zephaniah
3:17—Day 1

Zechariah
4:10—Day 262

Malachi
3:16—Day 251

New Testament

Matthew
3:4—Day 31
4:18–19—Day 210
4:19—Day 147, 229
5:10–11—Day 52
5:16—Day 348
5:44—Day 38
5:44–45—Day 112
6:7—Day 297
6:11—Day 222
6:19—Day 252
6:26—Day 233
6:28–29—Day 155
7:13–14—Day 286
7:18–20—Day 214
8:24—Day 204
10:14—Day 276
10:29, 31—Day 35
10:30—Day 193
13:3—Day 137
13:44—Day 228
14:29–30—Day 296
17:27—Day 218
18:11—Day 342
18:14—Day 172
22:37–39—Day 7

Mark
1:17—Day 241
4:9—Day 22
4:38–39—Day 126
16:15—Day 241

Luke
1:23—Day 82
2:7—Day 357
2:11—Day 358
5:4—Day 147
6:44—Day 235

6:47–49—Day 292
8:15—Day 169
8:24—Day 192
9:23—Day 130
9:33—Day 128
11:31—Day 62
12:31—Day 365
12:56—Day 117
19:39–40—Day 19
23:33—Day 194
23:43—Day 156

John
3:8—Day 362
4:14—Day 259
8:12—Day 346
10:14—Day 61
12:24—Day 97
13:15—Day 320
13:35—Day 350
14:6—Day 104
14:13—Day 261
15:3—Day 87
20:1—Day 88
20:26—Day 93
20:29—Day 134
21:15—Day 165
21:25—Day 268

Acts
2:17—Day 148
2:41—Day 131
12:5—Day 225
14:22—Day 11
16:6—Day 323

Romans
1:16—Day 314
1:20—Day 188
5:1—Day 304
9:16—Day 310
12:2—Day 45
13:12—Day 318

1 Corinthians
1:26—Day 2, 41
2:9—Day 197

3:14—Day 111
6:12–13, 15—Day 99
8:6—Day 343
10:12—Day 98
10:26—Day 142
13:12—Day 283, 318
13:13—Day 10
15:41—Day 53
15:58—Day 217

2 Corinthians
10:17—Day 9

Galatians
4:14—Day 49
6:7—Day 330
6:9—Day 201

Ephesians
1:9–10—Day 361
2:10—Day 96
5:1—Day 349
5:2–3—Day 349
5:14—Day 143
5:19–20—Day 329
6:13, 17—Day 168

Philippians
3:13–14—Day 260

Colossians
1:11—Day 150
1:16–17—Day 303
1:17—Day 170
3:12—Day 25
4:11—Day 264

1 Thessalonians
2:11–12—Day 103
4:11—Day 245

1 Timothy
1:12—Day 271
3:9—Day 284
4:13, 16—Day 359
5:8—Day 76
6:6—Day 187

6:9, 11—Day 14
6:10—Day 305

2 Timothy
4:5—Day 151

Titus
3:1—Day 333

Hebrews
4:16—Day 65
9:28—Day 209
10:25—Day 308
11:1—Day 134
11:9—Day 91
11:27—Day 363
12:1–2—Day 237
12:7—Day 29
13:2—Day 158

James
1:6—Day 154
1:12—Day 27
1:27—Day 206
3:5–6—Day 254
4:8—Day 190
5:4—Day 71

1 Peter
1:24–25—Day 281
2:25—Day 178
3:15—Day 72
5:4—Day 300
5:8—Day 60

2 Peter
2:9—Day 232

1 John
1:7—Day 180
4:4—Day 157
4:18—Day 270

3 John
2—Day 302

Jude

9—Day 167
Revelation
3:11—Day 135
3:14—Day 160
20:14–15—Day 208
21:6—Day 309
22:1—Day 199
22:1–2—Day 317
22:2—Day 255
22:17—Day 259
22:20—Day 360

Topical Index

Achievement
Day 11, 27, 32, 39, 57, 71, 75, 78, 344

Adams, Ansel
Day 188

Ant
Day 122, 233

Archery
Day 98

Art
Day 170

Aurora borealis
Day 322

Ayers Rock
Day 33

Badwater
Day 208

Birds
Day 6, 35, 36, 37, 38, 42, 46, 52, 60, 80,
106, 109, 127, 153, 157, 167, 174, 201,
231, 233, 240, 339, 354

Black Widow
Day 40

Boone, Daniel
Day 7

Butterfly
Day 66, 109

California condor
Day 21

Camping
Day 72, 73, 91, 135, 180, 205, 277

Carpentry
Day 111

Cathedral of the Pines
Day 58

Cave
Day 4, 65, 77

Climbing
Day 134, 159, 178, 234, 304, 314, 334

Clouds
Day 61

Custer, George Armstrong
Day 176

Darkness
Day 118, 291, 346

Death
Day 283, 311

Detail
Day 30, 34, 53, 61, 66, 92, 109, 117,
170, 249, 258, 262, 272, 301, 319

Dinosaur
Day 280

Disaster
Day 28, 67, 74, 108, 116, 123, 179, 215,
254, 274, 306, 342

Diving
Day 172

Drought
Day 102

Farming
Day 85, 90, 95, 102, 146, 169, 183, 269,
285

Fishing
Day 1, 9, 69, 70, 72, 113, 119, 124, 143,
147, 150, 155, 158, 165, 177, 187, 191,
210, 218, 229, 232, 236, 241, 251, 267,
275, 282, 298, 312, 326, 352

Fruit
Day 235, 239, 255, 278

Galaxy
Day 5, 53, 55, 70, 79, 100, 107, 160,
184, 193, 205, 268, 287

Golf
Day 133

Grand Canyon
Day 51, 197, 203, 349

Great Barrier Reef
Day 136

Grunion
Day 89

Halliburton, Richard
Day 15

Health
Day 302

Hiacoomes
Day 41

Hiking
Day 20, 27, 32, 39, 70, 71, 72, 75, 78,
81, 94, 106, 114, 118, 119, 129, 155,

159, 173, 178, 194, 201, 208, 209, 211, 237, 257, 265, 273, 277, 288

Horse riding
Day 87

Hunting
Day 14, 45, 50, 70, 80, 119, 132, 174, 186, 274, 278, 298, 329

Invention
Day 17, 224, 226, 245

Jungle
Day 101

Kayak
Day 130, 168, 189, 225, 263

Lake Kinneret
Day 121

Landmark
Day 33, 95, 161

Lost City of the Incas
Day 8

Machu Picchu
Day 8

Mammoth Cave
Day 4

Miracle
Day 144

Moon
Day 238, 335

Mount Everest
Day 24, 196

Mount Kilimanjaro
Day 32

Mount of Transfiguration
Day 128

Mount Rushmore
Day 8, 13

Mount St. Helens
Day 51

Mud
Day 96

Mystery
Day 284, 345

Niagara Falls
Day 131

Outdoor communion
Day 16, 22, 31, 34, 36, 55, 58, 63, 77, 84, 86, 88, 93, 105, 113, 124, 139, 141, 144, 163, 175, 190, 195, 207, 213, 230, 246, 248, 308, 312, 321, 336, 337, 338, 343, 365

Parachuting
Day 190

Paradise
Day 156, 157, 361

Park
Day 149

Pioneer
Day 7, 129, 277, 351

Rabies
Day 29

Rain
Day 25, 42, 48, 84, 102, 112, 122, 161, 166, 169, 204, 227, 243, 269, 292

Rocks
Day 3, 19, 33, 51, 213, 256, 299, 315

Salmon
Day 82

Seasons
Day 42, 47, 49, 54, 97, 105, 137, 222, 240, 243, 244, 247, 266, 275, 281, 293, 297, 303, 313, 353

Ship
Day 171

Smith, Jedediah Strong
Day 76, 151

Snorkeling
Day 44

Soldier
Day 12, 81, 224, 355

Sonar
Day 185

Space
Day 5, 10, 104

Sport
Day 140, 154, 219, 237, 253, 260, 271, 355

Standard Scientific Model for the Creation of the Universe
Day 83

Stewardship
Day 67, 142, 181, 220, 307, 316, 333

Storm
Day 18, 110, 117, 123, 126, 153, 162, 192, 204, 296

Survival
Day 23, 25, 35, 37, 42, 43, 104, 110, 120, 123, 178, 242, 300, 310

Sutter, Johann Augustus
Day 252

Temple
Day 99

Travel
Day 62, 76, 82, 87, 89, 114, 145, 182, 184, 197, 221, 257, 273, 286, 323

Treasure
Day 115, 228, 305, 331, 340, 341

Tumbleweed
Day 214

Van Orsdel, William Wesley
Day 270

Vision
Day 148

Water
Day 48, 59, 64, 74, 102, 112, 123, 126, 130, 131, 138, 146, 152, 154, 182, 192, 198, 199, 202, 206, 212, 217, 243, 259, 279, 294, 309, 317

Whitesides Mountain
Day 134

Wild animals
Day 6, 14, 26, 29, 35, 36, 37, 38, 42, 46, 52, 56, 60, 66, 68, 73, 103, 106, 116, 125, 135, 136, 164, 167, 200, 202, 216, 250, 256, 258, 264, 266, 276, 289, 290, 295, 330, 360

Wilderness
Day 7, 12, 16, 31, 43, 68, 88, 113, 120, 151, 186, 223, 324

Williams, Roger
Day 147, 328

Wind
Day 362

Winter
Day 42, 47, 49, 318, 320, 325, 332, 337, 347, 356, 358, 359

Yosemite National Park
Day 2, 188